Phenomenology and Pe

in Physical Education

Phenomenology is a philosophical approach to the study of consciousness and subjective experience. In recent years it has become a more prominent element of the social scientific study of sport and a core component of the important emergent concept of physical literacy. This book is the first to offer a philosophically-sound investigation of phenomenological perspectives on pedagogy in physical education

The book argues that phenomenology offers a particularly interesting theoretical approach to physical education because of the closely embodied relationship between the knowledge object (the actions, activities and practices of movement) and the knowing subject (the pupil). Drawing on the work of key phenomenological thinkers but also exploring the implications of this work for teaching practice, the book helps to illuminate our understanding of important concepts in physical education such as practical knowledge, skill acquisition, experience and ethics.

This is fascinating reading for any serious student or researcher working in physical education or the philosophy or sociology of sport.

Øyvind Førland Standal is Professor at the Department of Physical Education, Norwegian School of Sport Sciences. His teaching is in the area of movement activities for people with disabilities and inclusion in physical education. Øyvind is interested in pedagogy, phenomenology and qualitative research and has published articles on those topics in journals such as *Adapted Physical Activity Quarterly, Sport, Education and Society, Medicine, Healthcare and Philosophy* and *Sport, Ethics and Philosophy.* In addition to the research presented in this book, Øyvind has recently published research on practicum learning in physical education teacher education.

Ethics and Sport

Series editors
Mike McNamee
University of Wales Swansea
Jim Parry
University of Leeds

The Ethics and Sport series aims to encourage critical reflection on the practice of sport, and to stimulate professional evaluation and development. Each volume explores new work relating to philosophical ethics and the social and cultural study of ethical issues. Each is different in scope, appeal, focus and treatment but a balance is sought between local and international focus, perennial and contemporary issues, level of audience, teaching and research application, and variety of practical concerns.

Also available in this series:

Ethics and Sport
Edited by Mike McNamee and Jim Parry

Values in Sport
Elitism, nationalism, gender equality and the scientific manufacture of winners
Edited by Torbjörn Tännsjö and Claudio Tamburrini

Spoilsports
Understanding and preventing sexual exploitation in sport
Celia Brackenridge

Fair Play in Sport
A moral norm system
Sigmund Loland

Sport, Rules and Values
Philosophical investigations into the nature of sport
Graham McFee

Sport, Professionalism and Pain
Ethnographies of injury and risk
David Howe

Genetically Modified Athletes
Biomedical ethics, gene doping and sport
Andy Miah

Human Rights in Youth Sport
A critical review of children's rights in competitive sports
Paulo David

Genetic Technology and Sport
Ethical questions
Edited by Claudio Tamburrini and Torbjörn Tännsjö

Pain and Injury in Sport
Social and ethical analysis
Edited by Sigmund Loland, Berit Skirstad and Ivan Waddington

Ethics, Money and Sport
This sporting Mammon
Adrian Walsh and Richard Giulianotti

Ethics, Dis/Ability and Sports
Edited by Ejgil Jespersen and Michael McNamee

The Ethics of Doping and Anti-Doping
Redeeming the soul of sport?
Verner Møller

The Ethics of Sport Medicine
Edited by Claudio Tamburrini and Torbjörn Tännsjö

Bodily Democracy
Towards a philosophy of sport for all
Henning Eichberg

Ethics, Knowledge and Truth in Sports Research
An epistemology of sport
Graham McFee

Exercise and Eating Disorders
An ethical and legal analysis
Simona Giordano

The Ethics of Sports Coaching
Edited by Alun Hardman Carwyn Jones

Athletics and Philosophy in the Ancient World
Contests of virtue
Heather L. Reid

Doping and Anti-Doping Policy in Sport
Ethical, legal and social perspectives
Edited by Mike McNamee and Verner Møller

Watching Sport
Aesthetics, ethics and emotion for the spectator
Stephen Mumford

Phenomenological Approaches to Sport
Edited by Irena Martinková and Jim Parry

Olympic Legacies
Edited by Mike McNamee and Jim Parry

Sport and Art
An essay in the hermeneutics of sport
Andrew Edgar

Dispute Resolution in Sport
Athletes, law and arbitration
David McArdle

Philosophy and the Martial Arts
Edited by Graham Priest and Damon Young

Talent Development, Existential Philosophy and Sport
On becoming an elite athlete
Kenneth Aggerholm

On Sport and the Philosophy of Sport
A Wittgensteinian approach
Graham McFee

Phenomenology and Pedagogy in Physical Education
Øyvind Førland Standal

Phenomenology and Pedagogy in Physical Education

Øyvind Førland Standal

Routledge
Taylor & Francis Group
LONDON AND NEW YORK

First published 2015
by Routledge
2 Park Square, Milton Park, Abingdon, Oxon OX14 4RN

and by Routledge
711 Third Avenue, New York, NY 10017

First issued in paperback 2017

Routledge is an imprint of the Taylor & Francis Group, an informa business

British Library Cataloguing in Publication Data
A catalogue record for this book is available from the British Library

Library of Congress Cataloging in Publication Data
Standal, Oyvind.
Phenomenology and pedagogy in physical education : knowledge, experience and ethics / Oyvind Standal.
pages cm. -- (Ethics and sport)
Includes bibliographical references and index.
1. Physical education and training--Philosophy. 2. Phenomenology. I. Title.
GV342.S69 2015
613.7--dc23
2015011651

ISBN 13: 978-1-138-30866-4 (pbk)
ISBN 13: 978-1-138-02408-3 (hbk)

Typeset in Times New Roman
by Taylor & Francis Books

Contents

Figures

Acknowledgement

This book has been a work in progress for quite some time. There are number of people who have helped and encouraged me in the process of writing. First, I would like to thank Gunn Engelsrud, head of the Department of Physical Education at the Norwegian School of Sport Sciences where I work. Not only have you, Gunn, provided me with good working conditions and a sabbatical, but you have also been an inspirational and vital source of knowledge about phenomenology and physical education. During my sabbatical I was able to stay at the Centre for the studies of practical knowledge at Södertörns University. Thanks are due to Jonna Bornemark for facilitating my visit and to Fredrik Svenaeus for sharing his office space. In addition I would like to thank the participants at the seminar at Södertörn where we discussed my work. Several people have been reading and commenting on individual chapters in this book. Thank you to Gro Rugseth, Vegard Fusche Moe, Petter Erik Leirhaug and Gunn Engelsrud! Finally, thanks are due to my family: I love you!

1 Introduction

This book is about phenomenology and pedagogy applied to the context of school physical education. As such, it aims to fulfil a dual purpose, namely to contribute both to the *philosophy* of physical education as well as to the *pedagogy* of physical education. As an introduction to the topic, there is a need to do some conceptual groundwork by first providing an outline of the key concepts I will be working with: school physical education, pedagogy in relation to physical education, philosophy of physical education, and phenomenology. On the basis of this, I intend to argue for why this study into phenomenology and pedagogy in physical education is worthwhile and important. In outlining what 'physical education', 'philosophy of physical education' and 'pedagogy in physical education' might entail, I run the risk of derailing the whole project of studying phenomenology and pedagogy in physical education, because all these areas can be objects of a study in their own right. I will therefore be brief, thus inducing the risk of superficiality. However, I hope that in the course of developing my ideas and arguments throughout the book, I will be able to fill out the picture.

Physical education

There is a sense in which physical education can be understood as a broad process of induction, socialization, and learning to take part in the valued physical activities[1] of one's culture. The broad sense of 'physical education' includes – but is not limited to – school physical education. Physical education in a wide sense can be understood as the process of developing 'the body's intelligent capacities for movement and expression in physical culture, in all its varied forms' (Evans, 2004, p. 96). This book, however, is aimed at the school subject of physical education. Thus, my use of the term 'physical education' is restricted to the school subject. In the British context, Stidder and Hayes (2013) note that physical education 'relates specifically to the 76 hours (or 5%) of formal curriculum time devoted to the teaching and learning of physical education to all pupils in an academic year' (p. 2). In other words, the use of the term 'physical education' is restricted and distinguished from other school physical activities, for instance school sport programmes in the

UK (ibid.), and 'physical activity and health' in the Norwegian school context. The latter is an effort explicitly aimed at public health issues, where there is no curriculum and no requirement as to the competence of the person in charge of the activity. Although school sport and 'physical activity and health' fall within physical education in the broad sense, they are not part of physical education in the narrower sense in which I am interested.

Schools are diverse and situated in specific historical and cultural contexts. How physical education is practiced in schools in Norway today is surely different from the manner in which it was practiced in the 1950s. Also, the practice of physical education in Norway differs from how it is practiced in Japan, Nigeria, Afghanistan or in the USA. Indeed, it even differs between comparatively similar countries such as Norway, Sweden and Denmark (Annerstedt, 2008). Consequently, it is important to recognize that physical education means different things to different readers of this book. However, there may be some issues that, due to globalization and academization of the subject for instance, are quite similar across cultures and countries.

In *Physical Education Futures*, David Kirk (2010) develops what he calls the idea of the idea of physical education (abbreviated as 'id^2'). In order to capture what physical education means, Kirk relies on a social epistemological analysis rather than an analysis of various definitions of physical education. A social epistemological analysis implies that knowledge is socially constructed, but concedes at the same time that there must be some features that allow us to recognize 'when a practice is physical education and when it is something else' (p. 16). His perspective is that there are no essences of physical education that transcend time and place. But neither does he allow for a relativistic understanding where anything can pass as school physical education. For Kirk, the idea of the idea of physical education is expressed in terms of *physical education-as-sport-techniques*. This implies that it is the teaching and learning of various sport techniques which are central to the way physical education is currently practiced. This should not be taken as a simplistic conclusion about what physical education is. For one thing, Kirk points out that there are teachers who resist this idea, and teach the subject differently. In addition, he also points out that 'surrounding these techniques is a complex of other forces that gives the id^2 its considerable reach and durability' (p. 42).

There are four features of Kirk's analysis of physical education that I will highlight here. First, physical education is predominantly characterized by a multi-activity model where pupils are presented with a wide range of activities in which they should be active participants. This is a characterization of the curriculum which finds broad support in the research literature. For instance, Annerstedt (2008) made a comparative study of physical education in the Scandinavian countries and found that:

> The syllabi seem to have three dominating elements: physical activity, social learning and health. Through multi-activity programs of different physical and sporting activities, the pupils in Scandinavia are to learn

> about their bodies through the use of their bodies (Quennerstedt, 2006). Above all, pupils should develop a desire to perform life-long physical activity through experiencing the joy of movement during PE classes.
>
> (Annerstedt, 2008, p. 310)

It should be noted here that *active* in this context implies being physically active. Indeed, Annerstedt (2008) indicates that the focus in school physical education is 'more on activity than on learning' (p. 316), and questions the relationship between the idea of creating a life-long interest in physical activity and the actual learning outcomes of physical education lessons.

Second, in relation to physical education-as-sport-technique, Kirk (2010) highlights the distinction between technique and skill. Whereas techniques are decontextualized aspects of a sport or an activity, such as the dig in volleyball or the lay-up in basketball, skills are basically the same movements, but performed in context. That is, whereas the lay-up in basketball as a technique can be practised in isolation without reference to or interference from opponents, the lay-up skill takes place within the context of a game.

The third point I want to make about Kirk's 'id^2' of physical education is that the dominant form of teaching is an instructional style, which is directive and command oriented. Tinning (2010) similarly claims that the dominant pedagogical form of physical education is the so-called DEP-model, i.e. 'the sequence of demonstration, explanation and practice' (p. 43). One can therefore say that even though the pedagogical role of the physical education teacher has developed from the highly authoritarian command style of Swedish gymnastics, it is still very much modelled on a traditional instruction-based teacher role. The instructional style of teaching can be partly explained on the basis of the understanding of physical education-as-sport-technique, but also due to restrictions imposed on teachers by factors such as class size and timetabling.

The fourth point brought up by Kirk (2010) are four relational issues that the institutionalized practice of physical education must consider. These are physical culture, transfer of learning, standards of excellence, and social and cultural transmission. When it comes to physical culture – understood as the bodily practices of play, games, sports and 'other leisure physical activities that help define the social fabric of local and national communities' (Evans, 2004, p. 106) – one can analyse the relationship between the practice of physical education and the wider physical culture in which pupils (may) take part: To what extent does physical education engage young people's physical culture in contemporary society? Associated with this is the question of transfer of learning. Given that learning of sport techniques has a central place in the subject, to what extent is this learning transferable to pupils' lives here and now, and in a life-span perspective? According to Kirk (2010), the question of standard of excellence concerns how ability is understood and valued in the subject. As implied by Annerstedt (2008) and other researchers (e.g. Evans,

2004; Fitzgerald, 2005; Hay and Macdonald, 2009), it is skills in traditional masculine activities such as ball games that are valued. Therefore, it appears that excellence in these skills constitutes ability in physical education. This, then, leads to the fourth relational issue in Kirk's analysis, namely the social and cultural transmission of knowledge and values. As I will expand on later, this issue is about how hegemonies and inequalities are transmitted and reproduced through physical education with the effect of yielding benefits to some pupils but disadvantages to others.

In closing this section on what I talk about when I talk about physical education in this book, I want to make two points. First, one debate that physical education teacher educators, like myself, need to engage with is what physical education should be. This, however, will not be the main topic in this book. I nevertheless hope that my investigations into phenomenology and pedagogy in physical education give some guidance in future discussions about the normative question of what physical education should be like. Second, the analyses of Kirk (2010), Evans (2004) and Annerstedt (2008) point to the centrality of the body in physical education: the moving body is the knowledge object of physical education. That is, through developing skills, techniques or knowledge about physical activities, the moving body becomes a knowledge object. In addition, and of no less importance, the body is also the knowing subject of PE. The implication of the claim that the body is both the knowing subject and knowledge object of PE will be substantiated throughout the book.

Philosophy of physical education

Whereas philosophy of education is a burgeoning sub-discipline of philosophy with its own journals, conferences and international research associations, it appears that the philosophy of physical education is an unfashionable term. If this claim is true, then there is a history to this state of affairs, and some comments should be made about this history.

Morgan (2006) sees philosophy of physical education as a predecessor to philosophy of sport. He claims that up until 'the late 1960s or so' (p. 97), a pedagogical perspective informed philosophical approaches to various physical activities such as games, sport and physical education. This connection between physical education and philosophy of education was, however, severed with the invention of philosophy of sport. Indeed, he claims that '[philosophical work dealing with physical education] has been clearly dwarfed by the work devoted to sports' (ibid.). According to Morgan's analysis, this has meant that philosophically oriented research into physical education has been – and he also suggests that it will continue to be[2] – informed by philosophy of sport, rather than philosophy of education. In particular, he claims that 'much of this research will be centered on ethical inquiry into sports as opposed to the older epistemological research paradigm favored in philosophy of education circles' (p. 106).

Assessing the accuracy of Morgan's historical analysis is beyond the scope of this book, but two points can be made. First, the concept of fair play, which must be said to be a key concept in philosophy of sport (Loland, 2002), has found its way into the physical education curriculum in Norway (Kunnskapsdepartementet, 2006) and elsewhere (Kirk, 2010). The focus on fair play in physical education may indicate that Morgan to some degree is right in suggesting that ethical inquiry into sport informs physical education. Second, a literature search on the precise term 'philosophy of physical education' in the database *SportDiscus* gave seventy-five hits.[3] Of these, about two thirds were published before 1985. Thus, if this rather unstructured literature search is anything to go by, it seems that the heyday of philosophy of physical education was in the 1970s and 1980s, which is not so far from Morgan's claim.

One might wonder why philosophy of physical education seems to be a declining research area. Based on his perception of a 'yawning gap between the philosophy of PE, as articulated by academic philosophers, and PE as taught in a practical way by PE teachers', Green (1998, pp. 128–129) has researched the 'philosophies' of physical education teachers. By 'philosophies' Green does not mean the systematic thinking about concepts and practices, which is characteristic of philosophy as an academic study, but rather the ideologies that teachers of physical education hold about the nature and purpose of their subject. This gap between philosophy and the practicalities of PE identified by Green (1998) is also pointed out by McNamee (2005, p. 1):

> There has always been an air of suspicion about those who think philosophically about the nature and values of physical education. On the one hand, physical education teachers are apt to claim that theirs is essentially a practical vocation; a calling to the teaching of physical activities that can help students to live better lives. What need have they of a philosophy? On the other hand, philosophers of education, notably in the liberal-analytical tradition, have often sought to cast a dim light on physical education, thinking it valuable (on good days at least) – but not educationally so.

The gesture that McNamee makes towards liberal-analytical philosophy of education is important because this tradition has been highly influential on the philosophical debates that have taken place in the context of physical education. These debates centred on the justification of the subject in the school curriculum were set against the backdrop of the liberal-analytical philosophy of education advanced by Richard Peters and Paul Hirst. Their position was – stated very briefly – that education 'referred to the initiation of the unlearned into those intrinsically worthwhile forms of knowledge that were constitutive of rational mind' (McNamee, 2005, p. 2). By this account, physical education did not have educational value because it did not possess the cognitive qualities that were considered as the marks of education.

In a later chapter I return to some of the literature that aimed to argue for the inclusion of physical education into the curriculum. For now, suffice it to say that arguments were made against the restrictive view of education proposed by Hirst and Peters. The strategy was to argue for a broader understanding of knowledge in the sense that practical knowledge, which characterizes physical education, also has educational value. That is, in order to justify physical education as educationally worthwhile, a broadening of the concepts of education and knowledge was advanced. This work was, as McNamee (2005) notes, also situated within the analytical tradition, but it appears that the analytical philosophy of education and its relation to physical education has become unfashionable. I have already mentioned Green's (1998) work on teacher's philosophies, and quote him at length here in order to show what this dissatisfaction amounts to. Commencing with an interest in educational philosophy and physical education, Green traces his autobiographical development:

> I became increasingly concerned with academic PE philosophy itself; I focused entirely on the philosophical ideas themselves, abstracted from their social context, with the result that people (i.e. PE teachers themselves) 'disappeared'. [...] I had in effect been seeking to understand philosophies as though they were disembodied sets of ideas which could be understood without reference to the social lives of the people who generated and held those ideas. [...] My research had been in danger of becoming an *abstract* philosophical discussion of *abstract* philosophies – not, it should be noted, something which was without merit, but something, whatever its merits, provided little help in making sense of what PE teachers thought about PE, and why they thought it.
>
> (p. 129, italics added)

In a similar vein, Kirk (2010) argues that analytical philosophers' preoccupation with definition and conceptual analysis was situated in a 'purely logical space' that lacked references to the social forces in which the curriculum is situated. Kirk's project is a social epistemology where, if we want to understand what physical education means, we need to study what people do 'in the name of the subject' (p. 16).

The point I am making is that there seems to be a considerable scepticism towards thinking philosophically about physical education, not only among practising teachers (as argued by McNamee, 2005), but also among central scholars in the field. Philosophical thinking concerning physical education is diagnosed as abstract and out of touch with the practice of physical education. In all fairness, the point Green makes in the quote above is that philosophy of education is not without merits, but the double use of the word 'abstract' certainly carries with it unfavourable connotations. Nevertheless, if the argument is that sociological questions are not best answered by philosophical analysis, then it does not follow from this that thinking philosophically about physical education is irrelevant and without merit.

In light of the declining interest in 'philosophy of physical education', it was somewhat of a surprise to see a book-length treatment of this topic published in 2014 (Stolz, 2014). In this book Stolz gives the reader a comprehensive overview of the main sources dealing with philosophical questions concerning the place of physical education in educational institutions. He outlines the different traditions of physical education that have competed for hegemony when it comes to justifying physical education in school curricula. In particular, Stolz takes an interest in philosophies of the body from Aristotle, Aquinas and Descartes to Merleau-Ponty. Although the book is an impressive survey of philosophical work on physical education, I will refer here only to Stolz's concluding argument.[4] Stolz sees the different forms of legitimization of physical education as rival traditions that are 'essentially contested' (p. 156). By taking the philosophy of Maurice Merleau-Ponty as his starting point, Stolz advances a new tradition of physical education, namely embodied learning, and argues that his (i.e. Stolz's) position is educationally significant because

> the whole person is treated as a whole being, permitting the person to experience himself or herself as a holistic and synthesized acting, feeling, thinking being-in-the-world, rather than as separate physical and mental qualities that bear no relation to each other.
>
> (p. 163)

I am in full agreement with Stolz's emphasis on the role that movement and embodiment plays in learning in physical education and I am convinced of the importance of the experiential perspective on movement that Stoltz draws on. Although Stolz's arguments about the educational significance of the phenomenological perspective are persuasive, he does not draw out the pedagogical consequences of his proposed new tradition of physical education. That was not the intention of his book, but it is nevertheless an important task to inquire into how phenomenological perspectives on movement and embodiment can be enacted through pedagogical work in physical education. Therefore, the purpose of my book is to build further on Stolz's work by investigating the pedagogical consequences that phenomenology may have for physical education.

Pedagogy and physical education

No agreed-upon definition of pedagogy currently exists. Due to the different meanings that 'pedagogy' has in different languages and cultures, what passes for pedagogy in one context may not be thought of primarily as pedagogy in others (Tinning, 2010).

Etymologically, pedagogy is derived from the Greek word *paedagogus*, which referred to a person who walks with children. Pedagogy, as I employ the term in this book, is concerned with processes of teaching and learning. It is important to note that I do not think that pedagogy is only about teaching and learning; it has a broader scope than that, for instance through topics like socialization, curriculum studies and the raising of children. Neither do I believe that pedagogy and teaching/learning are synonymous.

In *Pedagogy and Human Movement*, Tinning (2010) claims that 'there is no Holy Grail of PE pedagogies' and that 'the possibilities for pedagogies will always be circumscribed by the foregrounded purposes to which PE is put, the nature of it being a physical/bodily subject matter and by the harsh realities of class size and available equipment' (p. 44). In his book, Tinning outlines what he calls four conceptual orientations in/on pedagogy, namely (i) pedagogy as the science of teaching, (ii) pedagogy and didactics, (iii) pedagogy and knowledge (re)production, and (iv) phenomenological pedagogy. In terms of the first, Tinning argues that in this orientation, researchers would investigate the effectiveness of various teaching strategies on pupils' learning. This orientation is therefore similar to the evidence-based movement, where the teachers' choice of pedagogical methods should be based on scientific studies of what works (Biesta, 2007).

Second, when Tinning (2010) outlines the relationship between didactics and pedagogy, he draws on Brent Davies, who maintains that there is a distinction between didactics concerned with instructional techniques and pedagogy as teachers' reflections on moral and ethical issues of their work. However, since the relations between teachers, learners and the subject matter that arises in teaching are fraught with ethical challenges, it is difficult to see that didactics and pedagogy can be separated in precisely that way. As Tinning points out, it is important to remember that terms are understood in different ways and vary between countries and languages. Whereas didactics in English seems to have negative connotation of mechanical instruction, it has a different and more positive connotation in French, where it is more broadly thought of as 'the practice of teaching and its methods' (Amade-Escot, 2006, p. 347). Third, Tinning describes pedagogy as knowledge (re)production as an orientation which is more or less consistent with critical pedagogy. Drawing on the Marxist tradition, particularly the work of Paulo Freire, this specific conceptual orientation sees pedagogy as a form of 'cultural politics' (p. 11) where the aim is to engage learners in reflections on socially unjust conditions in order to create empowerment and emancipation. According to Kirk, critical pedagogy is 'now common-place in the [physical education] research literature' (2010, p. 117).

Finally, Tinning also mentions phenomenological pedagogy as a conceptual orientation in physical education. Here, he refers to the work of Max van Manen, who arguably has made this approach known. However, Tinning points out that 'we have not seen much of the phenomenological focus on pedagogy in [human movement studies]' (p. 11). If Tinning is right in his assessment of phenomenological pedagogy – and I see no compelling reasons to think otherwise – then the project I undertake in this book fills a gap in the knowledge base of physical education pedagogy.[5]

Outline of the book

This chapter has provided an outline of three central backdrops for the present book, namely school physical education, philosophy of physical education, and pedagogy in physical education. Although brief and incomplete as a review of these three topics, enough has been said to state the purpose of this book, which is to provide a stronger philosophical account of phenomenology in physical education with the particular aim of drawing out the pedagogical consequences that phenomenology has in this subject.

Chapter 2 begins with a brief introduction to phenomenology as philosophy. The second part of the chapter surveys the literature on phenomenology in the context of physical education. The chapter takes a particular interest in the work on physical literacy (Whitehead, 2001; 2007; 2010). The main argument is that although this work is very valuable, it suffers from certain weaknesses in its philosophical groundwork. I also argue that physical literacy, as currently conceptualized, is too broad and all-encompassing to serve as a pedagogical model for physical education.

Chapter 3 seeks to establish a link between practical knowledge and phenomenology (Svenaeus, 2009). To have practical knowledge, from a phenomenological perspective, involves an acquaintance with meaning patterns of the lifeworld and to have the capability to move about in these meaning patterns in an effortless and skilled way. Through a detailed exposition of how Merleau-Ponty (1963, 1968, 2002) conceived of embodied learning, the chapter shows the closely embodied relationship between the knowledge objects (i.e. the actions, activities and practices of physical education) and the student as a knowing subject. Chapter 4 continues the exploration of the knowledge objects of physical education from a phenomenological perspective. More specifically, the notion of poise, which is central to the definition of physical literacy, is developed with the aid of the phenomenological philosophy of Samuel Todes (2001). Poise, in the phenomenological perspective, is understood as a qualitatively felt experience rather than a quantitative entity that one can have more or less of. Two problems with the phenomenological perspective on poise and skill are then noted, namely that it risks – perhaps surprisingly – making the body disappear from experience and that the perspective can be interpreted as being prejudiced against teaching. Chapter 5 deals with the two problems outlined in the previous chapter. It draws on resources from Martin Heidegger (1976), Loïc Wacquant (2004), and pedagogical theories such as situated learning (Lave and Wenger, 1991) and non-linear pedagogy (Chow et al., 2007) to argue for the importance of 'letting learn'. As a provisional conclusion to chapters dealing with the phenomenological perspective on practical knowledge, the chapter outlines *movement literacy* as pedagogical model for physical education. The word 'movement' is used instead of 'physical' to distinguish the pedagogical model from the broader work of Margaret Whitehead on physical literacy.

Chapter 6 outlines the phenomenological pedagogy of Max van Manen (1993; 1982). Although highly relevant to pedagogy in physical education because it argues that pedagogical work must start from the students' experiences in the educational situation, one shortcoming with van Manen's work is noted. While his emphasis is on teachers' understanding of the students' experience, it is also important to develop students' self-reflective understanding of their own experiences. The chapter therefore discusses how the body is always both an object and a subject of experience, and it questions the idea that objectifications of the body should be avoided. Chapter 7 discusses further the idea that the body can and should be objectified for educational reasons in physical education. Taking the place of the body seriously in physical education implies that we must attend to and reflect on the body as it appears to us in the movement experience. For that purpose, I suggest that pragmatism has useful contributions to offer physical education. In particular, the works of Shusterman (2008; 2012) and Dewey (1910; 1938) are discussed in relation to physical education.

Inclusion is an ethical challenge for physical education. Chapter 8 offers a phenomenological perspective on inclusion and difference. In this chapter I aim to refute the commonly held belief that phenomenology is unable to address certain issues that are highly relevant to inclusion, such as questions of power and how experiences are shaped by oppressive social structures. Drawing on the work of Iris Young (1998) and Sara Ahmed (2006), the chapter shows how queer phenomenology is of relevance to inclusive physical education. Queer phenomenology helps develop a critical aspect of the pedagogical model of movement literacy. Chapter 9 aims to draw out some normative implications of two related concepts, namely abilities and capabilities. I draw on the work of John Evans (Evans, 2004) and others (e.g. Hay and Hunter, 2006; Hay and Macdonald, 2009) who have been interested in how 'ability' is understood. Based on this work, I propose that there are certain normative implications for how physical education must be taught in order recognize individual differences among students. Building on this assertion, I also suggest that the capabilities approach as developed by Martha Nussbaum (2003; 2006; 2011) offers a good starting point for settling discussions of normative questions about how physical education should be taught.

Notes

1 It is important to note that I use 'physical activity' in a specific sense. A commonly used definition of physical activity is 'any bodily movement produced by skeletal muscles that results in energy expenditure' (Caspersen et al. 1985, p. 126). This definition, I would argue, is virtually meaningless for the physically active person. Of course it is not meaningless from a physiological perspective. For the moving subject, however, this definition literally implies that as long as the energy expenditure is equal, it doesn't matter whether you run on a treadmill with a gun to your head or if you enjoy a run in a beautiful sunset with your loved one. The point about this exaggerated comparison is that it highlights that physical activity by necessity also has meaning for the moving subject. The meaning dimension is a far more important perspective for phenomenological and pedagogical projects than energy expenditure.

2 I am, however, not completely convinced by Morgan's (2006) vision that philosophical work on physical education in the future will (or even should) come more from the philosophy of sport rather than from the philosophy of education. If philosophy of education is conceived of as 'the philosophical study of education and its problems' (Noddings, 2011, p. iii), then it would be quite strange if the subject of physical education could not benefit from such philosophical analyses.
3 The search was performed in October 2013. After dividing the results into decades the details are: 1959: 4; 1960–1969: 11; 1970–1979: 24; 1980–1989: 23; 1990–1999: 6; 2000–2013: 7. In addition, 16 of the 23 results from the 1980s were published in the first half of the decade.
4 I have reviewed his book more thoroughly on the online forum *Idrottsforum.org*: http://idrottsforum.org/staoyv_stolz150116/
5 A more thorough examination of pedagogy in physical education than I can provide here would make reference to work on how different pedagogical traditions, such as behaviourism, cognitivism, constructivism or socio-cultural approaches, have been applied to physical education. In addition, I would also have referred to work on learning theories in the subject (e.g. Macdonald, 2004; Quennerstedt et al., 2011).

References

Ahmed, S. (2006). *Queer phenomenology: Orientations, objects, others.* London: Duke University Press.

Amade-Escot, C. (2006). Student learning within the *didactique* tradition. In D. Kirk, M. O'Sullivan and D. Macdonald (eds), *Handbook of physical education* (pp. 347–367). London: Sage.

Annerstedt, C. (2008). Physical education in Scandinavia with a focus on Sweden: a comparative perspective. *Physical Education and Sport Pedagogy*, 13, 303–318.

Biesta, G. (2007). Why 'what works' won't work: evidence-based practice and the democratic deficit in educational research. *Educational Theory*, 57, 1–22.

Caspersen, C. J., Powell, K. E. and Christenson, G. M. (1985). Physical activity, exercise, and physical fitness: definitions and distinctions for health-related research. *Public Health Reports*, 100, 126–131.

Chow, J. Y., Davids, K., Button, C., Shuttleworth, R., Renshaw, I. and Arajo, D. (2007). The role of nonlinear pedagogy in physical education. *Review of Educational Research*, 77, 251–278.

Dewey, J. (1910). *How we think.* New York: D.C. Heath and Co.

Dewey, J. (1938). *Experience and education.* New York: Kappa Delta Pi.

Evans, J. (2004). Making a difference? Education and 'ability' in physical education. *European Physical Education Review*, 10, 95–108.

Fitzgerald, H. (2005). Still feeling like a spare piece of luggage? Embodied experiences of (dis)ability in physical education and school sport. *Physical Education and Sport Pedagogy*, 10, 41–59.

Green, K. (1998). Philosophies, ideologies and the practice of physical education. *Sport, Education and Society*, 3, 125–143.

Hay, P. J. and Hunter, L. (2006). Please Mr Hay, what are my poss(abilities): legitimation of ability through physical education practices. *Sport, Education and Society*, 11, 293–310.

Hay, P. J. and Macdonald, D. (2009). Evidence for the social construction of ability in physical education. *Sport, Education and Society*, 15, 1–18.

Heidegger, M. (1976). *What is called thinking?*New York: Harper and Row.

Kirk, D. (2010). *Physical education futures.* London: Routledge.
Kunnskapsdepartementet. (2006). *Læreplan i kroppsøving* [*The physical education curriculum*]. Retrieved from: www.udir.no/kl06/KRO1-03/
Lave, J. and Wenger, E. (1991). *Situated learning: Legitimate peripheral participation.* Cambridge: Cambridge University Press.
Loland, S. (2002). *Fair play in sport: A moral norm system.* London: Routledge.
Macdonald, D. (2004). Understanding learning in physical education. In J. Wright, D. Macdonald and L. Burrows (eds), *Critical inquiry and problem-solving in physical education* (pp. 16–30).
McNamee, M. (2005).The nature and values of physical education. In *Physical education: Essential issues* (pp. 1–20). London: Sage.
Merleau-Ponty, M. (1963). *The structure of behavior.* Pittsburg, PA: Duquesne University Press.
Merleau-Ponty, M. (1968). *The visible and the invisible.* Evanston, IL: Northwestern University Press.
Merleau-Ponty, M. (2002). *Phenomenology of perception.* London: Routledge.
Morgan, W. J. (2006). Philosophy and physical education. In D. M. D. Kirk and M. O'Sullivan (eds), *Handbook of physical education* (p. 97). London: Sage.
Noddings, N. (2011). *Philosophy of education.* Boulder, CO: Westview Press.
Nussbaum, M. (2003). Capabilities as fundamental entitlements: Sen and social justice. *Feminist Economics*, 9, 33–59.
Nussbaum, M. C. (2006). *Frontiers of justice: Disability, nationality, species membership.* London: The Belknap Press of Harvard University Press.
Nussbaum, M. C. (2011). *Creating capabilities: The human development approach.* London: The Belknap Press of Harvard University Press.
Quennerstedt, M., Öhman, J. and Öhman, M. (2011). Investigating learning in physical education: a transactional approach. *Sport, Education and Society*, 16, 159–177.
Shusterman, R. (2008). *Body consciousness: A philosophy of mindfulness and somaesthetics.* New York: Cambridge University Press.
Shusterman, R. (2012). *Thinking through the body: Essays in somaesthetics.* Cambridge: Cambridge University Press.
Stidder, G. and Hayes, S. (2013). Equity and inclusion in physical education: themes and perspectives for practitioners. In G. Stidder and S. Hayes (eds), *Equity and inclusion in physical education and sport* (2nd edn, pp. 1–16). London: Routledge.
Stolz, S. (2014). *The philosophy of physical education: A new perspective.* London: Routledge.
Svenaeus, F. (2009). Vad är praktisk kunnskap? En inledning til emnet och boken. In J. Bornemark and F. Svenaeus (eds), *Vad är praktisk kunnskap?* (pp. 9–36). Stockholm: Södertörn studies in practical knowledge.
Tinning, R. (2010). *Pedagogy and human movement: Theory, practice, research.* London: Routledge.
Todes, S. (2001). *Body and world.* Cambridge, MA: MIT Press.
van Manen, M. (1982). Phenomenological pedagogy. *Curriculum Inquiry*, 12, 283–299.
van Manen, M. (1993). *Pedagogisk takt* [*The tact of teaching: The meaning of pedagogical thoughtfulness*]. Bergen, Norway: Caspar Forlag.
Wacquant, L. (2004). *Body and soul: Notebooks of an apprentice boxer.* New York: Oxford University Press.
Whitehead, M. (2001). The concept of physical literacy. *European Journal of Physical Education*, 6, 127–138.

Whitehead, M. (2007). Physical literacy: philosophical considerations in relation to developing a sense of self, universality and propositional knowledge. *Sport, Ethics and Philosophy*, 1, 281–298.

Whitehead, M. (2010). The concept of physical literacy. In M. Whitehead (ed.), *Physical literacy: Throughout the lifecourse* (pp. 10–20). London: Routledge.

Young, I. (1998). Throwing like a girl. In D. Welton (ed.), *Body and flesh: A philosophical reader* (pp. 259–273). Oxford: Blackwell.

2 Phenomenology and physical education

This chapter begins on a personal note. My educational background is in physical education. During my graduate studies I read philosophical texts, and both my master's and doctoral theses were inspired by those texts. Even so, I always take care to point out that I am not a philosopher and I have never studied philosophy. I offer this caveat both out of respect for those who have made philosophy their professional work or study, and – I must admit – in self-defence. I want to avoid being faulted for pretending to engage in philosophy in the academic sense,[1] and I share these sentiments expressed by Sara Ahmed:

> It is a risk to read philosophy as a non-philosopher. When we don't have the resources to read certain texts, we risk getting things wrong by not returning them to the fullness of the intellectual histories from which they emerge.
>
> (Ahmed, 2006, p. 22)

Should this risk lead non-philosophers with an interest in philosophy such as myself to avoid using these texts? An argument can be made for this position. In the context of sport studies, for example, Martinkova and Parry (2011) have criticized what they consider to be sloppy use of the philosophical term phenomenology. Much of the work that celebrates the promise of phenomenology, they argue, has little philosophical relevance. Moreover, these scholars point out that many authors use philosophical terms completely incorrectly. Together with a colleague, I have examined the facile manner in which some writers in the sport sciences refer to differences in ontological and epistemological assumptions among phenomenological philosophers (Standal and Engelsrud, 2013). At the same, we observed that it is claimed, *with strength*, that non-philosophers with an interest in philosophy have an obligation to clarify our assumptions and declare which ontology and epistemology we apply: 'the debate between Husserl and Heidegger is about fundamental differences in ontology. It follows that research claiming to use a phenomenological approach must make explicit the ontological assumptions upon which it is based' (Kerry and Armour, 2000, p. 8).

That said, Engelsrud and I (2013) went on to argue that in the phenomenological tradition, the differences in ontological and epistemological assumptions are not as significant as they are sometimes claimed to be. In fact, these differences can be so nuanced that professional philosophers are still working out them out. Due to the vast amount of unpublished work (the so-called *Nachlass*) left behind by Husserl, the founder of phenomenology, his position on various philosophical topics is still emerging; to some extent, this research has revealed striking similarities between the work of Husserl and that of his successors (Zahavi, 2003a).

Certainly, I would not argue that anything goes as long as researchers do not pretend to be engaging in philosophy. One the other hand, I do not think that researchers who are not professional philosophers should avoid entering the philosophical terrain. Sara Ahmed (2006) makes the argument for the promise and perils of philosophy for us non-philosophers succinctly:

> the failure to return texts to their histories will do something. Of course, not all failures are creative. If we don't take care with the texts we read, if we don't pay attention, then the failure to read them 'properly' won't do very much at all.
>
> (pp. 22–23)

Striking this balance between not attempting to – or pretending to – engage in philosophy, yet reading and writing on philosophical subjects adequately is challenging, but it can also be productive.

In the case of physical education pedagogy, as Tinning (2010) has pointed out, the phenomenological perspective remains underdeveloped. In writing from this perspective, I hope that with this book I can serve the dual purpose of informing both the philosophy of physical education and the knowledge base of pedagogy. With this goal in mind, I will now offer a brief introduction to phenomenology.

Phenomenology as philosophy

As mentioned in the previous chapter, much of the work in the philosophy of physical education has been based on the analytical tradition. In this book, I take a different approach, inspired by McNamee's (2005) suggestion that Continental philosophy may have

> rich seams indeed for philosophers of physical education to plough. In particular, the work of phenomenologists and hermeneuticists has tremendous potential to offer understandings of our experiences in the activities that comprise physical education (whether in sport, games, play or even dance).
>
> (pp. 1–2)

An initial problem in trying to define[2] phenomenology is that it cannot be considered as one school of thought, in which philosophers are committed to a strict set of doctrines. It is, rather, a movement, which shares 'certain methodological commitments as well as closely related ideas about the proper domain of phenomenological research' (Luft and Overgaard, 2012, p. 1). As I understand it, phenomenology is a branch of Continental philosophy originating in the groundbreaking work of Edmund Husserl (1859–1938) that has had a profound influence on contemporary philosophy. The philosophical work of Husserl and philosophers who have been inspired by his work has also had great impact on other disciplines, including medicine, sociology and psychology. In addition, scholars have developed phenomenological research methods (e.g. Finlay, 2009; Giorgi, 1984; van Manen, 1990). Finally, Max van Manen has applied insights from phenomenological philosophy to develop a phenomenological pedagogy (van Manen, 1993; van Manen, 1982).

Despite all of this work, it is still not easy to define what phenomenology is. In an admittedly brief attempt to do so, I will begin by providing an introduction to phenomenology as a philosophy, first exploring the work of Edmund Husserl and the phenomenological methodology that he developed to make philosophy a rigorous science. I will then present a reading of the preface to Merleau-Ponty's (2002) *Phenomenology of Perception*, which begins with the question, What is phenomenology? In presenting Merleau-Ponty's ideas, I hope to show that the development of phenomenology has been a continuous process, encompassing Husserl and subsequent philosophers such as Merleau-Ponty.

Husserl's methodology

In *The Theory and Practice of Husserl's Phenomenology*, Reeder (2010) offers the following definition:

> Phenomenology is a philosophical movement based upon a self-critical methodology for reflectively (reflexively or introspectively) examining and describing the lived evidence (the phenomena) which provides a crucial link in our philosophical and scientific understanding of the world.
>
> (p. 21)

Simply stated, Husserl provided a new methodology for philosophy, which he believed would serve to ground all sciences. The object of his phenomenological studies was intended to be the lived evidence of experience. In other words, his project was to look at phenomena, i.e. the things that we have experiential access to. The point was not to examine a concrete experience *per se*, but rather to address the general and objective structures of that experience. Therefore, if you are concerned with the phenomenology of learning in physical education, you would not engage in an examination of my or your experience of that phenomenon. Rather you would try to investigate the general structure of what learning is like in physical education. Even if you began by examining your own experience, your purpose in using phenomenology would be to develop a general and objective description.

The methodology that Husserl developed and practised has three phases: retention, bracketing and eidetic reduction. *Retention* means to hold in presence a specific 'moment of a living trace (Husserl talks of sedimentation) of the moment just passed' (Reeder, 2010, p. 28). Phenomenological investigation is thus an examination of what is present in retentional experience. At this moment, you attend to your own experience. But, since phenomenology is expressly not about individual, subjective experience (it seeks to identify universal structures of a given experience), Husserl insisted on the adoption of the phenomenological attitude through *bracketing*. Reeder (2010) describes this as a metaphysically neutral attitude, in the sense that one does not assume anything about what caused the experience or what the experience in turn causes, but rather lets the experience simply appear in order to be described.

The final phase of Husserl's methodology involves a process called free variation in fantasy, which seeks to achieve *eidetic reduction*. This involves altering the structures of the experience of X to discern which of them are essential to experiencing precisely X. Take, for example, the experience of drinking a cup of tea or coffee[3] (see Reeder, 2010, pp. 75–77). One feature of that experience is the cup's colour (mine, for example, is green). The process of free imaginative variation is then to vary that feature of the experience to find out whether colour is an essential or contingent feature. I have no problem imagining that my cup is white, pink or any other colour. I would therefore conclude that colour is an essential feature of a cup, but the specific colour is only a contingent feature. However, I would also conclude that an invisible cup would not be possible. I might be able to imagine the existence of one, but I recognize that as a fantasy and not what we normally would expect. I could go on to examine other experiential features of the cup in a similar way, and through an arduous process, eventually identify the eidetic features of experiencing a cup.

Any attempt to describe Husserl's methodology for phenomenology in a few paragraphs is of course incomplete,[4] but I hope this introduction makes it clear that phenomenology was developed as an attempt to create a methodology for describing the structures of subjective experiences that would reveal the 'objective within the subjective' (Reeder, 2010, p. 82). Put simply, phenomenology attempts to provide an account of subjective experience, rather than a subjective account of experience (Gallagher and Zahavi, 2008).

Merleau-Ponty: what is phenomenology?

One of the most prominent philosophers who built on Husserl's foundation was Maurice Merleau-Ponty (1908–1961). In the preface to his principal work, *Phenomenology of Perception* (2002),[5] first published in 1945, Merleau-Ponty began by asking what phenomenology is, observing that 'It may seem strange that this question has still to be asked half a century after the first works of Husserl. The fact remains that it has by no means been answered' (p. vii). This preface, which is regarded as a good introduction to what phenomenology is (Zahavi, 2003b), presents its central themes, as Merleau-Ponty understood them. He identified five: phenomenology's relation to science, the phenomenological reduction, essences, intentionality, and the relation between subjectivism and objectivism.

Merleau-Ponty asserts that an important feature of phenomenology is that it represents a critique of the starting point of science.[6] Husserl began his academic career as a mathematician concerned with logic, but evolved into a critic of the psychologism of his time. The idea that logical laws are basically empirical laws of consciousness was one of his central preoccupations at the beginning of his career. Contra psychologism, he argued that even if the mind perceives a phenomenon, it does not necessarily follow that this phenomenon is purely mental. The phenomenological point of view is that a third-person science, such as the psychology in vogue at that time, cannot be seen as the foundation of all human knowledge. Following Husserl, Merleau-Ponty argues that this position fails to account adequately for subjectivity:

> The whole universe of science is built upon the world as directly experienced, and if we want to subject science itself to rigorous scrutiny and arrive at a precise assessment of its meaning and scope, we must begin by reawakening the basic experience of the world of which science is a second-order expression.
>
> (Merleau-Ponty, 2002, p. ix)

In this sense, phenomenology's critique of science is not so much a rejection of the possibility of science as it is a reminder about the conditions under which science is created: It is a human enterprise, in which human beings ask and answer questions.

One of the points where later phenomenologists, such as Merleau-Ponty, departed from Husserl (or at the very least the earlier Husserl texts) is on the question of phenomenological reduction. Merleau-Ponty believed that Husserl's transcendental idealism (Reeder, 2010) was too idealistic. A complete reduction, in which all our judgments about the world and our experiences are suspended, is impossible, according to Merleau-Ponty and other existential phenomenologists, because it would require that 'we were absolute mind' (Merleau-Ponty, 2002, p. xv). The existential perspective is that we can never become transparent to ourselves. For Merleau-Ponty, the phenomenological reduction involves putting aside our common sense and scientific understanding of the world; it can be described as *wonder* in the face of the world,[7] yet 'the most important lesson which the reduction teaches us is the impossibility of a complete reduction' (ibid.).

The existential dimension of phenomenology is also a theme in Merleau-Ponty's discussion of essences. He points out that a phenomenological investigation searching for the essences of an experience 'is not looking for what it is as an idea once it has been reduced to a theme of discourse; it is looking for what it is as a fact for us, before any thematization' (p. xvii). From this perspective, essences cannot be arrived at through a conceptual analysis (for instance, a conceptual analysis of what learning or education is). Rather, Merleau-Ponty argues that phenomenology puts essences back into existence. Perhaps more surprisingly, he goes on to claim that 'the eidetic method is the method of a phenomenological positivism' (p. xix). Both logical positivism and the positivism of psychology at that time were the targets of the phenomenological critiques. Merleau-Ponty's point is that positivism, which originally was aimed at grounding scientific studies in what is observable, is a fitting description for the phenomenological project. Indeed, Husserl himself remarked that we (i.e. phenomenologists) are the true positivists.

Another key topic in Merleau-Ponty's introduction is intentionality. Intentionality describes the directedness of consciousness, i.e. that all consciousness is consciousness of something. Reeder (2010) explains that intentionality is constituted by an ego-pole and an object-pole: My consciousness is always directed at objects. According to Merleau-Ponty (2002), the contribution of phenomenology is not the discovery of intentionality. Rather, its contribution is to expand intentionality from being characterized solely as a judgment, 'when we voluntarily take up a position' (p. xx). The contribution of Husserl was to ground intentionality at a more primordial level which he referred to as operative intentionality, 'which produces the natural and antepredicative unity of the world and of our life ... furnishing the text which our knowledge tries to translate into precise language' (ibid.). It is this embodied form of intentionality that Merleau-Ponty developed further in the *Phenomenology of Perception*, and which I will explore further in the next chapter.

In concluding his introduction, Merleau-Ponty claims that 'the chief gain from phenomenology is to have united extreme subjectivism and extreme objectivism' (p. xxii). The whole idea of phenomenology was to turn to experience in order to avoid the extremes of objectivism that Husserl and his immediate followers saw as a crisis plaguing the science of their time. However, even if phenomenology is concerned with subjective experience, it cannot be characterized as subjectivism: it seeks to develop descriptions of experiences that can be inter-subjectively validated – that is, descriptions of experiences that others could plausibly have. It is a way of mediating between the viewpoints of science and common sense, not taking for granted anything that people have 'learned or otherwise believe they know' (p. xv).

Husserl initiated the phenomenological movement and inspired others who have developed their own concepts in phenomenology. Even though they have been critical of various aspects of Husserl's work, it is still considered foundational. One reason for this is that when later phenomenologists developed their own versions of Husserlian terms, their contributions are informed by his work. The following section surveys phenomenological literature concerning physical education.

Phenomenology in physical education literature

The collection of essays published as *Sport and the Body: A Philosophical Symposium* (Gerber, 1972) can be considered an early expression of the growing interest in philosophical studies of sport and physical education. This book includes several essays of philosophers working in the phenomenological tradition, including 'The Body' by Sartre and 'The Lived Body as Phenomenological Datum' by Schrag. However, as the book's title suggests, its overall emphasis is more on sports than on physical education.

One of the first scholars to apply phenomenology to physical education extensively was P. J. Arnold. This is particularly evident in his book *Meaning in Movement, Sport and Physical Education* (Arnold, 1979), in which he highlights the crucial role that embodiment plays in human movement:

> [Embodiment] is the *sine qua non* of my existence and therefore of my consciousness. Secondly, it is my mode of experiencing the world, and therefore a prerequisite for discovering who I am. Embodiment allows me both to recognize my existence and at the same time permits me to explore my essence.
>
> (Arnold, 1979, p. 1)

Drawing on phenomenologists such as Marcel, Sartre, Merleau-Ponty and Zaner, Arnold (1979) argues that the phenomenological understanding of the constitution of the lived body could be relevant to the study of human movement. In developing the notion of 'actional movement', he also discusses how human movement is meaningful as lived experience. He distinguishes actional movements, which are conscious, voluntary and intentional, from reflexes or other non-voluntary movements, and suggests that they operate on three levels: the primordial, in which habits and skills are experienced as peculiarly *mine*; the contextual, in which meaning is generated from a broader movement situation, such as a given game; and the existential, which is perhaps more inspired by existentialism than phenomenology in the sense that moving and participating in sports can become expressions and fulfilments of personal choices.

Arnold's work was widely criticized in Britain, where it first appeared. As I will discuss at greater length in the next chapter, David Best (1978) asserted that Arnold's attempt to justify the inclusion of physical education in the school curriculum did not make a strong case for its educational value. Indeed, it seems that Arnold's work has fallen into disrepute in the British context, to the extent that scholars with a phenomenological perspective on human movement hardly refer to him. Even so, Arnold's (1979) work has recently enjoyed something of a revival in physical education literature (Brown and Penney, 2013; Brown, 2013); in particular, his focus on the meaning-making potential of movement.

Regardless of how Arnold's work is judged in contemporary scholarship, it is clear that the application of phenomenology to physical education is not new. Indeed, in an entry in the *Encyclopedia of Phenomenology*, Maureen Connolly (1997) argued that the change in terminology from 'physical training' to 'physical education' could in part be attributed to 'the influence of a non-dualistic approach to movement, gesture and expression' (p. 535). According to Connolly, this transition paralleled the development of the phenomenological movement. That is, even before scholars engaged in the philosophy of physical education came to think of their work as phenomenological, affinities with the ways in which phenomenology as a philosophical discipline looked at movement and the body had begun to emerge.[8] At the time, Connolly observes, this phenomenological orientation in physical education was more implicit than explicit, and had not really been actualized at the time her article appeared.

Connolly (1997) also made a distinction between three loose categories of phenomenological work in physical education: *phenomenology as a theoretical framework* for philosophical analysis of physical education; *phenomenological methods* used for researching topics in physical education; and *applied phenomenology*, which is the application of phenomenology in the practice of teaching physical education. An example of the latter category is that zeroing-in on 'eidetic features of a particular type of movement experience can make it clearer how to modify an activity so that persons with various capacities can all participate' (Connolly, 1997, p. 536). Connolly's own work on developing a movement curriculum for people with autism (2008) serves as an example in this regard.

Prior to writing this encyclopedia entry, Connolly (1995) had elaborated on the relationship between phenomenology and physical education. More specifically, she highlighted three sensitizing concepts – lived experience, intersubjectivity and insiders' stories – to develop the common ground shared between the philosophical tradition and the school subject. Drawing on the work of Maurice Merleau-Ponty and Max van Manen, she showed how the life-world existential elements of body, space, time and relations could be applied to teaching situations in physical education. The work of Connolly (Connolly, 1995; Connolly and Craig, 2002; Connolly, 1997; Connolly, 2008) is an important source of inspiration for the present work. In particular, I am inspired by the way in which she establishes a relationship between phenomenological philosophy, applied phenomenology and issues of teaching and learning.

Recent work on phenomenology and physical education

Thorburn (2008; 2007) has sought to develop a Merleau-Pontian phenomenology of physical education. Based on a study of high-stakes school exams in physical education, and their conceptual relationship to curricular issues (that is, the relationship between how the educational value of physical education is articulated, how the curriculum is structured and how pupils are tested). He argued that the 'problems [of bringing about rich practical learning environments and high levels of authentic attainment in high-stakes tests] are often exacerbated by trying to resolve conceptual coherence concerns through a narrow adherence to the structures of mind-body dualism' (2007, p. 181). Thus, Thorburn faulted physical education curricula that emphasize academic, theoretical knowledge about the body as an object (e.g. bio-mechanics, physiology) and overlook the practical, embodied character of knowledge on this subject.

In a subsequent work, Thorburn outlined a Merleau-Pontian phenomenological approach that integrates pupils' lived experiences of subject knowledge into high-stakes physical education examination awards (Thorburn 2008). He finds the work of Merleau-Ponty relevant due to its emphasis on the role of the body in perception and movement, and pays particular attention to two concepts, intentional arc and maximum grip (see the next chapter for an explanation of these terms). Drawing on the work of Hubert Dreyfus, an influential interpreter of Merleau-Ponty, Thorburn explores how phenomenology can serve as a foundation for understanding how experiential learning can 'resolve pragmatic difficulties about how the essence of personal experience can be captured within the assessment systems' (p. 267).

Thorburn (2008; 2007) takes up two issues also found elsewhere in the literature on phenomenology and physical education; the importance of embodied, practical knowledge and the possibilities for meaning-making in physical education. Although Arnold (1979; 1991) was also interested in phenomenology's contribution to an understanding of practical knowledge, it is mainly the meaning-making aspect of movement that has been explored in physical education literature.

Brown and Payne (2009) surveyed physical education literature concerning phenomenology of movement, and argued, like Tinning (2010), that phenomenological pedagogy to some degree is marginalized, noting that, 'despite 40 years of important but sporadic contributions to the literature … phenomenology of movement remains in a nascent stage of development' (p. 436). Their survey revealed four broad, to some extent interrelated themes: challenging assumptions about knowledge production; the importance of attending to the nature of the experiencer; shifts in locus and focus of inquiry and pedagogy; and examining the congruence 'between research approaches, aims, problems, design, and methodology' (p. 430).

One important contribution that phenomenology has made to physical education, according to Brown and Payne (2009), is to challenge assumptions of mind–body dualism. Such dualism is expressed, for instance, in an overemphasis on propositional, theoretical knowledge or a disembodied focus on movement as sheer physiology or bio-mechanics. This relates to their second point, which essentially highlights the positive contribution of phenomenology: If mind–body dualism is overcome by highlighting the importance of the lived body, they assert, then as a consequence one will discover the 'perceptual, sensory, kinaesthetic, and relational dimensions' of movement as experienced by the mover (p. 433). Indeed, they argue, such a perspective would shift the locus and focus of research in physical education towards meaning-making.

However, when it comes to the congruence of related research approaches, Brown and Payne refer to a problem raised by Kerry and Armour (2000), namely, that using the concepts of 'qualitative research' and 'phenomenological research' interchangeably is misleading, in the sense that the former is sometimes used to characterize research that does not share the ontological and epistemological assumptions of phenomenology.

A special 2013 issue of *Educational Theory and Philosophy* devoted to re-conceptualizing physical education contains a number of interesting articles relevant to philosophy of physical education. In Stolz's (2013) contribution on phenomenology and physical education, he argues that the lived body is central to physical education, observing that 'what makes phenomenology educationally desirable in this case is its capacity to take an explicit body-linked subject such as physical education and describe *how our embodiment has a significant role to play in student learning*' (p. 952, italics added). To make his case, he draws on the work of Maureen Connolly and Margaret Whitehead on physical literacy (see below) and of Hughson and Inglis (2002) on the phenomenology of soccer performance. In addition, Stolz (2013) applies the phenomenological approach of Merleau-Ponty to show that movement experiences are essential to becoming aware of spatial forms of activities (exemplified by a tennis swing) and, in turn, to develop skills in these activities. In addition, Stolz, like Brown and Payne (2009), asserts that meaning-making is an essential feature of physical education: without attending to the lived experiences of pupils, he argues, physical education inevitably falls short of its meaning-making potential.

Several of the articles cited above observe that insights derived from phenomenology have the potential to suggest and inform research into physical education. This position is consistent with other sport sciences literature that celebrates phenomenology's potential to increase our understanding of meaning-making and movement experiences, such as the work mentioned earlier by Kerry and Armour (2000) as well as contributions by Jacquelyn Allen-Collinson (Allen-Collinson, 2009; Hockey and Allen-Collinson, 2007). All of the studies on physical education reviewed here:

1. Its meaning-making aspect, i.e. due to the 'bodily nature' of physical education, phenomenological philosophy, with its emphasis on bodily experiences, is useful in conceptualizing and developing a theoretical framework for it;
2. Due to the practical nature of knowledge in physical education, phenomenology's commitment to an ontology that rejects body–mind dualism can be a particularly fruitful approach to examining it;
3. Justification, which is related to the other two themes. If education is conceived narrowly as a process of informing the rational mind, the focus will be on propositional and theoretical knowledge, and (potentially) exclude physical education. Drawing on the work of earlier phenomenologists, these authors highlight the educational value of meaning-making, bodily experiences and practical knowledge.

Physical literacy

One physical education researcher who has worked extensively within the phenomenological tradition is Margaret Whitehead. Since the mid-1980s, she has been developing the concept of physical literacy[9] (Whitehead, 2001; 2007; 2010). Like much of the other physical education literature inspired by phenomenology, her work is grounded in a dissatisfaction with what she has considered to be the dominant, dualist tendencies not only in the school subject, but in physical and movement activities more generally:

> Development of the debate regarding physical literacy was stimulated by the study of existentialist and phenomenological writers such as Sartre and Merleau-Ponty, who articulate a particular stance towards the nature of our human condition … [they] spell out a commitment *inter alia* to a monist or holistic view of the human condition, the centrality of our embodiment in existence and our nature as essentially beings-in-the world.
>
> (Whitehead, 2007, p. 283)

In addition to drawing on more traditional phenomenological literature, in her more recent work Whitehead has cited current neuro-scientific literature to support her argument that our embodied existence is fundamental and primordial (Whitehead, 2007).

The definition of physical literacy has developed and expanded over the years. In an edited collection on this concept and its application in different contexts, Whitehead defines it this way: 'as appropriate to each individual's endowment, physical literacy can be described as the motivation, confidence, physical competence, knowledge and understanding to maintain physical activity throughout the lifecourse' (2010, pp. 11–12). This definition is further delineated with respect to certain attributes that a physically literate person exhibits[10]:

(A) A disposition or motivation to capitalize on one's movement potential;
(B) Will move with *poise, economy and confidence* in different movement settings;
(C) Will be perceptive in reading all aspects of the environment and respond to possibilities for movement;
(D) Have an established sense of oneself as embodied being;
(E) 'Fluent self-expression through non-verbal communication' (p. 13), as well as empathic interaction with others;
(F) Have an understanding of the qualities of their movement performance as well as 'the principles of embodied health with respect to basic aspects such as exercise, sleep and nutrition' (p. 14).

Just as the traditional notion of literacy can be extended well beyond knowledge of grammar, reading and writing (i.e. functional literacy) to include an understanding of various genres and the abilities for self-expression, Whitehead's concept of physical literacy goes beyond a narrow focus on fundamental movement skills (for instance expressed in movement ABC) to include the dimensions of human movement expressed in points A to F. Physical literacy highlights the importance of developing one's capacities for movement in a variety of contexts (points A to C above). This is not so much about developing and mastering specific sets of skills, as it is about realizing the potential of each of us to express ourselves in and through movement – a point which is underscored by the significance Whitehead attaches to 'individuals' endowment' (p. 12). In that sense, physical literacy is not an absolute term with a universal end goal expressed, for instance, through descriptions of specific skills and skill levels. Rather, as I understand her, physical literacy is an ipsative term that must be seen in relation to the unique potential of each individual. Moreover, physical literacy is concerned with one's embodied sense of self, how one can express oneself in and through movement and how one can enter into empathic relationships with other movers (points D and E). Finally, it follows from point F that being physically literate also means that an individual understands principles of how movement performance can be enhanced, as well as 'the impact of activity on all-round health and well-being' (p.14).

The latter point is potentially problematic given the phenomenological underpinning of physical literacy. The strong focus in physical education on engaging in physical activity to promote health has been criticized for promoting a dualistic view of the body (e.g. Tinning, 2010). Whitehead (2007) herself has conceded that the kind of knowledge involved in this aspect of physical literacy 'moves towards dualism' (p. 292). However, she goes on to observe that ignoring these aspects of our embodied existence would be 'out of the question' (p. 294), and argue that incorporating both aspects is essential to create a robust concept of physical literacy.

Critical comments

Before closing this chapter, I want to raise two major criticisms of the literature on phenomenology and physical education. First, that some of this literature is based on a misinterpretation of phenomenology. Second, that Whitehead's concept of physical literacy suffers not only from this shortcoming, but has expanded to the point that it has lost clarity, particularly when applied to physical education.

The point that some of the literature on phenomenology and physical education has suffered from a misreading of its basic philosophical texts, has already been made by Irena Martinkova and Jim Parry (2011). One example they point to is the confusion of *intentionality* in the phenomenological sense and *intention* in the sense of purposiveness, such as in the term intentional movement. This mistake is found in both Brown and Payne (2009) and Thorburn (2008). Martinkova and Parry argue that this confusion represents a failure to differentiate between the ontological and the ontic: intentionality in the phenomenological sense means that consciousness is always directed at objects (i.e. that consciousness is transitive). This is one of its universal and ontological features. Thus a phenomenological exploration of intentional movements would be concerned with their eidetic structures, which is quite different from the various and particular intentions of the mover.[11] The point here is that a minimum requirement for utilizing phenomenology in the context of physical education must be that the work interprets its basic concepts accurately.

A second problem pointed out by Martinkova and Parry (2011) is an over-reliance on secondary sources, rather than expositions of original works by phenomenologists. Their analysis of two prominent texts on the potential value of phenomenology for the study of sport (Kerry and Armour, 2000, and Hockey and Allen-Collinson, 2007) shows that at times even the secondary literature cited is not sufficiently informed by philosophy. Their conclusion is harsh:

> it is useless to provide a sketchy introductory account of Husserl, Heidegger or Merleau-Ponty (especially when there is no direct textual reference to their work, or with reference only to commentaries) … Such accounts amount to mere ritual genuflections in the direction of authorities.
>
> (Martinkova and Parry, 2011, p. 195)

Both of the problems raised by Martinkova and Parry indicate that future work on phenomenology and physical education must have a stronger philosophical and conceptual foundation. This was also pointed out by Connolly (1997), who came to a similar conclusion.

The importance of this point can also be illustrated by examining Whitehead's development of the term physical literacy. As the quote from Whitehead (2007) above states, she claims that phenomenology has a 'monist' view of the human condition, which she contrasts to the dualism she identifies in traditional approaches to movement and physical education. Roughly, monism is a metaphysical claim that existence can be explained with reference to one substance, as opposed to the two-substance explanation of dualism. However, it isn't accurate to assert that all phenomenologists have been monists. Merleau-Ponty, for instance, explicitly denied that he was a monist, stating that the ontology he had developed was 'beyond monism and dualism' (Merleau-Ponty, 1968, p. 54).

The point here is not so much whether Whitehead is mistaken about the metaphysical claims of phenomenology, but rather that her work opens the door to rejection of phenomenological approaches to understanding human movement in general. For example, in an otherwise excellent article on how human movement can be understood from a post-structuralist perspective, Larsson and Quennerstedt (2012) argue that, 'the major problem with Whitehead's theorizing, from the poststructuralist point of view, *as is the case with phenomenologist approaches generally speaking*, is the preference for a monist approach to movement as an alternative to the dualist approach' (p. 293, italics added). Even if their critical comments about physical literacy are valuable and plausible (see below), their rejection of all phenomenological approaches to physical education and movement in general is unfounded.

Larsson and Quennerstedt go on to state that they 'are, instead, searching for an epistemological position that is neither dualist nor monist, but, rather, *pluralist*, and where human movement can be understood on the basis of the concrete social situation in which humans are moving, where any movement is performed by / performs some*body*' (p. 294, italics in original). I will argue that there is little reason to think that phenomenology does not open up the possibility of an epistemological understanding in which movement is always movement by somebody (see Standal and Engelsrud, 2013). It should also be noted that Larsson and Quennerstedt (2012) are not entirely consistent in their critique of phenomenology, since they also cite with approval Young's work, 'Throwing Like a Girl' (1998), which, contrary to what they seem to believe, is an example of phenomenology's potential to illuminate how human movement is always movement for somebody and cannot be divorced from the social situation in which it takes place.

Other salient criticisms can be levelled against the concept of physical literacy and how it has developed. One is the problematic connotations of the word 'physical'. As scholars have argued in the case of physical education (Arnold, 1979) and, more recently, physical literacy (Kentel and Dobson, 2007), inclusion of the word physical may suggest the dualism that the concept of physical literacy was intended to overcome. Kentel and Dobson (2007) propose *movement* literacy as a more appropriate term. This critique, however, might be seen as more semantic than substantive. Given the amount of space devoted by Whitehead to elaborate on the phenomenological foundation of physical literacy, it is a bit disingenuous to suggest that her use of the term physical literacy implies a dualistic approach.

Two other issues are, as far as I can see, much more pressing than the term applied to the concept. The first, which has also been raised by Larsson and Quennerstedt (2012), concerns the normativity that seems to underlie the concept of physical literacy. As they put it, if physical literacy is something that 'a person achieves and does not have from the beginning; the question can then be posed: literate/illiterate in relation to what?' (p. 294). It should be clear from Whitehead's work that physical literacy is not a congenital disposition or ability – it is something that is developed and learned. Therefore, the question, 'literate in relation to what?' must be answered. Whitehead's response is that physical literacy is not to be judged based on a universal standard. As noted above, she sees it in relationship to the endowment of each individual. However, a focus on endowment can create new problems. As I will discuss in a later chapter, we need to problematize ideas of 'endowment' or 'ability' that understand them primarily as characteristics of an individual. An illustration of the difficulties this perspective creates can be found in one of the chapters in the anthology on physical literacy, where Gately (2010) asserts that 'overweight and obese children would be considered to have lower levels of physical literacy … compared to their normal weight peers' (p. 98). First, assessing levels of physical literacy is in itself problematic; it is based on the premise that physical literacy is an ability (or set of abilities) that can be measured against a population norm that expresses how much physical literacy each individual is expected to have. Second, it is difficult to reconcile a focus on each individual's endowment and movement potential with the assertion that obese children by default have low levels of physical literacy.

The second critical point I want to highlight is that the definition of physical literacy has expanded greatly in the decade between 2001 and 2010 (see Whitehead, 2001; 2010). Her definition in the 2001 paper concerned only what became points B and C in the 2010 elaboration, i.e. to move with poise, economy and efficiency in a variety of challenging situations and to be perceptive in reading the movement environment.[12] This expansion may be a sign that the term lacks precision. How useful is a concept if its 'defining' characteristics are continually expanding? A related criticism is that some of these additional characteristics attributed to a physically literate person have more to do with public health concerns than with the development of what one normally thinks about in relation to moving with poise, economy and efficiency. For example, Whitehead now includes 'knowledge to maintain physical activity at an individually appropriate level throughout life' (Whitehead, 2007, p. 287). She also puts emphasis on sleep and nutrition as part of physical literacy. It could be objected that including this kind of knowledge at least to some extent blurs the focus on the lived, experiencing body. In addition, including health discourse in the context of physical education has been criticized for objectifying and disembodying pupils (see, e.g. Tinning, 2010) and, as the obesity example cited above shows, this focus on public health can undermine the very laudable approach of understanding physical literacy in relation to individual endowment, as opposed to a population norm.

A rebuttal to this critique could be that strengthening the case for the vital importance of physical literacy requires recognizing that physical activity is considered an appropriate tool for public health. One could also argue that even if this perspective is, in a sense, a form of objectification, the experience of being objectified is a lived, embodied experience (see Chapter 7). From this perspective, the notion of embodied health (Whitehead, 2010) can be seen as a productive engagement with the public health discourse, which would make sense if Whitehead's ultimate goal is to establish an integrated theoretical justification for physical education (see Loland, 2006).

Even if this is true, I think it is reasonable to argue that in expanding her definition of physical literacy, Whitehead is drawing on ideas and ways of thinking that do not comport with a phenomenological approach. From this perspective, I would argue that in the context of school physical education, her narrower 2001 definition of physical literacy is more useful. My reasoning is related to Kirk's (2010) discussions of alternatives to the multi-activity, physical-education-as-sport techniques that he asserts are standard practice in physical education. Kirk's alternative is a models-based physical education approach, in which different models such as sports education and health-based physical education are used to create a programme that pupils would consider both coherent and relevant. Kirk (2013) argues that physical literacy can be one such model, but that at present, it remains 'a philosophy in search of a pedagogical model' (p. 979). Serving as a useful theoretical framework would not require that physical literacy incorporate all forms of justification arguments. Rather, it might be more useful if its advocates focused on its strengths and left health issues to other physical education frameworks. Not only that, physical literacy might be a more influential concept if it were developed in depth rather than in breadth.

By going back to the phenomenological basis of physical literacy, this book attempts to provide both a strengthened philosophical foundation for this concept and guidance toward developing a pedagogical model based on it. I will, however, use the term 'movement literacy' rather than physical literacy to avoid potential misunderstandings related to the dualism use of the word physical might generate, and, more importantly, to distinguish my conceptual framework from Whitehead's more recent iterations of her concept of physical literacy. At the same time, my debt to her path-breaking work should be clear, beginning with her original definition of physical literacy:

> The individual moves with poise, economy and confidence in a wide variety of physically challenging situations. Furthermore the individual is perceptive in 'reading' all aspects of the physical environment, anticipating movement needs or possibilities and responding appropriately to these, with intelligence and imagination.
>
> (Whitehead, 2001, p. 131)

Notes

1 Philosophy is also sometimes used to mean some sort of personal orientation in life, but this is of course very different from the academic study of philosophy.

2 I must point out, however, that phenomenology does not find its expression in definitions, but rather in how it is applied in practice (Reeder, 2010).

3 There are lots of examples of drinking from cups in the phenomenological literature, perhaps because the coffee cup is very ready to hand for armchair philosophers. Husserl is supposed to have said, 'give me a cup of coffee and I shall make phenomenology out of it' (Moran, 2005).

4 In addition to Reeder (2010), Zahavi (2003a) and Moran (2005) are widely recognized as providing valuable introductions to the work of Husserl.

5 I use the 2002 edition of *Phenomenology of Perception*. A new English language translation of the book was published 2013, and for Merleau-Ponty aficionados there might be some nuances in the language. For the purpose of this book, these details shouldn't worry us.

6 Here, one should remember that 'science' at that time meant natural science.

7 Merleau-Ponty attributes this expression of wonder in the face of the world to Eugen Fink, one of Husserl's assistants.
8 According to Merleau-Ponty (2002), phenomenology can be thought of as a 'style of thinking, that existed as a movement before arriving at complete awareness of itself as a philosophy' (p. viii).
9 The term was not coined by Whitehead, who credits it to Ruth Morrison.
10 The same attributes also appear in Whitehead (2007), albeit in a slightly different order.
11 It is important to note here that we are talking about phenomenological in a philosophical sense. Conceivably, one could study student experiences of intentional, purposive movements using phenomenological research methods. Martinkova and Parry (2011) would be critical of the use of the term phenomenological to characterize empirical, qualitative research. In addition, the object of study is then not intentionality in the philosophical sense, but the experience that (some) students have when they engage in activities involving purposive movement.
12 More specifically: 'moves with poise, economy and confidence in a wide variety of physically challenging situations. Furthermore the individual is perceptive in 'reading' all aspects of the physical environment, anticipating movement needs or possibilities and responding appropriately to these, with intelligence and imagination' (Whitehead, 2001, p. 131).

References

Ahmed, S. (2006). *Queer phenomenology: Orientations, objects, others.* London: Duke University Press.

Allen-Collinson, J. (2009). Sporting embodiment: sport studies and the (continuing) promise of phenomenology. *Qualitative Research in Sport and Exercise*, 1(3), 279–296.

Arnold, P. J. (1979). *Meaning in movement, sport and physical education.* London: Heinemann.

Arnold, P. J. (1991). The preeminece of skill as an educational value in the movement curriculum. *Quest*, 43, 66–77.

Best, D. (1978). *Philosophy and human movement.* London: Allen & Unwin.

Brown, T. D. (2013). A vision lost? (Re)articulating an Arnoldian conception of education 'in' movement in physical education. *Sport, Education and Society*, 18(1), 21–37.

Brown, T. D. and Payne, P. G. (2009). Conceptualizing the phenomenology of movement in physical education: implications for pedagogical inquiry and development. *Quest*, 61, 418–441.

Brown, T. and Penney, D. (2013). Learning 'through' and' about' movement in senior physical education? The new Victorian Certificate of Education Physical Education. *European Physical Education Review*, 19(1), 39–61.

Connolly, M. (1995). Phenomenology, physical education, and special populations. *Human Studies*, 18, 25–40.

Connolly, M. (1997). Physical education. In L. Embree (ed.), *Encyclopedia of phenomenology* (pp. 535–537). Dordrecht, The Netherlands: Kluwer.

Connolly, M. (2008). The remarkable logic of autism: developing and describing an embedded curriculum based in semiotic phenomenology. *Sport, Ethics and Philosophy*, 2(2), 234–256.

Connolly, M. and Craig, T. (2002). Stressed embodiment: doing phenomenology in the wild. *Human Studies*, 25, 451–462.

Finlay, L. (2009). Debating phenomenological research methods. *Phenomenology and Practice*, 3(1), 6–25.

Gallagher, S. and Zahavi, D. (2008). *The phenomenological mind. An introduction to philosophy of mind and cognitive science.* London: Routledge.

Gately, P. (2010). Physical literacy and obesity. In M. Whitehead (ed.), *Physical literacy: Throughout the lifecourse* (pp. 83–99). London: Routledge.

Gerber, E. W. (1972). *Sport and the body: A philosophical symposium.* Philadelphia, PA: Lea & Febiger.

Giorgi, A. (1984). *Phenomenology and psychological research.* Pittsburgh, PA: Duquesne University Press.

Hockey, J. and Allen-Collinson, J. (2007). Grasping the phenomenology of sporting bodies. *International Review for the Sociology of Sport*, 42(2), 115–131.

Hughson, J. and Inglis, D. (2002). Inside the beatiful game: towards a Merleau-Pontian phenomenology of soccer play. *Journal of the Philosophy of Sport*, 14, 1–15.

Kentel, J. A. and Dobson, T. M. (2007). Beyond myopic visions of education: revisiting movement literacy. *Physical Education and Sport Pedagogy*, 12(2), 145–162.

Kerry, D. S. and Armour, K. M. (2000). Sport sciences and the promise of phenomenology: philosophy, method, and insight. *Quest*, 52, 1–17.

Kirk, D. (2010). *Physical education futures.* London: Routledge.

Kirk, D. (2013). Educational value and models-based practice in physical education. *Educational Philosophy and Theory*, 45(9), 973–986.

Larsson, H. and Quennerstedt, M. (2012). Understanding movement: a sociocultural approach to exploring moving humans. *Quest*, 64(4), 283–298.

Loland, S. (2006). Morality, medicine, and meaning: toward an integrated justification of physical education. *Quest*, 58(1), 60–70.

Luft, S. and Overgaard, S. (2012). Introduction. In S. Luft and S. Overgaard (eds), *Routledge companion to phenomenology* (pp. 1–14). Abingdon: Routledge.

Martinkova, I. and Parry, J. (2011). An introduction to the phenomenological study of sport. *Sport, Ethics and Philosophy*, 5(3), 185–201.

McNamee, M. (2005). The nature and values of physical education. In K. Green and K. Hardman (eds), *Physical education: Essential issues* (pp. 1–20). London: Sage.

Merleau-Ponty, M. (1968). *The visible and the invisible.* Evanston, IL: Northwestern University Press.

Merleau-Ponty, M. (2002). *Phenomenology of perception.* London: Routledge.

Moran, D. (2005). *Husserl: Founder of phenomenology.* Cambridge: Polity.

Reeder, H. P. (2010). *The theory and practice of Husserl's phenomenology.* Bucharest, Romania: Zeta Books.

Standal, Ø. F. and Engelsrud, G. (2013). Researching embodiment in movement contexts: a phenomenological approach. *Sport, Education and Society*, 18(2), 154–166.

Stolz, S. A. (2013). Phenomenology and physical education. *Educational Philosophy and Theory*, 45(9), 949–962.

Thorburn, M. (2007). Achieving conceptual and curriculum coherence in high-stakes school examinations in physical education. *Physical Education and Sport Pedagogy*, 12(2), 163–184.

Thorburn, M. (2008). Articulating a Merleau-Pontian phenomenology of physical education: the quest for active student engagement and authentic assessment in high-stakes examination awards. *European Physical Education Review*, 14(2), 263–280.

Tinning, R. (2010). *Pedagogy and human movement: Theory, practice, research.* London: Routledge.

van Manen, M. (1982). Phenomenological pedagogy. *Curriculum Inquiry*, 12(3), 283–299.
van Manen, M. (1990). *Researching lived experience: Human science for an action sensitive pedagogy.* Ontario, Canada: SUNY Press.
van Manen, M. (1993). *Pedagogisk takt* [*The tact of teaching. The meaning of pedagogical thoughtfulness*]. Bergen, Norway: Caspar Forlag.
Whitehead, M. (2001). The concept of physical literacy. *European Journal of Physical Education*, 6(2), 127–138.
Whitehead, M. (2007). Physical literacy: philosophical considerations in relation to developing a sense of self, universality and propositional knowledge. *Sport, Ethics and Philosophy*, 1(3), 281–298.
Whitehead, M. (2010). The concept of physical literacy. In M. Whitehead (ed.), *Physical literacy: Throughout the lifecourse* (pp. 10–20). London: Routledge.
Young, I. (1998). Throwing like a girl. In D. Welton (ed.), *Body and flesh: A philosophical reader* (pp. 259–273). Oxford: Blackwell.
Zahavi, D. (2003a). *Husserl's phenomenology.* Stanford, CA: Stanford University Press.
Zahavi, D. (2003b). *Fænomenologi.* Roskilde, Denmark: Roskilde Universitetsforlag.

3 Phenomenology and practical knowledge

In this chapter I will pursue the idea that phenomenology can be a useful resource for understanding practical knowledge in the field of physical education. I will proceed by examining the history of how practical knowledge has emerged as central to debates surrounding physical education, in particular when it comes to legitimizing its place in the school curriculum. Continuing from that, I will draw on Svenaeus' (2009) argument that phenomenology can be a theory for practical knowledge. An elaboration of Merleau-Ponty's phenomenological study of embodied learning will then be used to illustrate the relevance of phenomenology to the practical knowledge involved in movement.

Practical knowledge in physical education

Practical knowledge has been a theme of interest for philosophers of physical education for many years (e.g. Arnold, 1988; Carr, 1981; Parry, 1998; Reid, 1998; Stolz, 2014). One important reason for the interest in practical knowledge has been to provide arguments that can justify the value of physical education in school curricula. In particular, the work of the philosopher of education Richard Peters has had a profound influence on the thinking about the educational value of physical education and the knowledge claims that can be made on behalf of the subject.

According to the early work of Peters from the late 1960s, the subject matter of physical education did not have the necessary cognitive and theoretical content to be considered educationally valuable. Indeed, the claim was made that 'there is very little to know' about physical activity skills (Peters, 1970, p. 45, as quoted by MacAllister, 2013, p. 913). McNamee (2005) summarized Peters' thesis and its effect thus:

> education, properly conceived, referred to the initiation of the unlearned into those intrinsically worthwhile forms of knowledge that were constitutive of rational mind. Its shorthand was that education referred essentially to the development of rationality. Despite the hugely influential educational efforts of muscular Christianity, physical education enjoyed little more than a Cinderella existence, even in British education, throughout the

> twentieth century. And now, it was surely not to be invited to the ball. The hegemony of the great thesis cast physical education well and truly into the educational hinterland.
>
> (p. 2)

It should be mentioned that Peters developed a more positive position regarding the possibility of assigning educational merit to physical education in his later work (McNamee, 2005). Whereas Peters first dismissed physical education on the grounds that it had too little cognitive and theoretical importance to be of educational value, he later came to the conclusion that educational value could also be located in practical activities that 'are either transformed by theoretical understanding and/or contribute to the development of human excellence' (MacAllister, 2013, p. 914). As such, one could say that physical education was re-invited to the ball. However, even in quite recent discussions of the educational value of physical education, Peters' early liberal-analytical position on education is invoked and still interpreted as a foundation for potential threats to the legitimacy of physical education.

Peters' early thesis can be responded to in a variety of ways. One approach would be to admit its correctness and consequently give up the idea of physical *education*. The subject would then purely be a matter of physical training or exercise. Alternatively, one could change the content and methods of the subject to (if possible) meet the requirements of the thesis. Another option would be to argue that the thesis is wrong or that its definition of education is too restricted. The latter option is the avenue chosen by many of those who want to promote the value of physical education. In particular it has been the value of the practical nature of the knowledge involved in physical education that has been advanced.

One of the writers on physical education who has challenged Peters' thesis is P. J. Arnold (1979; 1988; 1991), who was introduced in the previous chapter. Arnold claimed that Peters' thesis was 'not only based upon dualistic assumptions, even if they are not always acknowledged, but has difficulty in seeing that the good life is made up of more than the pursuit of truth' (Arnold, 1979, p. 162). In other words, Arnold's critique was that Peters' thesis was too cognitive, in the sense that it over-emphasized the relative value of mental or intellectual activity. Thus, Peters' thesis could be characterized as dualistic in the sense of separating the mind from the body. Arnold's alternative was to draw on phenomenological philosophy in order to develop a more holistic understanding of both knowledge and people in physical education.

In particular, it is his tripartite distinction between education in, about and through movement that recently has attracted attention (Brown and Payne, 2009; Brown, 2013; Brown and Penney, 2013). Arnold argues that the *in* and *about* dimensions have intrinsic value, whereas education *through* movement – which is essentially the use of movement either to illustrate educational content in other subjects or to achieve external benefits such as health and fitness – has extrinsic value. The distinction between intrinsic and extrinsic value is important, because according to Arnold, it is the intrinsic values of physical education that give the subject its educational value.

To clarify the difference between the *in* and *about* dimensions, Arnold (1991) employed the distinction between knowledge and skill, where the former is associated with theoretical knowledge and the latter with practical knowledge. He argued that 'the prime responsibility of the teacher as educator is to get pupils on the inside of a selection of activities that they can explore and appreciate' (Arnold, 1991, p. 75). To get 'on the inside' implies getting a different perspective on the knowledge object than can be gained from a theoretical, spectator position. This participatory view of the moving agent was the perspective that Arnold had developed earlier with resources from phenomenological philosophy (Arnold, 1979). In addition, he linked the participatory perspective with practical knowledge and he claimed that practical knowledge (skills) 'must take precedence over theoretical knowledge' (Arnold, 1991, p. 75) as educational value in physical education.

Even though it is not clear if and how Arnold (1991) distinguished between skill and practical knowledge, the point here is that in an effort to legitimize the value of physical education, he emphasized practical knowledge of the subject matter. Others have made similar arguments (McNamee, 2005; Parry, 1998; Reid, 1998), but whereas Reid, McNamee and Parry all worked from a more analytical perspective, Arnold drew on phenomenology. Therefore (and despite the criticism Arnold has received, which I will return to below), Arnold's work is of interest. However, I see two problems with Arnold's account:

1 The relationship between practical knowledge and phenomenology is underdeveloped.
2 Arnold's explicit intention is to justify the value of physical education, but he runs the risk of going from one extreme (Peters' overly cognitive thesis) to another (extreme subjectivism).

The first point is that even though Arnold attempted to utilize phenomenology in developing arguments for the educational value of physical education, he left the relationship between practical knowledge and phenomenology under-explored in his writings. When Arnold employed phenomenology in the service of justifying physical education, it was the experiential, meaning-making aspects of physical education that he explored. This is also a contemporary approach to justifying physical education (see e.g. Brown and Payne, 2009; Loland, 2006; Stolz, 2014). However, as argued by Brown (2013), participation and engagement for the purpose of meaning-making alone is not sufficient for what Arnold called education 'in' movement. Developing practical knowledge is also an important aspect of education 'in' movement, but one which, according to Brown (2013), is an underdeveloped topic. Thus, I suggest that understanding the relationship between phenomenology and practical knowledge is a valuable direction for physical education pedagogy to take.

Second, Arnold's work received some heavy criticism. David Best (1978), for instance, was less than convinced by the arguments of Arnold and others who worked in the same line of research:

> It is ironic that such authors tend strenuously to deny that their work clearly reveals an underlying and incoherent preconception of a divided personality, or a dualist theory of mind, since it is this very conception to which they believe they are explicitly opposed in advancing their arguments in support of the value of physical education. Yet the irony is that the very formulation of their argument in those terms itself manifests precisely that misconception, since they inevitably have to presuppose separate entities or domains in order to argue that the supposedly desired 'wholeness' or 'integration' can be achieved ... It is precisely this synthesizing function to which Arnold appeals, supposing it to be the principal strength of his case.
>
> (p. 56)

In other words, Best is arguing that because Arnold's position is a negation of a specific conception of education (i.e. that of Peters), he tends to import the very assumptions he is critical of, thus ending up in an untenable position. This is a valid point, but Best's criticism of Arnold is also somewhat biased. In *Philosophy and Human Movement* it is evident that Best was – to put it diplomatically – sceptical towards phenomenology. He writes for instance of misconceptions 'encountered in discussions of the phenomenology of movement' (p. 81) and misapprehensions 'at the heart of phenomenological thought' (p. 93). It is well known that there has been, and to some degree continues to be, a hostile and crippling separation between analytical and phenomenological philosophy (Luft and Overgaard, 2012). Unfortunately, this long-standing disagreement could make any claim suggested by phenomenologists sound like an unintelligible misapprehension for the analytical philosopher Best (1978). However, Best might also be correct in his claim that the writers he criticized misconstrued phenomenological philosophy, thus making their case unintelligible. Clearly, one of Best's main points in *Philosophy of Human Movement* is that not everything which was labelled philosophy in the context of human movement studies deserved that label:

> there is a great deal of pretentious verbosity which passes for the 'philosophy' of sport, physical education and dance, and which has to be eradicated before a constructive genuinely philosophical enterprise can realize the potential of the discipline in this field of study.
>
> (p. 87)

Without having studied the original texts that Best criticizes, it seems clear that his scepticism is towards authors who employ phenomenology in opposition to the objectivism of so-called hard science (see for instance chapters 5 and 6 in *Philosophy of Human Movement*). This strategy clearly runs the risk of falling into the other extreme: subjectivism. However, settling the score between Best and his phenomenological opponents is beyond the scope of this book.

Perhaps due to Best's critique, Arnold's work has fallen into disrepute in British educational studies. Those who have sought to make claims for the educational value of physical education have based their work on analytical philosophy. Notwithstanding this, Arnold's work continues to wield influence in physical education literature, for instance in recent work in the Norwegian (Ommundsen, 2013) and Australian contexts (Brown and Penney, 2013; Brown, 2013). Be that as it may, one important lesson to take away from Best's critique is that when one argues against a specific thesis, one runs the risk of replacing that thesis with a new one which is only a negative version of the original – thus retaining the problems one originally sought to address. Instead of studying practical knowledge in physical education in its own right, it appears to have been studied mostly in order to justify the value of physical education in the school curriculum. Thus, I suggest that it can be beneficial to approach the question of practical knowledge in physical education without at the same time trying to justify the educational value of the subject.

The rest of this chapter will be devoted to pursuing the link between phenomenology and practical knowledge. First, I will provide some general arguments suggesting that phenomenology can be a theory for practical knowledge. Second, I provide an account of learning (of embodied skills) as laid out by Merleau-Ponty.

Phenomenology as a perspective on practical knowledge

How does practical knowledge look from a phenomenological perspective? Husserl and other philosophers following in his wake have argued that by examining the lifeworld through the first person perspective, we will detect meaning patterns which uphold the lifeworld. As presented in Chapter 2, it is the purpose of phenomenological reduction and phenomenological philosophy to uncover and elucidate these meaning patterns. However, in the normal course of events we live and deal with these meaning patterns without explicitly attending to them.

Svenaeus (2009) argues that to 'have practical knowledge involves being acquainted with meaning patterns (whether one can describe them or not) and to be able to move about in them in an effortless and skilled way' (p. 26). Furthermore, Svenaeus argues that the phenomenological perspective provides a way of describing and putting into terms practical knowledge. In order to show how phenomenology can be a theory of practical knowledge in the context of physical education, I will in now outline Maurice Merleau-Ponty's phenomenological analysis of learning.[1] His analysis is relevant for the present purpose because of his interest in the moving, human body. As a philosopher, he also held a chair as professor in child psychology and pedagogy at the

Sorbonne, so he was well versed in the pedagogical and psychological theories of his time.

Merleau-Ponty's relation to behaviourism

In his first doctoral thesis, *The Structure of Behavior*, Merleau-Ponty engaged at length with the subject of learning. At the time of writing (the late 1930s), contemporary learning theory in psychology was more or less synonymous with behaviourism, a theory that tried to explain the acquisition of new behaviours by linking an external stimulus to the release of a given response. Between the stimulus and the response there exist only external and causal relations:

> Learning and development … only transfer to certain stimuli the power of releasing certain movements, the motor conditions of which are considered as given in advance. The development of behavior consists only in different associations of pre-existing elements. … The conditioned reflex theory presents stimulations and responses which succeed each other in an organism like a series of events external to each other and between which no relations can be established other than those of immediate temporal contiguity.
>
> (Merleau-Ponty, 1963, pp. 94–95)

Merleau-Ponty emphasizes a distinction between (i) the physical event that the stimulus is in itself, and (ii) the situation taken as a whole for the organism, in which the stimulus as a physical event is just one part. This distinction is not taken into account by behaviourism. Indeed, for behaviourism it is only (i) that can explain behaviour: It is the external, physical event that causally leads to the release of behaviour. For the behaviourists, (ii) would be an explanation attributed to the situation by a human observer. That is, (ii) is an anthropomorphism without relevance to the experimental situation, and which therefore has no explanatory power in behaviourism.

For Merleau-Ponty on the other hand, the situation taken as a whole is not something merely attributable to a combination of stimuli, because these stimuli are integrated into structural processes that play a regulating role: 'they establish *a relation of meaning* between situation and response … It is to the extent that relations of this kind emerge and become efficacious by themselves that the progress of behavior is explicable' (Merleau-Ponty, 1963, p. 103, italics added).

What Merleau-Ponty suggests here is a critique of the atomism that lies at the heart of behaviourism, where any situation can be – indeed must be – decomposed into its constitutive parts in order to find the stimulus that causally leads to the release of behaviour. Against atomism Merleau-Ponty evokes the notions of 'form' or 'structure' that he takes from the gestalt psychologists.[2] As opposed to atomism, gestalt psychology holds that the whole of a system is not equivalent to the sum of its isolated parts, but is rather 'defined as total processes which may be indiscernible from each other while their "parts", compared to each other, differ in absolute size … the systems are defined as transposable wholes' (Merleau-Ponty, 1963: 47). According to Merleau-Ponty, the notion of gestalt can help us to better understand how a relation of meaning is established between the total situation and the response, rather than between the stimulus and the response.

A second critical point is that behaviourism places the stimuli and the response after one another in a linear, temporal process. The stimulus and the response are two externally linked moments following each other in time. Merleau-Ponty questions this linear relation: 'Situation and reaction are linked internally by their common participation in a structure in which the mode of activity proper to the organism is expressed. Hence they cannot be placed one after the other as cause and effect' (Merleau-Ponty, 1963, p. 130). Behaviour, for Merleau-Ponty is not a matter of external causation between two isolated events, but rather an internal participation in the structure of a situation. Merleau-Ponty is questioning the conceptualization of time employed by behaviourism:

> [Behavior] does not unfold in objective time and space like a series of physical events; each moment does not occupy one and only one point in time; rather, at the decisive moment of learning, a 'now' stands out from the series of 'nows', acquires a particular value and summarizes the groupings which have preceded it as it engages and anticipates the future of the behavior.
>
> (Merleau-Ponty, 1963, p. 125)

In behaviourism, time is conceived as an objective phenomenon, where each second disinterestedly overtakes the previous one. Merleau-Ponty, on the other hand, calls attention to lived time, in which the *decisive now* summons the past in a projection towards the future. Thus, Merleau-Ponty takes behaviour and learning out of the order of strict objectivity and sees them as a

> projection outside the organism of a possibility which is internal to it. The world, in as much as it harbors living beings, ceases to be a material plenum consisting of juxtaposed parts; it opens up a place where behavior appears.
>
> (Merleau-Ponty, 1963, p. 125)

Through his critique of behaviourism, Merleau-Ponty shows how organisms – both animals and human beings – react to the total constellation of a situation, rather than to isolated physical or chemical stimuli. If behaviourism was successful in isolating certain stimuli that produced given responses, this was only possible in the conditions found in a laboratory setting. The conditions of life are different, because here the organism displays 'a sort of prospective activity' (Merleau-Ponty, 1964, p. 4), not reckoned with in laboratory conditions. This means that the organism, for example the human body, does not wait for external forces to set it in motion, but rather orients itself towards the meaning of the current situation.

The critique of a behaviouristic conception of learning has so far been a negative one. But Merleau-Ponty also points to a positive description of learning. Against behaviourism, Merleau-Ponty says that 'to learn never consists in being capable of repeating the same gesture' (Merleau-Ponty, 1963, p. 96), for instance pressing levers to get food or finding a way through a maze, as the animals in the behaviorists' experiments must do. Rather, to learn consists of 'providing an adapted response to the situation with different means' (ibid.). To learn is not to be able to repeat the same gesture over and over again. Rather, the response must be more flexible than automatic: 'There must be a *principle in the organism* which ensures that the learning experience will have a general relevance' (Merleau-Ponty, 1963, p. 99, italics added). One way of understanding what this general principle or function is, involves attending to Merleau-Ponty's notions of body and habit.

Habits of the body

Habits have a bad reputation. Crossley (2001) notes that Gilbert Ryle – a British philosopher who in many respects shared Merleau-Ponty's interest in practical knowledge ('knowing how' as Ryle termed it) – was sceptical towards habits, which he saw as simple and mechanical behaviours acquired through mindless drilling. Ryle preferred the notion *disposition* to cover the flexible and situationally attuned tendencies towards actions that are performed without explicit thoughts and deliberate reflection prior to action. Dispositions, to Ryle, 'entail an intelligent and strategic adaptation to contextual exigencies and are purposive' (Crossley, 2001, p. 53) in ways that habits are not thought to be.

Likewise, Hubert Dreyfus (cf. Dreyfus, 2002) values what he calls 'skill' and 'skilful coping' over 'habit' for precisely the same reasons as Ryle: 'rigid behavior,' which connotes habit, says Dreyfus, 'is exactly what Merleau-Ponty is trying to distinguish from the flexible and situation-sensitive skills that make up *l'habitude*' (p. 145, italics in original). *L'habitude* is the word used in the French text of *Phenomenology of Perception*, and which is translated as 'habit' in the English edition. But, the notion of habit, to Dreyfus, is so infused with undesirable connotations that the use of the word 'habit' destroys the intended meaning of *l'habitude*. Dreyfus therefore prefers the terms 'skill' or 'absorbed coping'.

However, despite habit's bad reputation, Crossley points out that the English connotations of the word habit refer to a 'corrupted form of habit' (Crossley, 2001, p. 54) and he holds that what Ryle calls dispositions and Dreyfus calls skills are similar to what English translations of Merleau-Ponty call habits. I will therefore use the term habit, following the English translations of

Merleau-Ponty's texts and denote by it a flexible, situational, and adjustable ability to act.

Merleau-Ponty was interested in the notion of habit for the same reasons that he was interested in behaviour and movement: they are phenomena that can be properly understood neither by intellectualism nor empiricism. Empiricism would equate habit with the conditioned reflexes, i.e. the behaviourist programme of establishing causal links between stimuli and responses. The intellectualist account of habit would be the automatism of mental representations, where the proper mental representation is called up and the movement executed without conscious monitoring of the acting subject. Merleau-Ponty rejects both these explanations: 'Habit has its abode neither in thought nor in the objective body, but in the body as mediator of the world' (Merleau-Ponty, 2002, p. 167). It is not in thought (intellectualism) or in the objective body (empiricism) that we find the home of habits. It is to be found in the body itself as a subject of knowledge.

In terms of practical knowledge, it is also interesting to note the epistemological status of habits. Merleau-Ponty pursues this question using the example of people who are skilful at typewriting. He states that these people are not in possession of knowledge of the place of each letter among all the others on the keyboard. Neither have they acquired a conditioned reflex for each one. What, then, is the epistemic status of habits?

> [Habit] is *knowledge in the hands*, which is forthcoming only when bodily effort is made, and cannot be formulated in detachment from that effort. The subject knows where the letters are on the typewriter as we know where one of our limbs is, through a *knowledge bred of familiarity* which does not give us a position in objective space.
>
> (Merleau-Ponty, 2002, p. 166, italics added)

Thus, for Merleau-Ponty habit is a form of 'knowing how' rather than 'knowing that'. It is embodied knowledge, hence it is referred to as knowledge in the hands.[3] The body involved in these habits is to Merleau-Ponty, 'the third term', the alternative to the intellectualists' and empiricists' account of the body, and the body does not primarily find its place in objective space. The spatiality of the body-in-action is the spatiality of a situation rather than a spatiality of a position (Merleau-Ponty, 2002, p. 115).

Habits and embodied learning

How does Merleau-Ponty think that the body-subject acquires habits? He does not accept the intellectualists' account of learning, because he states that learning should not be conceived of as an intellectual synthesis, neither does he accept the empiricist account, because 'the subject does not weld together individual movements and individual stimuli' (Merleau-Ponty, 2002, p. 164). Rather, his summary of how motor habits are acquired is presented in this quote:

> A movement is learned when the body has understood it, that is, when it has incorporated it into its 'world', and to move one's body is to aim at things through it; it is to allow oneself to respond to their call, which is made upon it independently of any representation. Motility, then, is not, as it were, a handmaid of consciousness, transporting the body to that point in space of which we have formed a representation beforehand.
>
> (Merleau-Ponty, 2002, pp. 160–161)

By elucidating this quote we can understand Merleau-Ponty's conception of the learning of motor habits.[4]

In order for us to say that a movement is learned, it is required that the body-subject must *understand* the movement. The understanding we are talking about here is not formed through an intellectual analysis: 'it is the body which "catches" (*kapiert*) and "comprehends" movement. The acquisition of a habit is indeed the grasping of a significance, but it is the motor grasping of a motor significance' (Merleau-Ponty, 2002, p. 165, italics in original). To explain what this means, Merleau-Ponty uses the example of a woman with a feather on her hat. The woman is continuously aware of the position of the feather in the same manner that she is aware of where her head is. The feather has become an extension of the body, which is taken account of without thinking about it, so that when she walks through a door she bows her head in order to avoid breaking the feather.

More generally, Merleau-Ponty says that 'to understand a movement is to experience the harmony between what we aim at and what is given, between the intention and the performance' (Merleau-Ponty, 2002, p. 167). Therefore, movement is not a matter of applying representations formed and stored in the mind. Dreyfus (2002) points this out, saying that the world is presented *to* the learner rather than represented *in* the learner. The presentation of the world to the learner takes place through 'the intentional arc', a feedback loop between body-subject and world:

> the life of consciousness – cognitive life, the life of desire or perceptual life – is subtended by 'an intentional arc' which projects round about us our past, future, our human setting, our physical, ideological and moral situation, or rather which results in our being situated in all these respects.
>
> (Merleau-Ponty, 2002, p. 157)

The projection of the present situation – facilitated by the intentional arc – is given to the body-subject as a gestalt, where certain aspects and features of the situation stand out and call for action (e.g. bowing the head so as to not break the feather). This gestalt figure is harmonious insofar as it solicits a performance that matches the intention of the body-subject (Dreyfus, 2002). Thus, Merleau-Ponty could say that *to move is to respond to the call of the world*.

Learning movements is therefore to continually enrich the intentional arc, which takes up past experiences and future expectations in the projection of the present situation (Dreyfus, 2002). Movement is, as Merleau-Ponty says, not primarily a matter of *I think*, but of *I can*. The *I* must not be thought of as a fully constituted subject, where the body is an object for the *I can*. Indeed, the *I* in *I can* is the body-subject. This means that the *I can* is something acquired through effort, in which habitual strategies are developed by the body-subject to deal with its environment (Dillon, 1997). This points towards a basic intentionality, which Merleau-Ponty refers to as operative intentionality (Merleau-Ponty, 2002, p. xx). The operative intentionality is directed towards the world as it is being presented in experience and is prior to the thetic intentionality that can be equated with our thoughts *about* the world. At the same time, we must bear in mind that the *I can* always also entails the possibility of being thematized. It is this possibility that both frees from us from being doomed to live only in the concrete and actual, and provides us the opportunity to 'undertake movements in the human space of possibility' (Dillon, 1997, p. 137). Thus, the *I can* entails an openness towards becoming otherwise.

Finally, it is stated that for a movement to be learned, it must be incorporated into the body schema.[5] Learning is therefore a form of incorporation, a 'rearrangement and renewal of the corporeal schema' (Merleau-Ponty, 2002, p. 164). The body schema is not a fixed entity, but something that is continually open for revision. We can therefore say that a movement is not learned until it is incorporated into the body schema. Given that Merleau-Ponty argues that what can be said about motor habits is true of habits in general, all habitual learning requires a rearrangement of our body schema.

One problem with this presentation of the acquisition of habits is that, on the one hand there is a perceived world, which is projected by the body-subject. But on the other hand the body-subject is responding, as if by remote attraction, to the calls from the perceived world. It is hard to see which is more primary: the perceived world projected by the body-subject or the perceiving subject responding to calls from the world. This is in essence a chicken and egg situation: which came first? The perceived world or the perceiving subject? This problem, however, presupposes that one of these entities has a privileged position over the other. But, for Merleau-Ponty 'the most basic unity of experience is that of a figure-on-a-background and if analysis seek to reduce this fundamental complex into something simpler, it can arrive only at constructs' (Dillon, 1997, p. 60). For Merleau-Ponty, the question of which is most primary – the subject or the world – is misguided, because both belong to the foundational gestalt figure.

Learning and being-in-the-world

In one of the working notes that Merleau-Ponty left behind after his death, he wrote that the 'original layer above *nature* shows that *learning* is *In der Welt*

Sein and not at all that *In der Welt Sein* is *learning* in the American sense or in the cognitive sense of Brunswik' (Merleau-Ponty, 1968, p. 212, italics in original). One should be careful when interpreting Merleau-Ponty's working notes, because they are unfinished and sometimes even incoherent.[6] Nevertheless, it might be fruitful to try to understand what Merleau-Ponty can have meant by saying that learning is *In der Welt Sein*, or being-in-the-world.

First, I would just point out what I think the latter part of the quote (i.e. 'not at all that *In der Welt Sein* is *learning* ...') suggests: it is quite easy to see that this is the traditional Merleau-Ponty strategy of pointing out how his favourite opponents, empiricism and intellectualism, fail. As theories of learning, behaviourism (i.e. 'learning in the American sense') and intellectualism (represented by cognitivism in this quotation) fail because they are committed to objective thought and are thus unable to 'grasp consciousness in the act of learning' (Merleau-Ponty, 2002, p. 33). Empiricist and intellectualist accounts of learning make subjective, everyday experience secondary to objective thought. For Merleau-Ponty on the other hand, objective thought is a derivation of being-in-the-world, and this seems to be his reason for saying that being-in-the-world is not learning in the behaviouristic or cognitive sense.

The context of the quote under consideration is a discussion of cultural perception and wild perception.[7] Our perception comes already interpreted, that is, perception is always already oriented by cultural systems, so that what we perceive is not raw sense data, but meaningful impressions. Thus, above nature there is a layer of perception, which is 'a dilation of perception ... which obliges us to put in continuity the perceptual openness to the world ... and the openness to a cultural world (acquisition of the use of instruments)' (Merleau-Ponty, 1968, p. 212). With this continuity between the natural and the cultural as the context for saying that learning is being-in-the-world, we have the framework for understanding how learning could be being-in-the-world.

Being-in-the-world is a term coined by Heidegger and taken up by Merleau-Ponty and other phenomenologists. The term expresses the fundamental intertwining of human beings with their world. In order to understand how learning is being-in-the-world, I will attend to a quite practical example of the football player's relation to the pitch, his team mates and opponents, given by Merleau-Ponty in *The Structure of Behavior*: For the player, the football field is not an object, says Merleau-Ponty. This means that the measures that the player takes of the field are not those of objective, geometrical space. It means that a player does not locate another player to be, say, 5 metres in front himself, 25 degrees to the left and travelling at the speed of 5 m/s. Rather,

> [the field] is pervaded by lines of force (the 'yard lines'; those which demarcate the 'penalty area') and articulated in sectors (for example, the 'openings' between the adversaries) which calls for a certain mode of action and which initiate and guide the action as if the player were unaware of it. *The field itself is not given to him, but present as the immanent term of his practical intentions*; the player becomes one with it and feels the

> direction of the 'goal', for example, just as immediately as the vertical and horizontal planes of his body.
>
> (Merleau-Ponty, 1963, p. 168, italics added)

The phenomenal (football) field is internal to the player's practical intentions. This is because there is a dialectic between the field and the actions of the player, so that 'each maneuver undertaken by the player modifies the character of the field and establishes in it new lines of forces which in turn unfold and are accomplished, again altering the phenomenal field' (Merleau-Ponty, 1963, p. 169). There is thus an interdependence between the body-subject's intentions and movements on the one hand and the phenomenal field on the other.

We can therefore see that the structure or gestalt of the field is not imposed solely by the bodily intentions of the player, because the field – by virtue of its set limits – is already configured, at least to some extent. The configuration of the field is, however, not exhausted by the demarcations. Rather, the lines of forces and the possibilities open for play, are continually changing as moves are made. The player's bodily intentions are therefore complicit in the organization of the field, at the same time as the performance of the player's intentions is restricted by his abilities. 'The body's freedom is circumscribed by phenomenal space, time, and objects around it which serve both to ground and to limit its "I can"' (Dillon, 1997, p. 147).

With this elaboration of Merleau-Ponty's conception of embodied learning, in particular through the final example of a typical sport skill, I hope I have shown how phenomenology can provide a theoretical understanding of practical knowledge. I have illustrated how the body-subject is immersed in meaning patterns that are partly created and partly given. This chapter has also explained how the knowledge object of practical knowledge, i.e. the ability to take part in and perform movement activities, is closely linked to the knowing subject, i.e. the person moving. This point, and its consequences for pedagogy in physical education, will be expanded upon.

Notes

1 This is a slightly reworked version of a chapter in my doctoral dissertation (Standal, 2009).

2 It is interesting to note that the French word *structure* is usually used to translate *Gestalt* from German to French (Priest, 1998). This gives a clear indication of what kind of structure Merleau-Ponty is investigating in *The Structure of Behavior*.

3 Here is an experiment you can do for yourself in order to see how this is so: Can you tell which finger you use to press the letter F on the keyboard of your computer? Most people who are somewhat proficient at typing would not. But if they sit at their keyboard, the finger will find the letter immediately without the intervention of thought.

4 There seems to have been a slide in focus here, from talking about habits in general, to talking about motor habits specifically. One must therefore ask whether what is said here about motor habits holds true for habits in general. Merleau-Ponty suggests that it is so: 'just as the analysis of bodily spatiality foreshadowed that of the

unity of one's own body, so we may extend to all habits what we have said about motor ones' (Merleau-Ponty, 2002, p. 175).

5 The body schema is a term that Merleau-Ponty takes up from the neurologist Henry Head, as distinct from the body image. Put briefly, the difference between body schema and image is that with body image 'one is consciously attending to body', whereas with the body schema one is 'marginally aware of the body' (Gallagher, 2005, p. 27). The body is more of a fully fledged object in the body image than is the case with the body schema. The body schema, according to Gallagher, does its work 'before we know it' (2005, p. 5), thus structuring our experiences of the body-in-action. See Chapter 7 for a further elaboration.

6 As Dillon (1997) points out, the danger is that 'in philosophy as in astrophysics, paucity of data typically results in speculative extravagance' (p. 155).

7 Wild, and sometimes brute, are parts of a new terminology that Merleau-Ponty began to work out in *The Visible and the Invisible*, where he wanted to get at the ontological layers of 'experiences that have not been "worked over" that offer us all at once, pell-mell, both "subject" and "object", both existence and essence, and hence give philosophy resources to redefine them' (Merleau-Ponty, 1968, p. 130).

References

Arnold, P. J. (1979). *Meaning in movement, sport and physical education.* London: Heinemann.

Arnold, P. J. (1988). Education, movement, and the rationality of practical knowledge. *Quest*, 40, 115–125.

Arnold, P. J. (1991). The preeminece of skill as an educational value in the movement curriculum. *Quest*, 43, 66–77.

Best, D. (1978). *Philosophy and human movement.* London: Allen & Unwin.

Brown, T. D. (2013). A vision lost? (Re) articulating an Arnoldian conception of education 'in' movement in physical education. *Sport, Education and Society*, 18(1), 21–37.

Brown, T. D. and Payne, P. G. (2009). Conceptualizing the phenomenology of movement in physical education: implications for pedagogical inquiry and development. *Quest*, 61, 418–441.

Brown, T. and Penney, D. (2013). Learning 'in', 'through' and 'about' movement in senior physical education? The new Victorian Certificate of Education Physical Education. *European Physical Education Review*, 19(1), 39–61. Carr, D. (1981). Knowledge in practice. *American Philosophical Quarterly*, 18(1), 53–61.

Crossley, N. (2001). *The social body: Habit, identity and desire.* London: Sage.

Dillon, M. C. (1997). *Merleau-Ponty's ontology* (2nd edn). Evanston, IL: Northwestern University Press.

Dreyfus, H. L. (2002). Intelligence without representation: Merleau-Ponty's critique of mental representation. *Phenomenology and the Cognitive Sciences*, 1, 367–383.

Gallagher, S. (2005). *How the body shapes the mind.* Oxford: Clarendon Press.

Loland, S. (2006). Morality, medicine, and meaning: toward an integrated justification of physical education. *Quest*, 58(1), 60–70.

Luft, S. and Overgaard, S. (2012). Introduction. In S. Luft and S. Overgaard (eds), *Routledge companion to phenomenology* (pp. 1–14). Abingdon: Routledge.

MacAllister, J. (2013). The 'physically educated' person: physical education in the philosophy of Reid, Peters and Aristotle. *Educational Philosophy and Theory*, 45(9), 908–920.

McNamee, M. (2005). The nature and values of physical education. In *Physical education: Essential issues* (pp. 1–20). London: Sage.

Merleau-Ponty, M. (1963). *The structure of behavior.* Pittsburg, PA: Duquesne University Press.

Merleau-Ponty, M. (1964). *The primacy of perception.* Evanston, IL: Northwestern University Press.

Merleau-Ponty, M. (1968). *The visible and the invisible.* Evanston, IL: Northwestern University Press.

Merleau-Ponty, M. (2002). *Phenomenology of perception.* London: Routledge.

Ommundsen, Y. (2013). Fysisk-motorisk ferdighet gjennom kroppsøving: et viktig bidrag til elevenes allmenndanning og læing i skolen [Physical-motor skill through physical education:– an important contribution to children's learning and education]. *Norsk Pedagogisk Tidsskrift,* 97(02), 155–166.

Parry, J. (1998). Reid on knowledge and justification in physical education. *European Physical Education Review,* 4(1), 70–74.

Priest, S. (1998). *Merleau-Ponty.* London: Routledge.

Reid, A. (1998). The value of education. *Journal of Philosophy of Education,* 32(3), 319–331.

Standal, Ø. F. (2009). *Relation of meaning: A phenomenologically oriented case study of learning bodies in a rehabilitation context.* Oslo, Norway: Norwegian School of Sport Sciences.

Stolz, S. (2014). *The philosophy of physical education: A new perspective.* London: Routledge.

Svenaeus, F. (2009). Vad är praktisk kunnskap? En inledning til emnet och boken [What is practical knowledge? An introduction to the topic and the book]. In J. Bornemark and F. Svenaeus (eds), *Vad är praktisk kunnskap?* (pp. 9–36). Stockholm: Södertörn studies in practical knowledge.

4 The knowledge objects embodied

Following from the previous chapter, I will here argue that in physical education (and in movement activities more generally), there is a close embodied relationship the *knowledge objects* of practical knowledge and the *knowing subjects*. I will make this argument through a series of reflections on the objects of practical knowledge, on poise as an important element in movement literacy, and finally through a reflection on skill acquisition and Merleau-Ponty's conception of habits. The chapter concludes with a question mark regarding the role of experience, expertise and teaching in the Skill model (Dreyfus, 2002). My purpose is to highlight a problem that arises to some extent in any approach of teaching practical knowledge.

The knowledge objects of practical knowledge

First, I want to clarify what is meant by the term *knowledge object*. According to David Carr (1981), a central difference between theoretical and practical knowledge is that 'whereas the objects of theoretical knowledge are something like statements and propositions, practical knowledge is directed towards action [...] knowing how concerns the mastery of practices' (pp. 54–55). More formally, in order for someone to have practical knowledge three conditions must be satsified:

A knows how to φ only if:

1 A may entertain φ-ing as a purpose
2 A is acquainted with a set of practical procedures necessary for successful φ-ing
3 A exhibits recognizable success at φ-ing (Carr, 1981, p. 58)

Practical knowledge is therefore purposive (condition 1), has a specific form of rationality of its own (condition 2) and can be inter-subjectively validated and confirmed via the demonstration of a reasonable degree of success (condition 3).[1] Based on this formulation, Carr (1981) defines the objects of practical knowledge in physical education as action, activities and practices.

The Norwegian physical education curriculum provides some examples illustrating Carr's points.[2] This curriculum has two parts. The first outlines the overall objectives for physical education from grade 1 (6-year-olds) through the third year of secondary school. It states, for example, that 'pupils shall develop competence through a wide selection of play and different kinds of activities' and that 'the subject shall contribute to humans' sensing, experiencing, learning and creating with the body' (quotations are from Utdanningsdirektoratet, 2012). The second part of the curriculum provides detailed descriptions of learning outcomes that should be attained by the time a pupil completes the 4th, 7th and 10th grades, as well as after each year of secondary school. These competency objectives are set out using verbs such as 'perform', 'play', 'take part in', 'practise',[3] and 'make functional use of'. All of these verbs denote the active doing of something. Therefore, it could be said that Norwegian physical education is concerned with practical knowledge in the form of actions (e.g. 'use basic techniques and simple tactics in some selected individual sports'), activities (e.g. 'swim the breaststroke/crawl and backstroke and dive') and practices (e.g. 'practise some activities with roots in Sami traditions').[4]

In the previous chapter, I outlined a phenomenological perspective on practical knowledge and presented arguments for its value, drawing on the work of Svenaeus (2009). This approach implies that the person possessing practical knowledge is acquainted with relevant meaning patterns and is 'able to move about in them in an effortless and skilled way' (p. 26). Merleau-Ponty provides a phenomenological analysis of habits and their acquisition; in other words, skills and skill-learning. His perspective is well summed up in his example of the football player[5]: the meaning patterns emerge through the player's movements, within certain constraints. These constraints can be artificial, such as the size and shape of the playing field, rules of the game and so on. Other constraints are imposed by the limits of the body. For example, the location of our eyes at the front of our head inhibits our freedom to move in other directions.[6] Following from this, as we learn new habits or refine old ones we come to see the world differently. Our habits make the world meaningful for us (Crossley, 2001); by extension, acquiring and refining habits opens up the world: 'Habit expresses our power of dilating our being-in-the-world' (Merleau-Ponty, 2002, p. 166).

Based on this reflection, we can conclude that in physical education, the pupil as a knowing subject embodies the knowledge objects (i.e. the knowing how to take part in actions, activities and practices). The relationship between the knowledge objects and the knowing subjects is therefore embodied.

Poise: a re-interpretation of 'what' there is to learn in physical literacy?

In Chapter 1, I referred to the frequent criticism of current physical education practices that they are more concerned with keeping pupils physically active than with ensuring that they learn something (Annerstedt, 2008). If physical education is a subject 'where learning something is not a matter of importance and where the pedagogic idea seems to be keeping the pupils physically active' (Nyberg and Larsson, 2014, p. 126), then *what* could be learned will be of lesser concern. This is, of course, problematic, as it raises questions about the educational dimension of physical education.

Recall the definition of physical literacy cited earlier which was centrally concerned with to move with poise, economy and efficiency (Whitehead, 2001). Here, I will focus on the practical knowledge – i.e. what there is to learn – in physical education related to the notion of poise. My purpose is twofold: To elucidate a central aspect of movement[7] literacy and to further elaborate on the argument that physical education requires a close and embodied relationship between the knowledge objects and the knowing subjects.

Samuel Todes' view of poise

The notion of poise is a central concern in Samuel Todes' book *Body and World* (Todes, 2001). Until its publication in 1991, this book, which was written as Todes' dissertation in philosophy from Harvard, circulated as a sort of underground classic (Strong, 2015). Like Merleau-Ponty, Todes was not interested primarily in the moving body *per se*, but in its significance as part of a larger philosophical project.[8]

In movement, Todes argued, we come into contact with the world and we enter into relationships with things and other people:

> In beginning to act, the human subject does not first perceive his [*sic*] body, then take it up and use it, as he does an umbrella on a rainy day. Rather, when active, he becomes aware of objects only as they are brought to his attention as relevant to what he (inseparable from his body) is doing. It is not merely his body that he is moving or is prepared to move, that he perceives to come into new relationships with objects; it is *himself* that he perceives to come into these new relationships through his bodily movement.
>
> (p. 43, italics in original)

Put simply, things appear to us through the movement of our bodies. In this sense, the world of our immediate surroundings – our movement-environment – is embodied. It might be argued that the term 'objects' as used here differs from what I have earlier called knowledge objects. At least, if we want to say that the meaning of 'objects' in this quote and 'knowledge objects' as I have used it above are equivalent, then we have to understand the term 'objects' as referring to meaning patterns involving things and other people, as well as more immaterial things such as rules of games. Also, what Todes is saying does not preclude the body from being an object for the human subject. Indeed, it assumes that the active human subject has a sense of her body.

Todes distinguishes different ways in which the body can be an object for the human subject. First, it can appear as an object for me when I, say, locate an itch in my finger. In that situation I am an immobile observer of my own body. Even while moving it is possible to maintain the attitude of locating a feeling in a specific body part, for instance, through visual or proprioceptive attention to the position of my elbow during a forehand stroke in tennis. In such cases, Todes would say that I am moving the specific body part. But his primary interest is the human subject as a self-moved mover, i.e. situations where I move my whole body as a unity, coordinated and operating with reference to external objects.[9]

From this perspective, our movements occur in a spatio-temporal field that we generate by moving. The field is spatially oriented by virtue of being embodied. There is a left and right, up and down; what is close or far away is determined not by geographical distance as measured in meters, but by the degree to which the object is ready-to-hand, to use Heidegger's expression.[10] It is also temporal in the sense that the body has a back and a front: In front of us we have the future and the 'back leaves behind what has appeared … so that the front-back body distinction makes possible the passage of time' (p. 49). Therefore, we produce the spatio-temporal field through our movements. Just like the football player in *The Structure of Behavior* (Merleau-Ponty, 1963), our production of the spatio-temporal field is dependent on our movement skills.[11] Todes refers to this as anticipatory knowledge: 'To develop a habit in respect to something, I must be able to anticipate its presence … each person has some such threshold of expectability, some minimal reaction-time, which sets a limit to his ability to respond' (p. 63).

Before turning to the notion of poise as outlined by Todes, consider again the aim of 'moving with poise, economy and efficiency', as well as of 'being perceptive in reading the environment'. According to Todes, a phrase like 'reading the environment' is to some extent misleading. The phenomenological perspective on practical knowledge applied here implies that the mover is at the same time both reading *and writing* the environment. In fact, an element of what is required to move with poise is precisely what Todes calls anticipatory knowledge. Without that knowledge, you are acting without being aware of 'what you are going to do before you do it' (p. 63). In reading and writing the environment, the moving human subject is responding to anticipated objects. These responsive acts are the acts 'by which we first make the world habit-able' (p. 65). In this sense, movement literacy's aim of being perceptive in reading (and writing) the environment is actually an effort to make our world of movement habit-able, a place to live. This is a positive description of what Merleau-Ponty described negatively when he claimed that 'motility, then, is not, as it were, a handmaid of consciousness, transporting the body to that point in space of which we have formed a representation beforehand' (Merleau-Ponty, 2002, p. 161). According to Merleau-Ponty, habits or skills are learned when they become part of the life-world – a habit-able place – and *moving skilfully is to move with poise.*

Anticipatory knowledge is expressed through poise, which can be seen as a response to a felt need for movement, an indeterminate deprivation or lack of something that calls for a certain response. To continue moving is therefore a way of making the need more determinate.

> The success of poise is not in its *execution*, but in its very *existence* by which the body is, to begin with, knowingly in touch with the objects around it [...] Poise is not merely a matter of internal bodily coordination, but also of skill in handling things (and persons) about us. Thus, when one fails in what he is attempting to do, one necessarily loses his poise and is, at least momentarily, thrown off balance, however quickly one may recover his balance and poise.
>
> (Todes, 2001, p. 66, italics in original)

Poise, then, is an expression of how the moving subject knowingly is in contact with the knowledge object; the specific movement project she is involved in. Skills are not *in* the body, but in a relationship between the moving agent and the environment. Importantly, this environment is produced by the moving subjects. However, this does not indicate that through movement we create the environment all on our own – as if we simply write on a blank slate without reading the environment. Even when we move alone just for our own sake, we are constrained by gravity and our bodily contingencies. As Gunnar Breivik (2008) points out, engaging in a sport is essentially playing within with these constraints.

Poise as a qualitatively felt experience

Whitehead suggests that poise is an embodied capability that encompasses 'capacities such as balance, coordination, flexibility, agility, control, precision, strength, power, endurance and the ability to move at different speeds' (Whitehead, 2007, p. 287). What I have presented here, however, is a philosophical clarification of the term poise from a phenomenological perspective. As Todes argues (2001), moving with poise involves being knowingly in touch with one's circumstances. Importantly, Todes also describes poise as a qualitatively felt experience. This means that one cannot have more or less of it. In this respect, poise is a qualitative rather than a quantitative term.

This formulation calls for a clarification regarding poise's relation to the notion of skill. At least in the context of sports, skill is usually thought of as something you have more or less of, something that can be acquired in a kind of linear development. Similarly, in the context of fundamental motor skills, skill is commonly considered to be a quantitative entity, again something you can have more or less of. Furthermore, it is possible (and in some instances also considered desirable) to measure a child's motor skills through tests like Movement ABC. Such tests can be used to measure the level of motor skill, i.e. its quantity, and determine how a particular child scores in comparison to a norm. That is, the tests imply a strong normativity, in which a child's performance is compared to an idea of what a 'normal' child can do. (The idea of 'the normal child' will be problematized in Chapter 9. Suffice it to say that in quantitative terms 'normal' is average.)

Even though the development of motor skills is one of the claimed benefits of physical education (Bailey et al., 2009), it is perhaps more correct to say that in physical education, the major component is sport skills or techniques. David Kirk (2010), for instance, argues that physical education can be thought of as the teaching of sport techniques. Further, as Bailey et al. (2009) suggest, physical education is 'organised around short taught "blocks" of a limited range of physical activities, particularly team games, which are not necessarily lifelong activities' (p. 8). Just as with motor skills, sports are associated with normative ideals of how they should be performed.[12] These techniques, like motor skills, can be interpreted quantitatively, and it is possible to distinguish between those who are more or less technically proficient.

If, then, it is the case that skill – whether motor or sports – is a quantitative concept in physical education, then adopting the concept of poise as it is developed by Todes requires a reorientation in how skill is understood. Since poise in a phenomenological perspective is a qualitatively felt experience, you cannot have more or less of it, and it cannot be norm-referenced. Thus, describing poise as Whitehead does (2007) becomes problematic because that definition is likely to be understood quantitatively: You can have more or less endurance; you can have more or less flexibility. I would, therefore, argue that a decision to make poise, in the sense of a qualitatively felt experience, an object of knowledge in physical education presents significant challenges to traditional ideas about 'what there is to learn' in this subject.[13]

At first glance, it would appear that if poise is defined as a qualitatively felt experience, then there appears to be very little that can be learned. Put differently: if poise is not a quantity – as is the case with sports techniques and motor skills – it is hard to see any room for learning and development. Viewing poise as a qualitative felt experience implies that as long as pupils can claim to have that experience, they have no need to learn more: Why should they put any effort into moving differently when their way is already as good as anyone else's? In contrast, the norms imposed by more established approaches to skill learning have the advantage of facilitating the establishment of standards that pupils can measure themselves against. Techniques can be honed and perfected; there is always more to learn. As I will return to in the next chapter, my counter-argument would be that the emphasis on experience and on the embodied relationship between the knowledge objects and the knowing subject in physical education means that the learning involved in poise is to develop knowledge and understanding about oneself as an embodied human being.

Before continuing the elaboration of the learning outcomes of movement literacy, I want to point out some further problems when it comes to learning of movements in a phenomenological perspective. These problems will be highlighted by a critique of the so-called Skill model (Dreyfus, 2002; Dreyfus and Dreyfus, 1986), which has had considerable influence in philosophy of sport.

The Skill model

The Skill model is based on the work of Maurice Merleau-Ponty and Martin Heidegger, and applies the phenomenological philosophy of movement presented above. This model has had some influence within the philosophy of sports, where it has been used to advance a phenomenological understanding of skilful actions and skill acquisition (Breivik, 2007; Breivik, 2013; Eriksen, 2010; Moe, 2007; Sutton et al., 2011). The model has also been subjected to criticisms (Breivik, 2013; Selinger and Crease, 2002; Standal and Moe, 2011) which highlight challenges that movement literacy must overcome if it is to be a pedagogical model for physical education. More specifically, the Skill model appears to have an inherent bias against teaching or coaching (Selinger and Crease, 2002) and the skilled mover may be portrayed as somewhat zombie-like (Breivik, 2007; Breivik, 2013). Without a clear role for the teacher and a concept of the value of experience, it is hard to envision how and by whom pedagogies can be carried out.

The literature on the philosophy of sports includes many discussions of the phenomenology of skill acquisition. Moe (2005), for example, has criticized the information-processing theory that underlies the cognitivist perspective on skilled motor behaviour. This perspective views the individual as a computer-like system who relies on mental representations and explicit rules to learn and perform actions. The alternative posited by Moe is based on philosophical theories of Hubert Dreyfus and John Searle. The work of Dreyfus and the phenomenological philosophy he developed have become a particularly influential paradigm for understanding the phenomenology of skilled sports performances, as well as of learning the requisite skills (Breivik, 2007; Sutton et al., 2011).

The Skill model of Dreyfus and Dreyfus (cf. Dreyfus, 2002; Dreyfus and Dreyfus, 1986) describes a five-step progression of skill acquisition, from novice to expert.[14] This is a process in which learners gradually advance from being dependent on decontextualized and explicit rules and instructions through an intermediate phase in which they become increasingly involved in the situation, but still remain dependent on detached rule-following for coping with the learning situation. As they become more proficient, their 'theory of the skill, as represented by rules and principles, will [...] gradually be replaced by situational discriminations accompanied by associated responses' (Dreyfus, 2002, p. 370). In other words, experience, the right feedback, and personal involvement in the learning situation can gradually free the learner to perform a skill without having to follow explicit rules.

Both Moe (2004) and Eriksen (2010) point out that the structure of the Skill model is similar to that of more traditional, cognitive models of skill acquisition. In both, the learner moves from being dependent on rules provided by a teacher to enter a state in which these rules fade out. Whereas in the cognitivist model the mental representations of rules become automatized, in the phenomenological Skill model the expert performer acts without any mental representations:

> What one has learned appears in the way the world shows up; it is not represented in the mind and added on to the present experience. That is, according to Merleau-Ponty, what the learner acquires through experience is not *represented* in the mind at all but is *presented* to the learner as a more and more finely discriminated situation, which then solicits a more and more refined response.
>
> (Dreyfus 2002, p. 373, italics in original)

As this quote makes clear, the foundation of the Skill model is the phenomenology of Merleau-Ponty, together with the work of Heidegger. Dreyfus has also cited the work of Todes: 'Todes agrees with Merleau-Ponty, who maintains that, in absorbed coping, the agent's body is led to move so as to reduce a sense of deviation from a satisfactory gestalt' (p. 396). That is, Dreyfus suggests that both Merleau-Ponty's notion of maximum grip and Todes' concept of poise express how the moving agent accomplishes movements in response to situational needs without explicitly attending to the body. These quotes encapsulate their views:

- Merleau-Ponty: '[the body] is *the darkness needed in the theatre* to show up the performance [...] one's own body is the third term, always tacitly understood in the figure-background structure' (2002, p. 115, italics added).
- Todes: When active, 'things appear to the human subject through his body, *but his body does not itself appear to him as an object*' (2001, p. 45, italics added).

From this perspective, the body is a tacit background presence in skilled movement actions and the learning process is designed to put the body there. Through bodily intentionality – or motor intentionality, as Merleau-Ponty called it – we are knowingly in contact with the spatio-temporal field around us. Once we accept this, it can also be argued that the knowledge objects are embodied.

The problem with 'expertise'

The Skill model describes a development from novice to expert, in which expert performance is characterized as 'what must be done, simply is done' (Dreyfus, 2002, p. 372). The expert doesn't need to think or mentally represent either the situation or the action. Dreyfus characterizes the expert's performance as *absorbed coping*. To convey this point, he cites various types of skills (chess and car driving being the most common), as well as the ability to open doors and the performance of basketball players such as Larry Bird. Several commentators (e.g., Breivik, 2013; Standal and Moe, 2011) have pointed out, however, that Dreyfus' use of examples illustrates a problem with his notion of expertise. He does not make a distinction between simple, everyday behaviours such as opening doors and driving to work and the high-level, very demanding skills required to be an Olympic swimmer or a player in the NBA.[15] As Montero (2013, p. 305) puts it:

> You may be a good driver but most likely you are not recognized as an expert driver, and sad to say, after learning the basics you probably did not engage in strenuous efforts to improve. So as I understand the notion of expert, everyday skills do not count as expert skills.

It follows from this critique that expertise is a misleading characterization of habit (Merleau-Ponty) or poise (Todes). For them, habit is more a matter of qualitatively felt experiences of movements. In contrast, skills, defined as expertise, assume an exclusive normativity. On one level, this objection to the Skill model does not pose much of a problem, in so far as physical education is not intended to produce expert performers in the exclusive, normative sense, nor would it ever be likely to do so. This ambiguity in the Skill model's use of the notion of expertise highlights the importance of making a distinction between skill as a quantitative and normative entity and as a qualitative, felt experience available for personal development.

The prejudice against teaching

One feature of the Skill model is that teaching takes place at the first three stages, in which the learners rely on rules and maxims for behaviour provided by a teacher or a coach. At the higher levels, the teacher or coach disappears. The learner is basically expected to learn via the intentional arc, as described earlier. Selinger and Crease (2002) find this division problematic:

> A lived, embodied subject lacks an objective purchase on its own performing process. Though Dreyfus would clearly disagree, the performing of that subject is always, therefore, in principle open to being better disclosed to outsiders, whose intercessions may then help the subject to perform better. This is not to say, of course, that the outsider's insights are achieved because of an objective stance; rather, it is because the outsider is situated differently.
>
> (p. 260)

Selinger and Crease also point out that the Skill model mischaracterizes teaching as 'a dispensing of rules in a standardized way' (p. 259), a method of passing on rules and maxims for how to perform the skills being taught. They observe that effective teaching 'involves modeling and demonstration and is addressed to the specific performances of specific embodied learners. Since these performances differ from body to body, the knowledge embodied in [teaching] cannot be reduced to rules of thumb' (ibid.).

The problem with embodied experience

Gunnar Breivik (2013) has criticized the Skill model for painting a picture of expert performances as being zombie-like:

> I disagree with Dreyfus, who thinks that athletes' bodies are just automatically drawn toward the right solution so as to reduce a certain tension in relation to a Gestalt-like pattern. The athletes are much more in hand with what they are doing.
>
> (p. 103)

According to Breivik, Dreyfus and others go too far in their portrayal of the role of absorbed coping in athletic performance. Somewhat paradoxically given the anti-dualistic basis of phenomenology, Breivik (2013) sees them as describing the expert performer as a body-subject who merely reacts to stimuli in the environment in an almost behaviouristic manner. In a similar critique, Zahavi (2013) goes even further by suggesting that 'it is hard to see why Dreyfus's account [of absorbed coping] should merit the label "phenomenology"' (p. 334). Zahavi reads Dreyfus as claiming that absorbed coping takes place non-consciously, for instance when he likens Olympic swimmers to sleepwalkers (a view also criticized by Breivek, 2013). Consequently: without any conscious experience, no phenomenological access to expert performance.

Dreyfus' notion of absorbed coping is not alone in viewing mindedness as antithetical to skill acquisition. More traditional cognitive approaches share this perspective, as Eriksen (2010), Moe (2005) and Montero (2013) have pointed out. These approaches posit that the aim of the learning process is automatization, a level that transcends reflection and thinking, as in the proverb 'thinking is stinking'. In both cases, what Jean Lave (1996) calls 'the telos of learning'[16] seems to be to forget the body. I would argue that this view of the experience of moving is not satisfactory in general, and is particularly problematic for physical literacy, which 'directs attention to the role of our embodiment in human experience' (Whitehead, 2007, p. 286). This debate touches on central topics in philosophy of mind that merit further attention.[17]

Summary

This chapter has further developed the argument that phenomenology can serve as a theory for practical knowledge in physical education. In this chapter, it has been argued that the knowledge objects of physical education – that is, the actions, activities and practices which pupils are supposed to learn – are embodied. This idea was refined through a discussion of the notion of poise as it is outlined by Todes (2001). Poise is also a central part of the definition of movement literacy, and Todes provides a new perspective on its centrality. Poise as Todes defines it is a qualitative, felt experience, which is antithetical to more quantitative understandings of sport skills, as well as fundamental motor skills. From a qualitative perspective, all pupils are inherently competent (this also why the notion of expertise is not of relevance to movement literacy and physical education). For sure, there will be differences between pupils, but these differences do not represent deficits. Rather, the 'focus of analysis is upon the "present tense," on what can be achieved in the here and now' (Evans and Penney, 2008, p. 43). In contrast, a quantitative perspective on skills would emphasis the external output displayed by pupils. More specifically, the focus would be on any deficiencies they might exhibit relative to a norm (e.g. a certain level of motor skills).

Perhaps unfairly, I have also used the Skill model to illustrate two problems that might arise in a phenomenological perspective on movement and movement learning. One is that, if poise is a felt experience and movement literacy is centrally concerned with embodied experiences, it might be considered problematic that the body is turned into *a darkness*, almost inaccessible to phenomenological experience. I will argue that this is not a necessary consequence of the phenomenological perspective on movement, and in Chapter 7 I will show that attending to bodily experiences of learning movement can be incorporated into movement literacy and physical education.

I also disputed the position of Dreyfus and Dreyfus on the role of teaching in the Skill model. Their view that teaching is a matter of passing on rules for how to perform specified skills is actually quite similar to the current method used to teach physical education in schools. As Tinning (2010) and Kirk (2010) have observed, the emphasis is on demonstration, explanation and practice (DEP). Both approaches assume that the teacher's role is to pass on rules for actions that the pupils must try out, and in both cases the telos of learning (Lave, 1996) is to forget the body and to automatize the skill. However, there might be room for developing the pedagogy for teaching movement skills in physical education, and I will attend to this in the next chapter.

Notes

1 It is common to distinguish between practical knowledge in its weak and strong senses, the latter requiring fulfilment of all three conditions. Practical knowledge in a weak sense, according to Carr (1981), exists when someone is acquainted with the practical procedures, but unable to perform them. One example might be a ballet dancer who is unable to perform due to either injury or age.

2 As argued in Chapter 1, the approach to physical education is broadly similar in many countries. Therefore, I believe that examples from the Norwegian context are relevant elsewhere.

3 I want to note the distinction between practise with an s and practice with a c. As Aggerholm (2014) notes, practise implies more than simply taking part in a social practice. It has connotations to the German *Übung* and Norwegian *øving*. The notion of 'being practising' is important in physical education (the Norwegian name for physical education is *Kroppsøving*, which would be directly translated to *Body practising*). I will not follow up on this etymological lead here, but the perceptive reader will understand that practising, as it is developed by Aggerholm, is highly relevant to the pedagogical model I am developing in this book.

4 This is not to imply that the theoretical knowledge component, which is not discussed here, is irrelevant or of lesser value. The Norwegian curriculum mandates the acquisition of propositional knowledge in areas such as health, healthy behaviour, how aerobic exercise affects the body and so on (e.g., 'explain the relationship between physical activity, life style and health').

5 '[the field] is pervaded by lines of force (the "yard lines"; those which demarcate the "penalty area") and articulated in sectors (for example, the "openings" between the adversaries) which call for a certain mode of action and which initiate and guide the action as if the player were unaware of it. The field itself is not given to him, but present as the immanent term of his practical intentions; the player becomes one with it and feels the direction of the "goal", for example, just as immediately as the vertical and horizontal planes of his body' (Merleau-Ponty, 1963, p 168).

6 Note that socio-cultural factors influence this as well. The freedom to move is not something determined by bodily conditions alone. Put another way, the environment includes socio-cultural and attitudinal dimensions that limit individual freedom. I will return to this point in Chapter 8.

7 Recall that when I write about *movement* literacy, I am referring to a concept based on Whitehead's *physical* literacy that I propose in this book. As noted earlier, I use a different term to emphasize the distinction between my concept and the broader notion of physical literacy developed by Whitehead. Her concept of physical literacy is broader in two respects: it is intended to cover a much broader area than physical education and its application too has a broader focus on topics such as health and nutrition. Movement literacy is concerned only with the physical education model.

8 In *Body and World*, Todes' project is a critique of dominant figures in the history of philosophy, such as Hume, Kant and Leibniz, who – in different ways – held that intelligibility is a matter of 'objectifying our experience by bringing it under concepts' (Dreyfus, 2002, p. 393). Contrary to these philosophers, Todes argues that perception involves non-conceptual forms of judgment that are nevertheless objective.

9 A loss of the basic feeling of bodily unity, argues Todes (2001), involves at the same time a loss of coordination: 'The person who lacks a feeling of the unity and wholeness of his body can act only by moving parts of his body at a time. He is thus awkward, ridiculous and jerky in his movements' (p. 46). An exception to this is the dance form *popping*, which is a coordinated and rhythmic form of movement where one part of the body is moved and the others isolated, held still.

10 See also Toombs (1995), who illustrates how *here* and *there* change when one is struck by illness or disability.

11 As the mover 'accumulates skills proven effective by his past perceptual experience, *his* perceptual field (evidently generated by *his* capacity to perceive) must reflect this enrichment. To *have* a determinate perceptual field (of one's own) *is* to have evidence of one's general, though not unerring, capacity to effectively determine objects with one's present skills' (Todes, 2001, p. 79, italics in original).

12 The dominant teaching model in the subject, which Tinning (2010) calls DEP, seems to confirm this. DEP stands for demonstration, explanation and practice,

and implies that an ideal or correct movement pattern is presented visually, followed by explanations of how to do it and then a process of trying it out followed by correction of errors.

13 A definition of poise similar to the one suggested here existed more than half a century ago in 'Movement Education', as described, for example, in the English physical education curriculum *Movement and Growing,* published in 1952 (Evans and Penney, 2008). As Jan Wright (2000) points out, however, the approach is based on 'the work of Laban and female educators in the UK,' and got 'criticised and eventually marginalised in physical education because of their failure to conform with the scientific approaches to motor skill acquisition gaining prominence in the 1950s' (p. 35). As Wright (2000) and Kirk (2010) point out, 'Movement Education' was marginalized by other approaches. In this sense, the concept of poise as qualitative rather than quantitative is not new.

14 Although Dreyfus and Dreyfus generally present a five-level model, this was modified in one text to include sixth and seventh levels: mastery and practical wisdom (Dreyfus, 2001), but in most texts from Dreyfus and Dreyfus, the model has five steps. This is also true for a text published after the inclusion of the extra steps (Dreyfus, 2002).

15 National Basketball Association, the world's premier basketball league.

16 Telos of learning refers to 'the change implied in the notions of learning' (Lave, 1996, p. 156). The telos of learning should not be understood merely as a form of goal-directed activity; it refers to the trajectory learners follow in the process of learning.

17 In particular, see the edited volume *Mind, Reason, and Being-in-the-World: The McDowell-Dreyfus Debate* (Schear, 2013).

References

Aggerholm, K. (2014). *Talent development in sport: On becoming an elite athlete.* London: Routledge.

Annerstedt, C. (2008). Physical education in Scandinavia with a focus on Sweden: a comparative perspective. *Physical Education and Sport Pedagogy,* 13(4), 303–318.

Bailey, R., Armour, K., Kirk, D., Jess, M. and Pickup, I. (2009). The educational benefits claimed for physical education and school sport: an academic review. *Research Papers in Education,* 24(1), 1–27.

Breivik, G. (2007). Skillful coping in everyday life and in sport: a critical examination of the views of Heidegger and Dreyfus. *Journal of the Philosophy of Sport,* 34(2), 116–134.

Breivik, G. (2008). Bodily movement: the fundamental dimensions. *Sport, Ethics and Philosophy,* 2(3), 337–352.

Breivik, G. (2013). Zombie-like or superconscious? A phenomenological and conceptual analysis of consciousness in elite sport. *Journal of the Philosophy of Sport,* 40(1), 85–106.

Carr, D. (1981). Knowledge in practice. *American Philosophical Quarterly,* 18(1), 53–61.

Crossley, N. (2001). *The social body: Habit, identity and desire.* London: Sage.

Dreyfus, H. L. (2001). *On the internet.* London: Routledge.

Dreyfus, H. L. (2002). Intelligence without representation: Merleau-Ponty's critique of mental representation. *Phenomenology and the Cognitive Sciences,* 1, 367–383.

Dreyfus, H. L. and Dreyfus, S. E. (1986). *Mind over machine: The power of intuition and expertise in the era of the computer.* New York: The Free Press.

Eriksen, J. (2010). Mindless coping in competitive sport: some implications and consequences. *Sport, Ethics and Philosophy*, 4(1), 66–86.

Evans, J. and Penney, D. (2008). Levels on the playing field: the social construction of physical ability in the physical education curriculum. *Physical Education and Sport Pedagogy*, 13(1), 31–47.

Kirk, D. (2010). *Physical education futures.* London: Routledge.

Lave, J. (1996). Teaching, as learning, in practice. *Mind, Culture and Activity*, 3(3), 149–164.

Merleau-Ponty, M. (1963). *The structure of behavior.* Pittsburg, PA: Duquesne University Press.

Merleau-Ponty, M. (2002). *Phenomenology of perception.* London: Routledge.

Moe, V. F. (2004). How to understand skill acquisition in sport. *Bulletin of Science, Technology and Society*, 24(3), 213–224.

Moe, V. F. (2005). A philosophical critique of classical cognitivism in sport: from information processing to bodily background knowledge. *Journal of the Philosophy of Sport*, 32, 155–183.

Moe, V. F. (2007). Understanding intentional movement in sport: a philosophical inquiry into skilled motor behavior. Doctoral thesis. Oslo:Norwegian School of Sport Sciences. Montero, B. (2013). A dancer reflects. In J. K. Schear (ed.), *Mind, reason, and being-in-the-world: The McDowell-Dreyfus debate* (pp. 303–319). London: Routledge.

Nyberg, G. and Larsson, H. (2014). Exploring 'what' to learn in physical education. *Physical Education and Sport Pedagogy*, 19, 123–135.

Schear, J. K. (ed.) (2013). *Mind, reason, and being-in-the-world: The McDowell–Dreyfus debate.* London: Routledge.

Selinger, E. M. and Crease, R. P. (2002). Dreyfus on expertise: the limits of phenomenological analysis. *Continental Philosophy Review*, 35(3), 245–279.

Standal, Ø. F. and Moe, V. F. (2011). Merleau-Ponty meets Kretchmar: sweet tensions of embodied learning. *Sport, Ethics and Philosophy*, 5(3), 256–269.

Strong, T. (2015). Bodies and thinking in motion. *Janus Head*, 7(2), 516–522.

Sutton, J., McIlwain, D., Christensen, W. and Geeves, A. (2011). Applying intelligence to the reflexes: embodied skills and habits between Dreyfus and Descartes. *Journal of the British Society for Phenomenology*, 42(1), 78–103.

Svenaeus, F. (2009). Vad är praktisk kunnskap? En inledning til emnet och boken [What is practical knowledge? An introduction to the topic and the book]. In J. Bornemark and F. Svenaeus (eds), *Vad är praktisk kunnskap?* (pp. 9–36). Stockholm: Södertörn studies in practical knowledge.

Tinning, R. (2010). *Pedagogy and human movement: Theory, practice, research.* London: Routledge.

Todes, S. (2001). *Body and world.* Cambridge, MA: MIT Press.

Toombs, S. K. (1995). The lived experience of disability. *Human Studies*, 18, 9–23.

Utdanningsdirektoratet (2012). *Læreplan i kroppsøving* [*Physical education curriculum*]. Retrieved from www.udir.no/kl06/KRO1-03/

Whitehead, M. (2001). The concept of physical literacy. *European Journal of Physical Education*, 6(2), 127–138.

Whitehead, M. (2007). Physical literacy: philosophical considerations in relation to developing a sense of self, universality and propositional knowledge. *Sport, Ethics and Philosophy*, 1(3), 281–298.

Wright, J. (2000). Bodies, meanings and movement: a comparison of the language of a physical education lesson and a Feldenkrais movement class. *Sport, Education and Society*, 5(1), 35–49.

Zahavi, D. (2013). Mindedness, mindlessness and first-person authority. In J. Schear (ed.), *Mind, reason, and being-in-the-world: The McDowell–Dreyfus debate* (pp. 320–343). London: Routledge.

5 Teaching embodied knowledge

The previous chapter discussed the ambiguity concerning the role of the teacher in the Skill model. My purpose was not to criticize the Skill model *per se*, but to highlight a problem that arises to some extent in any approach to teaching practical knowledge. Put simply: If movements are performed pre-reflectively, then knowledge of movement is – at least to some extent – a form of tacit knowledge. If practical knowledge to some degree cannot be put into words, what role does this leave the teacher?

Letting learn

In a series of lectures in 1951–52, Heidegger endeavoured to teach his students what thinking means.[1] These lectures have been published as *What Is Called Thinking?* (Heidegger, 1976). The text includes this response to the problem outlined in the introduction to this chapter: 'We shall never learn what "is called" swimming ... or what it "calls for" by reading a treatise on swimming. Only the leap into the river tells us what is called swimming' (s. 21). From a safety standpoint, Heidegger's pedagogical approach is not advisable: we can't just throw our pupils into the deep end so they can learn how to swim (or sink). This is not Heidegger's intention, however. His point is that some forms of knowledge lie outside the discursive realm, at least to some extent. Put differently, some forms of knowledge cannot be adequately expressed in language.

The French sociologist LoïcWacquant's book *Body and Soul: Notebooks of an Apprentice Boxer* (Wacquant, 2004) presents an interesting approach to the pedagogy of embodied learning. Wacquant originally set out to study the Afro-American communities of Southside Chicago. While searching for a vantage point for his research, he came across and joined a boxing club. *Body and Soul* partly outlines the 'carnal' sociology that he subsequently conducted: methodologically speaking, 'a sociology not only *of* the body ... but also *from* the body, that is, deploying the body as tool of inquiry and vector of knowledge' (p. viii). More importantly for this discussion, however, is Wacquant's analysis of his induction into what he calls the sweet science of boxing, culminating in his debut in the ring. Over the course of his field work, the French sociologist – with 'minimal athletic abilities' (Wacquant, 2005, p. 448) – morphed into the pugilist 'Busy Louie'.

Becoming apprenticed

In a comment relevant to the previous chapter and the debate over whether or not skilled movement involves thinking, Wacquant (2004) holds that 'to learn how to box is to imperceptibly modify one's bodily schema, one's relation to one's body and to the uses one usually puts it, so as to internalize a set of dispositions that are inseparably mental and physical' (p. 95). The question is not so much whether one is thinking in action or acting intuitively, since for Wacquant, 'the riddle solves itself as soon as one realizes that a boxer's ability to cogitate and reason in the ring has become *a faculty of his undivided organism* – what John Dewey would call his "body-mind complex"' (p. 97, italics added).

This point is further illustrated through an instance in which Wacquant, in traditional academic fashion, had gone to the university library early in his field work and found a book on boxing entitled *The Complete Workout of the Boxer*. When he asked his coach if he thought the book would be helpful, the coach reacted with scorn. In response to Wacquant's suggestion that at least reading the book wouldn't hurt, the coach replied that it certainly would, especially since he was a novice boxer.[2] The coach's philosophy was the same as Heidegger's: Reading a treatise on a specific movement skill will not teach you how to perform that skill. Here is the problem with the written text, as Wacquant sees it:

> its effect of totalization and detemporalization. The virulence of [the coach's] reaction reveals practically the antinomy that exists between the abstract time of theory (that is, of contemplation) and the time of action … to uproot it [i.e. boxing or more generally movement] from its proper time and tempo, is to impose on it an alteration that destroys it as such.
>
> (p. 101)

By depicting movements in diagrams and drawings, textbooks function as a temporal suspension of movement – and, I would suggest, a disembodied representation as well. The coach's disdain is understandable. The temporal and embodied dimensions of movement are absolutely crucial, because even the most technically perfect movement is meaningless unless it is incorporated into 'the tempo of the exchange and suited to the style of the boxer' (p. 102).

Wacquant describes the alternative to the bookish study of learning how to box as a visual and mimetic apprenticeship as a 'transmission and mastery of bodily knowledge through practical osmosis and visual mimesis, the silent pedagogy of enskilled organisms in action' (2005, p. 454). This pedagogy was largely implicit and collective. Although Wacquant acknowledges that he benefitted from overt and verbal instructions at the gym, he insists that this explicit form of pedagogy was a less powerful source of initiation than the collective teaching provided through the gym's overall organization. He describes a temporal coordination of the training in which the coach keeps track of time (three minutes of effort, one minute pause) so that each individual boxer works on his own, but still in a group. This type of training 'apprenticed' Wacquant by giving him access to role models who were both more and less skilled than he was. Through this 'dialectic of corporeal mastery,' he observes, you can begin to 'understand what you have to do, you watch the others box, but you do not truly see what they are doing, unless you have understood a little with your eyes' (p. 118).

This form of embodied learning through apprenticeship requires abilities of inter-corporeal awareness, i.e. not only awareness of your own body, but the bodies of others, as well as imitation and turn-taking, for instance in the form of observation-then-practice (Sheets-Johnstone, 2000). Sheets-Johnstone asserts that apprenticeship is a fundamental way of learning movement skills, and not only in the sense that we are from birth apprentices of our own bodies:

> skill-learning is rooted in the capacity of one bodily presence to be attentive to another and to pattern movement along the lines of the other, imitating the way in which the other performs something, but also selecting the occasions on which one will and will not perform according to the methods of another.
>
> (p. 359)

Heidegger (1976) also cites apprenticeship as an important way of learning. The apprentice carpenter, he notes, is not merely learning a practice through gaining knowledge about the things he must build. Rather, he must learn to 'answer and respond above all to the different kinds of wood and to the shapes slumbering within the wood – to wood as it enters into man's dwelling with all the hidden riches of its nature' (p. 14). Without being related to the wood in this manner, 'the craft will never be anything but empty busywork' (p. 15). That is, without relatedness to the material, the craft is something done solely for the sake of income, thus lacking any personal investment on the part of the craftsperson. In a similar manner, Wacquant is critical of the fitness industry for appropriating movements that simulate the movements of boxing; taking them out of their context, he observes, robs them of their relationship to the craft of boxing.[3] To be truly apprenticed involves not only learning the actions of the activity, but also learning to participate in its social practices.

Situated learning

Situated learning is a theory that emphasizes learning as a form of social practice (Lave and Wenger, 1991; Wenger, 1998). A key feature of this approach and other theories that view learning as situated action is that actions are not explained and understood in light of the mental states of the individual, but rather 'in terms of what goes on between individuals, and between individuals and situations' (Marton and Booth, 1997, p. 11). Lave and Wenger developed situated learning based on their analysis of studies of apprenticeship learning.[4] Despite this specific origin, they caution that their 'historical-cultural theory of learning should not be [seen as] merely an abstracted generalization of the concrete cases of apprenticeship' (p. 37). Although they agree that apprenticeship is a historical form of learning that is highly variable through time and space, in their view situated learning merits more general application.

In situated learning, the notion 'situated' carries a broader meaning than the obvious fact that learning always takes place in a specific place at a specific time. It also involves more than the social sense of being situated, i.e. that learning involves the presence of, and interaction with, other people. Furthermore, it goes beyond the notion of learning as situated in practical activity (e.g. learning by doing). Rather, the situatedness implied by the term means that 'learning is an integral and inseparable aspect of social practice' (Lave and Wenger, 1991, p. 31). The notion 'situated' thus subsumes practical activities, interaction with others and the place and time of learning, but it is reducible neither to any of these, nor to an aggregate of them.[5]

Situated learning has attracted some interest in the physical education pedagogy field (Kirk andMacPhail, 2002; Kirk and Macdonald, 1998; Kirk andKinchin, 2003). Kirk and Macdonald (1998) have argued that this concept has the potential to become a theory that could integrate diverse constructivist approaches to learning in physical education. These approaches emphasize the active involvement of individuals in the learning process, as well as their interrelationship with the environment and other individuals. Kirk and Kinchin (2003, p. 223) have asserted that situated learning 'is useful to think with in relation to school PE'. Finally, Kirk and MacPhail (2002) have discussed situated learning in relation to the pedagogical model known as Teaching Games for Understanding[6] (TGfU). Here, they summarize their argument:

> When learning to play games is understood as a form of situated learning, we suggest that it becomes possible for teachers to explicitly address aspects of learning that have hitherto at best been understood only intuitively. So, for example, through a situated learning perspective, teachers may be able to address explicitly the authenticity and meaningfulness to children of the experience of learning to play games in school settings.
>
> (p. 189)

Even though Kirk and MacPhail (2002) credit situated learning with providing a theoretical foundation for the TGfU approach to skill acquisition, they believe its major contribution would be to highlight the importance of meaningful participation. This argument touches upon a crucial distinction made in theories on situated learning which, as I noted earlier, is also essential to apprenticeship learning; namely, the link between learning as acquisition of a skill and learning as increased participation in social practices.

Sfard (1998) has presented a theoretical basis for the distinction between the acquisition and participation metaphors. The acquisition metaphor, she maintains, implies that learning is a process of 'gaining ownership over some kind of self-sustained entity' (Sfard, 1998, p. 5). Knowledge is seen as the property of an individual learner, something she 'possesses'. The participation metaphor, in contrast, describes a more action-oriented process of knowing: 'talk about states has been replaced by attention to activities ... the permanence of *having* [knowledge] gives way to the constant flux of *doing*' (Sfard, 1998, p. 6, italics in original). The telos of learning associated with these opposing concepts differs: The acquisition metaphor is based on the premise that knowledge (both theoretical and practical) is stored in the individual, whereas the participation metaphor assumes that learning changes the individual's possibilities for participation in social practices.

The power of the acquisition and participation metaphors is evident in examining the work of theorists such as Kirk who have discussed situated learning and similar pedagogical approaches to physical education. In Kirk's more recent work (2010), he emphasizes two points relevant to these metaphors. First, he criticizes physical education for teaching decontextualized sports techniques, and second, he calls for the development of a relational analysis that puts the practice of physical education more into alignment with the physical culture that young people move about in. If the objects of practical knowledge in physical education are action, activities and practices (see Chapter 4), then situated learning illuminates the problem that arises when techniques and activities introduced in physical education are practised without any reference or connection to the social practices in which they are applied.

Nonlinear pedagogy

The essence of Kirk's critique of current physical education pedagogy, I believe, is that pupils are exposed to a series of introductory lessons in which they are taught fundamental techniques of the various sports included in the curriculum. These lessons follow a pattern in which the techniques are broken down into drills isolated and decontextualized from authentic game situations. As the previous section concluded, not only does this approach lack authenticity and meaning, it also diminishes learning. This observation is also supported by research in motor skill acquisition:

> Undoubtedly, the technique approach is reasonably successful in inducing short-term performance gains among early learners in physical education

> (Rink, 2001), and teachers often mistakenly confuse such temporary improvements with long-term behavioral changes (learning).
>
> (Davids et al., 2008, p. 122)

Physical education-as-sports-technique can be labelled a linear approach, based on the premise that techniques can be broken down into sub-techniques; once learned they can be reassembled into the full skill. The line of development goes from simple to complex, from isolated drills to execution in a real game.

Recently, some experts in the field have called for a nonlinear pedagogical approach to physical education (e.g. Chow et al., 2007; Davids et al., 2008). Theoretically, this approach is based on using dynamic system theory as a framework for skill acquisition. This theory posits that each individual is located in a reciprocal system involving the environment and the particular movement task at hand. The system is dynamic in the sense that changes in one part of the system influence all other parts of the system. Constraints (i.e. the features that shape the emergence of behaviour by a learner who is seeking a stable state of organization (Chow et al., 2007)) can both limit and enable potential movements of the learner. Such constraints can be related to the individual (e.g. age, skill level, anatomical and physiological make-up, or cognitive capacities), to the environment (e.g. physical factors such as surface, light, gravity, or socio-cultural factors such as influence of peer groups, norms or cultural expectations), or to the specific task (e.g. rules of the game, equipment, playing area and so on).

Whereas the linear model of skill acquisition emphasizes teacher-led instruction, the central idea of a nonlinear pedagogy is to facilitate independent learning through exploitation of constraints (Davids et al., 2008) The role of the teacher is to identify and manipulate relevant constraints that can aid the learner in developing particular movements through explorations of the environment. The practitioner of nonlinear pedagogy is considered to be a hands-off pedagogue, whose task is to 'create a learning environment for the discovery of optimal solutions by manipulating constraints, interpreting movement variability and nurturing learners in their search activities' (Davids et al, 2008, p. 100) and 'call forth' a movement pattern that fits each individual pupil. Less importance is attached to an ideal movement pattern that all learners should strive towards, and teachers are not expected to devote much attention to correcting errors in movement.

Although dynamic system theory is to some extent derived from the ecological psychology of J. J. Gibson, rather than phenomenology, the two approaches share fundamental assumptions. Sanders (1993) has observed that 'the internal logic' in the work of Merleau-Ponty and the work of Gibson 'is extraordinarily close' (p. 288). He points out that both scholars drew on the gestalt psychologists and their critique of the atomism of behaviourism. In addition, both understood perception as an activity, rather than a passive response to sensations, rejecting strict bifurcations between subject and object, perceiver and the perceived: 'What is out there – what we respond to – is a function, to an important degree, of us' (Sanders, 1993, p. 289).

The role assigned to the teacher is also similar in nonlinear pedagogy and the phenomenological perspective. Both Heidegger and Wacquant stress the importance of teaching without explicit, prescriptive instructions. So do advocates of nonlinear pedagogy. As Davids et al. (2008) have pointed out, this does not mean that the role of the teacher is diminished, or limited to 'rolling out the ball', as suggested in the caricature of physical education as organized recess. As Heidegger points out, the role of the 'hands-off' teacher is quite demanding:

> Teaching is even more difficult than learning. We know that; but we rarely think about it. Why is teaching more difficult than learning? Not because the teacher must have a larger store of information, and have it always ready. Teaching is more difficult than learning, because teaching calls for this: to let learn. ... If the relation between the teacher and the taught is genuine, therefore, there is never a place in it for the authority of the know-it-all or the authoritative sway of the official.
>
> (Heidegger, 1976, p. 15)

How tacit is it, really?

The storyline of this chapter has taken us from the philosophical and sociological works of Heidegger and Wacquant to apprenticeship and situated learning and then to nonlinear pedagogy. Applied to physical education, all of these perspectives start from the premise that the objects of practical knowledge are embodied and to some extent beyond the discursive realm. In this perspective, pupils will derive more benefits from a hands-off pedagogy, rather than the teacher-centred and instruction-oriented DEP model traditionally employed in physical education. Critics of this approach might question whether it gives too much weight to the tacit dimension of practical knowledge.

The notion of the tacit dimension was developed by Michael Polanyi, a Hungarian scientist and polymath who became a professor of social sciences at Manchester after fleeing the Nazis. Polanyi argued that scientific laboratory work, such as the processes of making and interpreting experiments, involves a great deal of unarticulated knowledge. This knowledge, he argued, is taught and learned via practical exercises and apprenticeships in a laboratory setting (Polanyi, 1962).

The relevance of Polanyi's ideas to movement activities is exemplified by his use of bicycle riding as a standard example of tacit knowledge:

> If I know how to ride a bicycle ... this does not mean that I can tell how I manage to keep my balance on a bicycle ... Nor can it said that I know how to bicycle ... and yet do not know how to coordinate the complex pattern of muscular acts by which I do my cycling.
>
> (Polanyi, 1962, p. 4, as quoted by Collins, 2010, p. 101)

Polanyi's famous phrase 'we know more than we can tell' implies that we cannot produce an exhaustive explanation of how we go about performing an activity such as riding a bike. A corollary of this observation is that knowledge of the bio-mechanical laws of bicycling does not tell us how to balance on a bike. (Polanyi's explanation of tacit knowledge is much more elaborate, but beyond the scope of this chapter.[7])

In his work *Tacit and Explicit Knowledge*, Collins (2010) offers an important critique of Polyani and the standard way his work has been interpreted, asserting that 'a heavy diet of examples of tacit knowledge that turn on the abilities of the body has not been helpful' to our understanding of the concept (p. 11). Even though the body is clearly important in the acquisition of knowledge, Collins argues, this 'says less about the *nature of knowledge* than has been assumed; what it does indicate is something about the nature of human beings and how they acquire knowledge' (p. 8, italics in original).

Usually, tacit knowledge is thought of as that which cannot be made explicit or explicable. However, as Collins (2010) points out, the terms 'explicated' and 'cannot' are both equivocal. He lists eight different meanings of 'cannot', ranging from the logically impossible (it cannot rain and not rain at the same time) to contingent (I cannot tell because it is a secret) (pp. 88–91). Collins' project is to define and explain the explicit and then to classify the tacit. By explicit, Collins means the various ways that strings[8] impact on things through physical impact, inscription or communication. Explicit knowledge is knowledge that to some extent can be transferred through the use of strings under circumstances that enable communication. Though interesting, Collins' discussion of explicit knowledge is less relevant here than his fine-grained classification of tacit knowledge.

Collins divides tacit knowledge into three categories, differentiated by their degree of resistance to being made explicit. Weak or relational tacit knowledge is knowledge that is not made explicit for purely contingent reasons – secrets, for instance. Any individual piece of relational tacit knowledge can in principle be made explicit, but for logistical reasons all of it cannot be made explicit at once.

Medium or somatic tacit knowledge is the kind of knowledge that Polanyi refers to when he discusses bicycling. According to Collins, this kind of knowledge is possible to explicate in principle, but this explication would be of little use to someone who embodies or wants to acquire it. In other words, the bio-mechanical laws for balancing on a bike can be made explicit through scientific explanations, but this would be useless to an imbalanced bike rider, because she would not be able to compute the formula and in that way improve her balance. Collins calls this 'somatic-limit' tacit knowledge, since it is our bodily facticity that prevents us from making use of it. Collins also talks about *somatic-affordance* tacit knowledge. This is knowledge that humans may have that could not be used by other creatures or machines even if explicated, because there is something about our bodily facticity that enables us to apply that knowledge in a way other creatures could not, since they are not like us.

The third form is strong or collective tacit knowledge, which is comprised of those issues that 'we do not know how to make explicit and that we cannot foresee how to explicate' (p. 85). This is knowledge that is located in society and can only be transferred through social practice. The distinction between bike *balancing* and bike *riding* is significant in this regard. While bike balancing is context-free and can be explicated using bio-mechanical models (i.e. somatic tacit knowledge), riding a bike in traffic requires that we understand social conventions that are not available in explicit rule books and vary in different locations. To understand the biking conventions in Oslo, Copenhagen, New York, New Delhi or Beijing, we would have to ride in that city.

Collins' distinctions, particularly between somatic and collective, provide helpful tools to think with in relation to the topic of this chapter. His description of somatic tacit knowledge, for example, makes it clear that this is a kind of knowledge that can be conveyed. Coaching rules like 'it is harder to balance when you are going slowly' promote the development of 'tacit knowledge-laden skills' (p. 63). These pointers or hints are more like rules of thumb than rules of law. When Polanyi talks about explicit knowledge of bike balancing, he is referring to the bio-mechanical law for correcting an imbalance. Collins, in contrast, shows that coaching pointers can convey explicit knowledge without it being knowledge that is scientifically explainable. Even though Wacquant's boxing coach is right in saying that he wouldn't learn how to box by reading a book from the university library, certain boxing skills might still be conveyed through textbooks and coaching pointers. However, this does not negate Wacquant's emphasis on the importance of the collective and of apprenticeship learning, if it is understood that boxing is an activity that involves a great deal of collective tacit knowledge as well as somatic tacit knowledge. It is the social practice of the sport that concerns Wacquant, which probably explains why he ends up describing a pedagogy of 'practical osmosis and visual mimesis' (Wacquant, 2005, p. 454). He is right, according to Collins (2010), to argue that boxers require knowledge that is tacit in the strong sense, but they also benefit from knowledge that is tacit in the medium and weak senses.

Movement literacy as a pedagogical model for physical education

One objective of this book is to refine the notion of movement literacy and explore its relevance to physical education. In concluding this chapter, I will begin to explore how movement literacy can be a pedagogical model contributing to models-based physical education. More specifically, I will address the implications that Chapters 3 and 4 and the first half of this one might have for movement literacy, pedagogically speaking.

One alternative to the traditional, multi-activity, sport-centred curriculum that has been proposed in recent years is models-based physical education.[9] This approach is based on the work of Ann E. Jewett, who outlined and discussed 'curriculum models', and Michael W. Metzler, who did the same for 'instructional models' (see Haerens et al., 2011; Kirk, 2013). As Haerens and co-authors (2011) have observed, focusing on 'curriculum models' puts too much emphasis on the subject matter and concentrating on 'instructional models' puts too much emphasis on the teacher. In contrast, making *pedagogical* models the subject for examination, 'highlights the interdependence and irreducibility of learning, teaching, subject matter and context' (Haerens et al., 2011, p. 324).

The vision of models-based physical education is that the use of several models with distinct features and specific learning outcomes can meet the need for varied forms of physical education. In addition, models-based approaches provide strong arguments for the inclusion of physical education in the school curriculum, with different models offering different forms of support:

> A models-based approach to physical education would make use of a range of pedagogical models, each with its *unique and distinctive learning outcomes* and its *alignment of learning outcomes with teaching strategies and subject matter*, and each with its *non-negotiable features* in terms of what teachers and learners must do in order to faithfully implement the model.
>
> (Kirk, 2013, p. 979, italics added)

In evaluating the appropriateness of movement literacy as a pedagogical model, it is therefore useful to explore its learning outcomes, how these outcomes are aligned with teaching strategies and subject matter, and what non-negotiable features would be.

Learning outcomes

Key points raised in previous chapters are particularly relevant to an exploration of the learning outcomes that could be attained by applying movement literacy as a pedagogical model. In particular, I would argue that the phenomenological perspective, in this book represented by the work of Maurice Merleau-Ponty (1963; 2002; 1968) and Samuel Todes (2001), shows that the knowledge objects of physical education are embodied. This means that the knowledge object and the knowing subject are umbilically connected. The ontology of movement literacy is thus non-dualistic. This represents a subtle but important difference from Whitehead's (2007; 2010) monist approach to physical literacy. In developing the concept of movement literacy, one of my primary goals is to provide a stronger philosophical foundation for two learning outcomes that I have argued should be essential elements of movement literacy: moving with poise, and reading and writing the environment perceptively.

It might be mere coincidence that both Whitehead (2001) and Todes (2001) use the word poise. But the decision of both to use this term might also express something vital about movement activities and movement experiences. For Todes, poise is intended to cover the felt experience, 'the very existence by which the body is, to begin with, knowingly in touch with the objects around it' (Todes, 2001, p. 66). As discussed in Chapter 4, he argues that moving with poise makes the environment of movement habit-able. In contrast with a more traditional understanding of a skill as something one measures and compares to a standard or a norm, he presents poise as a qualitatively felt experience; it is not possible to have more or less of it. Thus Todes' notion of poise is fundamentally different from the approaches to motor skill acquisition (e.g. fundamental motor skills or movement ABC) that predominate in physical education curricula, as well as from the Olympic slogan employed in competitive sports: 'faster, higher, stronger'. Consistent with Todes' perspective, I would argue that Whitehead's (2001) definition of physical literacy should not include the terms economy and efficiency, as both have the connotation of being quantitative, measurable attributes.

The second learning outcome that I believe merits attention is being perceptive in reading and writing the movement environment. One could say that this attribute and poise are opposite sides of the same coin, since poise requires a determination of the perceptual field.[10] We can then consider 'reading the environment' as the capacity to search for and identify opportunities for movement. In my discussion in Chapter 3 of how the notion of embodied learning was developed in the work of Merleau-Ponty and in particular his description (1963) of a football player's relation to the field, I offered support for his position that learning should be taken out of the order of strict objectivity and causality, and placed in the life-world: Embodied learning is not a matter of responding to stimuli, but of being affected by the meaning of the situation taken as a whole. As we learn, we come to see the world differently. In addition, we may come to see ourselves differently. This is one of the implications of the embodied relationship between knowledge objects and the knowing subject that I would argue should be a guiding principle in physical education.

In a non-dualistic ontology, the environment of movement is not completely fixed, since an embodied subject is moving. Thus, 'writing the environment' can be considered as the capacity to create and make changes in the environment that enable the mover to express herself. In other words, 'writing the environment' expresses the moving subject's capacity for shaping the knowledge object to create opportunities for movement. Consistent with this perspective, movement literacy assumes that knowledge objects cannot be predetermined in the form of an ideal movement pattern that learners must incorporate.

It must be noted that the concepts of skill and poise present a challenge for movement literacy here. Todes (2001) argues that poise relies on anticipatory knowledge, which is an expression of the ability to be perceptive in reading the movement environment. An individual possesses this knowledge thanks to an accumulation of

> skills proven effective by his past perceptual experience, *his* perceptual field (evidently generated by *his* capacity to perceive) must reflect this enrichment. To *have* a determinate perceptual field (of one's own) *is* to have evidence of one's general, though not unerring, capacity to effectively determine objects with one's present skills.
>
> (p. 79, italics in original)

Clearly, for Todes, skill level influences how the movement environment is perceived. In other words, increasing your skills allows you to see more possibilities for future actions. However, as I understand Todes (2001), the *experience* of moving with poise is independent of the skill level of the mover. Therefore, I would argue that in movement literacy, the inevitable differences in pupil's skill levels are not a concern in movement literacy. What counts is each individual's experience.

Alignment with teaching strategies

A pedagogical model must constructively align desired learning outcomes with teaching strategies. Most of this chapter has been devoted to an attempt at outlining these teaching strategies. The teaching style of movement literacy assumes that pupils learn best through a hands-off pedagogy. According to dynamic system theories of motor learning, this requires a nonlinear methodology in which the construction of learning landscapes allows pupils to explore and discover different ways of moving.

How this might work is illustrated by a study conducted by Næss and other researchers (Næss et al., 2014). Their action research looked at whether a high school physical education programme can enable pupils to (re)learn to enjoy running. After a group of eight pupils shared their experiences with running in a physical education context, they took part in an eight-week programme in which they explored *how* they would like to run (fast, slow, long, short, as long as they spent 45 minutes doing it), *with whom* (alone or in a group) and *where* (on forest trails, tarmac or a combination of the two). Every lesson ended with the pupils reflecting on their experiences of running that day. The programme made it clear that these experiences were what was important, rather than the pupil's technique, pace or distance covered. Although not couched in phenomenological language, the study was designed to encourage pupils to explore how and where they found poise while running. In contrast to their previous physical education programmes, in which running was introduced only in warm-ups or to test aerobic capacity, this one provided opportunities for the pupils to learn something about themselves as runners and what it would take for them to make the world of running habitable. This small-scale study showed positive results in terms of how the pupils began to think differently about running.

The more general point to be taken from this example relates to my earlier discussion of the role of the teacher: Movement literacy requires a hands-off pedagogue. But being hands-off does not mean being distant or disengaged from the pupils' learning process. On the contrary, the pedagogue must construct a learning environment in which pupils have options and are able to explore their own movement desires and potential. To be effective, a hands-off pedagogue must follow the movement experiences of each pupil closely (see next chapter's discussion of phenomenological pedagogy) and attempt to understand how each pupil interprets those experiences. In addition, the hands-off pedagogue is responsible for encouraging pupils to become self-reflective about their own movement experiences.

Subject matter

A pedagogical model must also say something about subject matter, with the understanding that any specifications should be flexible enough to allow for local adaptations (Haerens et al., 2011). As should be clear from the earlier discussions of poise and the emphasis on valuing individual differences, a curriculum based on movement literacy would exclude activities promoting a strict and normative ideal of how movements should be performed. Put differently, standardization of movements is an ideal that falls outside the domain of movement literacy. Similarly, movement literacy would not include activities that involve competition and ranking of pupils, including traditional team sports. For some, this may sound like a crazy form of physical education: surely, sports and team games are natural ingredients in the subject! My view is that excluding traditional sports and team games from movement literacy illustrates the strength of a models-based approach to physical education, which assumes the curriculum will include multiple models. Some of these models, such as Sports Education or TGfU might include competitive sports and team games.

The particular activities included in the movement literacy model are less important than the way they are practised. The running programme described above (Næss et al., 2014) illustrates this concept: Although the activity of running can be introduced normatively by teaching pupils that there is one ideal way of performing a running stride, in movement literacy the goal would be to encourage each pupil to find her own way of running. In this regard, movement literacy shares the fundamental assumptions of what Brian Pronger has termed post-sport and that Michael Atkinson (2010) has further developed empirically through a study of yoga, parkour and fell-running:

> Post-sports are sinewy and connected athletic practices that are decisively anticommercial, *co-operative over competitive, rejectionist of advanced material technology, socially inclusionary rather than hierarchical, process-oriented, holistic and internally differentiated in their orientation and engagement.* A post-sport physical culture values human spiritual, physical and emotional expression through athleticism beyond medical-technical or power and performance terms.
>
> (p. 125, italics added)

Movement literacy's alignment of learning outcomes with subject matter and teaching strategies promotes the inclusion of activities and practices that facilitate explorations of pupils' movement possibilities and emphasize collaboration rather than competition. It calls for a pedagogy that encourages learning through the creation of learning landscapes that facilitate specific explorations, with the teacher posing questions rather than providing ready-made answers.

I have earlier referred to several authors who have questioned the current practice of physical education where keeping the pupils happy and busy is more important than that they learn something (Annerstedt, 2008; Kirk, 2010; Nyberg and Larsson, 2014). The emphasis on poise as a qualitatively felt experience and on avoiding the normativity of motor and sport skills may create the impression that movement literacy is just another participatory approach to physical education in which it doesn't matter whether or not pupils learn anything so long as they are happy and enjoy taking part in physical activity. However, although movement literacy is concerned with participation, it is also intended to promote learning. Consistent with its foundation in phenomenology, with particular emphasis on the idea that the knowledge object and the knowing subject are interwoven, movement literacy assumes that pupils can and should learn something about themselves as moving subjects. Pedagogies based on the premise that learning in movement activities should focus on skill acquisition or development of performance – achievements that can be measured through pre- and post-testing – do not include subjective experiences as a learning objective. In contrast, learning how to read and write the movement learning environment opens up the possibility that a pupil will learn about her own potential as a moving subject in the world.

Non-negotiable features

I began this chapter with a quote from Martin Heidegger about swimming. The point Heidegger was making was not about skill acquisition. In his view, at its worst, skill acquisition (or technique training) is an objectifying practice that does not facilitate the development of a personal relationship to the activity in question.[11] Heidegger's point is that if we want to know what it means to be swimming or what it means to be a swimmer, we have to engage in the activities and practices of swimming. With this in mind, I will now suggest that the following features are essential elements of any pedagogical model that could be considered a form of movement literacy:

1. Emphasize the qualitatively felt experience of moving, rather than a linear understanding of skill. Avoid normative ideals of performance where pupils are compared with each other or with norms.
2. Emphasize a teaching style that encourages exploration of each pupil's individual potential. Avoid demonstrations intended to convey a 'correct' way of moving that pupils should imitate.
3. Emphasize collaboration between pupils, as opposed to competition.

Notes

1 In the introduction to *What Is Called Thinking*, the translator, J. Glenn Gray, points out that for Heidegger, thinking is not the same as forming an opinion, reasoning or thinking in scientific terms. Even though thinking depends to a great extent on the thinker's will and wishes, it is also something that happens to us as a response on our part to a call which issues from the nature of things [...]

> Thinking is determined by that which is to be thought as well as by he who thinks [...] It is a gathering and focusing of our whole selves on what lies before us and a taking to heart and mind these particular things before us in order to discover in them their essential nature and truth.
>
> (p. xi)

Heidegger's conception of thinking is therefore deeply connected to his conception of being-in-the-world, and his approach to philosophy and philosophizing.

2 This approach is starkly different from the one advocated in the Skill model, in which skill acquisition begins with the teacher providing de-contextualized rules and maxims.

3 'The private forms of pugilistic practice that the new entrepreneurs in body management, always on the lookout for exotic exercises with which to renew a chronically overcrowded fitness market, tried to popularize for a time have nothing in common with boxing but the name' (Wacquant, 2004, p. 100). I would suggest that the same could be said about yoga, which traditionally was a completely different practice from the yoga practiced in fitness centres today.

4 Lave and Wenger (1991) used case studies of a broad range of activities in the book: tailors in Africa, traditional midwives in Mexico, becoming a non-drinking alcoholic, naval quartermasters learning to navigate, and butchers.

5 A full account of the theory of situated learning, in particular key concepts such as community of practice and legitimate peripheral participation, is beyond the scope of this book.

6 TGfU was proposed by David Bunker and Rod Thorpe as an alternative to traditional technique-led approaches to teaching games. In TGfU games are modified to suit the developmental level of the pupils in terms of rules, playing area and equipment. Another feature of TGfU is that it suggests simple games can be used to teach the basics of several different more elaborate games. For example, football, basketball and ice hockey are all based on players invading the territory of the other team to score and defending their own territory to prevent opponents from scoring. A generic invasion game incorporating these similarities could teach tactics common to all three.

7 Hopsicker (2009) has applied Polanyi's theory to analyse skilled motor behaviour. For those interested in a more detailed account of how Polanyi's work is relevant to (philosophy of) sports, that article provides a useful introduction.

8 Strings are 'bits of stuff inscribed with patterns' (Collins, 2010, p. 9). The dark spots that are on this page are examples of strings. They form a pattern that we recognize as letters and that can be physically transformed into vibrations in the air when the letters, words and sentences are read out loud.

9 I referred to Kirk (2010) and his critique of the practice of physical education-as-sport-techniques in Chapter 1.

10 'A percipient can have a determinate perceptual field only by being *poised* in it ... *Our poise is sensuous proof that the perceptual experience of our immediate future conforms to that of our immediate past, and without poise, no determinate perception is possible*' (Todes, 2001, p. 79, italics in original).

11 Or actually facilitates a personal distaste for the activity (Kirk, 2010).

References

Annerstedt, C. (2008). Physical education in Scandinavia with a focus on Sweden: a comparative perspective. *Physical Education and Sport Pedagogy*, 13(4), 303–318.

Atkinson, M. (2010). Fell running in post-sport territories. *Qualitative Research in Sport and Exercise*, 2(2), 109–132.

Chow, J. Y., Davids, K., Button, C., Shuttleworth, R., Renshaw, I. and Arajo, D. (2007). The role of nonlinear pedagogy in physical education. *Review of Educational Research*, 77(3), 251–278.

Collins, H. (2010). *Tacit and explicit knowledge*. Chicago: University of Chicago Press.

Davids, K. W., Button, C. and Bennett, S. J. (2008). *Dynamics of skill acquisition: A constraints-led approach*. Champaign, IL: Human Kinetics.

Haerens, L., Kirk, D., Cardon, G. and De Bourdeaudhuij, I. (2011). Toward the development of a pedagogical model for health-based physical education. *Quest*, 63 (3), 321–338.

Heidegger, M. (1976). *What is called thinking?*New York: Harper & Row.

Hopsicker, P. (2009). Polanyi's 'from-to' knowing and his contribution to the phenomenology of skilled motor behavior. *Journal of the Philosophy of Sport*, 36, 76–87.

Kirk, D. (2010). *Physical education futures*. London: Routledge.

Kirk, D. (2013). Educational value and models-based practice in physical education. *Educational Philosophy and Theory*, 45(9), 973–986.

Kirk, D. and Kinchin, G. (2003). Situated learning as a theoretical framework for sport education. *European Physical Education Review*, 9(3), 221–235.

Kirk, D. and Macdonald, D. (1998). Situated learning in physical education. *Journal of Teaching in Physical Education*, 17, 376–387.

Kirk, D. and MacPhail, A. (2002). Teaching games for understanding and situated learning: rethinking the Bunker-Thorpe model. *Journal of Teaching in Physical Education*, 21(2), 177–192. Lave, J. and Wenger, E. (1991). *Situated learning: Legitimate peripheral participation*. Cambridge: Cambridge University Press.

Marton, F. and Booth, S. (1997). *Learning and awareness*. Mahwah, NJ: Lawrence Erlbaum Associates.

Merleau-Ponty, M. (1963). *The structure of behavior*. Pittsburg, PA: Duquesne University Press.

Merleau-Ponty, M. (1968). *The visible and the invisible*. Evanston, IL: Northwestern University Press.

Merleau-Ponty, M. (2002). *Phenomenology of perception*. London: Routledge.

Næss, H. S., Säfvenbom, R. and Standal, Ø. F. (2014). Running with Dewey: is it possible to learn to enjoy running in high school physical education? *Qualitative Research in Sport, Exercise and Health*, 6(2), 301–315.

Nyberg, G. and Larsson, H. (2014). Exploring 'what' to learn in physical education. *Physical Education and Sport Pedagogy*, 19, 123–135.

Polanyi, M. (1962). *Personal knowledge: Towards a post-critical philosophy*. London: Routledge.

Sanders, J. T. (1993). Merleau-Ponty, Gibson, and the materiality of meaning. *Man and World*, 26(3), 287–302.

Sfard, A. (1998). On two metaphors for learning and the dangers of choosing just one. *Educational Researcher*, 27(2), 4–13.

Sheets-Johnstone, M. (2000). Kinetic tactile-kinesthetic bodies: ontogenetical foundations of apprenticeship learning. *Human Studies*, 23, 343–370.

Todes, S. (2001). *Body and world*. Cambridge, MA:MIT Press.
Wacquant, L. (2004). *Body and soul: Notebooks of an apprentice boxer*. New York: Oxford University Press.
Wacquant, L. (2005). Carnal connections: on embodiment, apprenticeship, and membership. *Qualitative Sociology*, 28(4), 445–473.
Wenger, E. (1998). *Communities of practice: Learning, meaning and identity*. Cambridge: Cambridge University Press.
Whitehead, M. (2001). The concept of physical literacy. *European Journal of Physical Education*, 6(2), 127–138.
Whitehead, M. (2007). Physical literacy: philosophical considerations in relation to developing a sense of self, universality and propositional knowledge. *Sports Ethics and Philosophy*, 1(3), 281–298.
Whitehead, M. (2010). The concept of physical literacy. In M. Whitehead (ed.), *Physical literacy: Throughout the lifecourse* (pp. 10–20). London: Routledge.

6 Phenomenological pedagogy and embodied experiences

In this chapter, I will present the phenomenological pedagogy developed by Max van Manen and discuss the ways it can contribute to the movement literacy model for physical education, particularly in relation to embodied experiences. If physical literacy is a 'philosophy in search of a pedagogical model' (Kirk, 2013, p. 979), then I suggest that phenomenological pedagogy could be a useful place to start, because of the common ground in phenomenology it shares with movement literacy.

Phenomenological pedagogy

Before describing phenomenological pedagogy as outlined by Max van Manen, I will first briefly discuss in what sense it is phenomenological. Also, I will discuss the relevance of phenomenological pedagogy for physical education.

In what sense is phenomenological pedagogy phenomenological?

Max van Manen is a Dutch-Canadian, former professor of education at the University of Alberta, Canada. Even though he did not invent phenomenological pedagogy (see below), his name is very much linked to it, because he has both developed and made it accessible to the English-speaking world. Before attending to the contents of this pedagogical approach, it is worth inquiring in what sense it is phenomenological.

In an earlier chapter, I discussed Martinkova and Parry's (2011) critique of the superficial use of the term *phenomenological* in qualitative research. Briefly re-stated, their critique was that in sport literature, there is a tendency to use the term phenomenological in inappropriate ways, where the usage departs from the philosophical project of phenomenology. One argument is that phenomenology as philosophy seeks to uncover the ontological and not the ontic, i.e. the 'modes and structures of the being of entities, not in the particular entities themselves' (p. 189). Qualitative phenomenological research on the other hand, can only gain knowledge about the ontic, because it studies personal, individual experiences. This, according to Martinkova and Parry, does not qualify as phenomenological, because it is not strictly philosophy.

Thus, Martinkova and Parry's advice is to 'beware phenomenological flag-waving!' (p. 199).

On the basis of this critique one might wonder whether phenomenological pedagogy is just another such instance of unjustified flag-waving. In one sense, van Manen (1996) actually agrees with Martinkova and Parry when he states that in education 'there has been a virtual explosion of studies that purport phenomenological and hermeneutical affiliations, but often these writings bear little resemblance to the insightful interpretive texts of the original phenomenological tradition' (p. 40). On the other hand, this quote also reveals a difference from Martinkova and Parry (2011), because whereas their focus is mainly on the phenomenology developed by Husserl in order to investigate transcendental subjectivity, van Manen's emphasis is on the more existential aspects of phenomenological philosophy developed by later phenomenologists such as Sartre and Merleau-Ponty.

When van Manen (1996; 1978) traces the origin of phenomenological pedagogy, he refers to the so-called Utrecht School, a group of educators, psychologists and psychiatrists who were educated in phenomenological philosophy. According to van Manen, this group of scholars was influenced by phenomenologists such as Husserl and Heidegger, and also hermeneutic philosophers like Dilthey, Schleiermacher and Gadamer. This is a constellation of philosophers that broadly falls under the notion of *Geisteswissenschaften*, i.e. an approach to science which holds that human phenomena must be studied using methods different from those applied to the study of natural phenomena. The Utrecht School was also inspired by Husserl's turn to the life-world, but sought to establish 'a pedagogy on phenomenological principles' (van Manen, 1978, p. 50) by drawing more on the work of the existential and hermeneutical thinkers already mentioned. More specifically,

> The Utrecht School adopted from Husserl the desire to develop a science of subjectivity, of the life-world. Therefore, the emphasis in phenomenological pedagogy is on the concept of the life-world and educational situations. The difference between Husserl and his followers at the Utrecht School is that the latter accepted Husserl's theme of the natural attitude and the life-world as an avenue that would lead to a new pedagogy and a new psychology. However, like the existentialists, they did not (and do not now) want to follow Husserl on his path to the creation of a transcendental phenomenology wherein all subjectivity would be formalized – cut off from its concrete and existential referents.
> (p. 56)

There is of course an issue here about the degree to which there is a marked break between Husserl's idealistic phenomenology and the later existentialists. Some hold that there is a sharp distinction between the two (e.g. Priest, 1998), whereas others, such as Zahavi (2003) claim that studies of the so-called *Nachlass* (i.e. the large body of unpublished work of Husserl) indicate that 'it is certainly striking how many similarities there are between Husserl's account of the relation between self, world, and other, and the accounts to be found among the later phenomenologists (Heidegger, Sartre, and Merleau-Ponty)' (p. 77). In any case, the point here is that the Utrecht School, as well as van Manen himself, are interested in the practical and reflective method of phenomenology rather than phenomenology as professional philosophy (i.e. in the sense of a philosophical discipline). Indeed, in van Manen's (2014) latest work, he argues that in some cases, professional philosophers who are working with phenomenology are not doing phenomenological work. His point is that these philosophers are caught up in exegesis and technical discourse that has lost touch with the originary experiences that phenomenology set out to study. As a consequence, phenomenological pedagogy should not be taken as an attempt to practice academic philosophy, but rather as a way of being oriented by phenomenological philosophy in one's practice as a pedagogue.

The pedagogy

Being oriented[1] by phenomenology means approaching a given area of interest (in this case pedagogical practice) with an awareness of its phenomenological potential. Van Manen describes the phenomenological orientation towards pedagogy with reference to Merleau-Ponty's preface to the *Phenomenology of Perception*. The phenomenologist is 'a perpetual beginner' (Merleau-Ponty, 2002, p. xv), someone who approaches each situation with an attitude of not wanting to let previous experiences and knowledge determine what she sees in the present situation. This means that the phenomenologist's task is to describe a situation before analysing it. A pedagogue with a phenomenological orientation attempts to describe what it is like to have a certain experience in a given pedagogical situation. In this sense, phenomenological orientation provides a specific way of knowing the world, where the pedagogue is 'mindful of the ease with which we tend to rely on a reconstructed logic in our professional endeavors. We read theories into everything' (van Manen, 1982, p. 296).

We read theories into everything is a good starting point for outlining phenomenological pedagogy. Throughout his entire work, van Manen has been concerned with an opposition to 'calculative rationality' (van Manen, 2007, p. 20) as the foundation for pedagogical practice. His preferred approach suggests a different way of knowing the world:

> Coming to an understanding is a sense-making and an interpretative enterprise. In this context, practical knowledge does not consist of technical-practical recommendations derived from empirical-analytical theory and research. Practical knowledge, in a communicative sense, is provided by those phenomenological and interpretive bodies of knowledge and literature that help the teacher gain access to the *Verstehende* reality of humans' lifeworlds.
>
> (van Manen, 1977, p. 220)

The link between phenomenology and pedagogy that van Manen has developed since the 1970s is based on an interpretative approach to the realities of teaching and raising children.

Van Manen wants to get away from a pedagogy where the teacher or parent's methods are based entirely on pre-determined facts, theories or ideologies. Put differently: van Manen is worried that an overly theoretical and empirical-analytical approach to the act of teaching hinders the pedagogue from grasping the lived qualities of the pedagogical situation. By technical approach, van Manen means 'an instrumental preoccupation with techniques, control, and with means-ends criteria of efficiency and effectiveness' (ibid., p. 209). In other words, van Manen has from the start of his academic career been proposing an alternative to the modern idea of evidence-based practice (Standal, 2008).

Van Manen also expresses his opposition to technical approaches to pedagogical work in his discussion (1996) of the work of Nicolaas Beets, a member of the Utrecht School. Beets outlined the difference between medical and pedagogical thinking about children, arguing that a medical, diagnostic way of thinking about children conflicts with a pedagogical orientation. Whereas medical thought is concerned with 'the (almost moral) idea of the (statistical) average or normal pattern' (p. 13), the fundamental pedagogical question is 'what is it like for the child to experience a situation like this?' (p. 11). Pedagogical thinking of the phenomenological kind does not reduce the child to its medical diagnosis, instead considering the child's concrete and particular situation. It is this difference between attending to the child's specific experience of a concrete situation rather than to diagnostic categories that shows more generally van Manen's opposition to theoretical or analytical approaches to pedagogy. Instead, he favours an approach that emphasizes describing rather than explaining.

The phenomenological pedagogue begins her work in the facticity of a social situation by describing and clarifying the details of the situation and the background in which the situation occurs. The concept of *situation analysis* was therefore important to the members of the Utrecht School (van Manen, 1977). In terms of pedagogical practice, the Utrecht School restructured social situations based on their situational analysis in order to create an improved educational situation. This transformation of social situation into educational situation comes about through the active intervention of a pedagogue.

Van Manen views pedagogy as primarily a relationship between an adult and a child,[2] and argues that in every pedagogical situation there is a 'relation of influence' (1996, pp. 44–45) in the sense that the adult – the pedagogue – is the one who is responsible for the situation. Only gradually, van Manen notes, does the child begin to assume more responsibility. This asymmetrical relationship within pedagogy introduces to it a normative and ethical dimension. If pedagogy is understood as a practical knowledge of acting in certain concrete situations, then the pedagogue also needs to be able to distinguish between the appropriate and the inappropriate, between right and wrong actions.

A key notion in phenomenological pedagogy is *tact*, which has three central meanings (van Manen, 1993). Etymologically, tact refers to the sense of touch or feeling. This suggests that tact has something to do with touching or being in touch, such as in the word tactile. Further, tact is used in music to describe the orchestration of several instruments, and in addition, tact connotes the ability to deal carefully with delicate situations. In a related sense, teacher's tact refers to a pedagogue's ability to be in touch with the teaching situation, to find the rhythm of the pupils, and to create learning situations in ways that are precisely suited to their needs. According to van Manen, tact is a teacher's ability

> *to see* a situation calling for sensitivity, *to understand* the meaning of what is seen, *to sense* the significance of this situation, *to know* how and what *to do*, and to actually do something right.
>
> (1993, p. 132, italics added)

It is clear from the verbs in the quote that tact unfolds through acts of pedagogy, i.e. it is an ability to interact with others in a pedagogical relationship. This also indicates that for van Manen, pedagogy is a form of practical knowledge, the meaning of which must continually be redeemed (van Manen, 1982). In other words, true pedagogy is not attained via a course certification, a teaching licence or even being employed as a teacher/pedagogue. Instead, the concept of pedagogy must be understood performatively through doing; one becomes a pedagogue through active participation in specific pedagogical relationships.

How?

The aim of phenomenological pedagogy seems clear enough; the teacher should be sensitive to the lived experiences of pupils in specific learning situations *and* be capable of responding to them in an appropriate, ethical and effective way. However, one might ask how these skills can be put into practice. Is there any such thing as a how-to guide to phenomenological pedagogy?

In fact, van Manen resists answering the question of how. Perhaps due to his opposition to technical guidelines for teaching, he is reluctant to offer specific answers to such questions. Instead, he addresses the question in this manner:

> As teachers and researchers we are interested in the promise that phenomenology can make to practice. But Heidegger warns that phenomenology 'never makes things easier, but only more difficult' (2000, p. 12). He agrees with those who feel that phenomenology lacks effectiveness or utility if one hopes to do something practically useful with it.
>
> (van Manen, 2007, p. 13)

Phenomenological pedagogy does not provide us with anything useful; it actually makes things harder for us! If we can't do anything with it, then what is the point? Following Heidegger, van Manen argues that even if we can't do anything with phenomenology, that doesn't make it useless. On the contrary, the usefulness of phenomenology and phenomenological pedagogy is the effect they have on the pedagogue. Instead of providing how-to guides, phenomenological pedagogy 'aims to open up possibilities for creating formative relations between being and acting, between who we are and how we act, between thoughtfulness and tact' (van Manen, 2007, p. 13). Van Manen refers to this as *pathic knowledge* (van Manen, 1996; van Manen and Li, 2002). The teacher's practical knowledge is pathic in the sense that it depends on 'presence, relational perceptiveness, tact' and other aspects of 'pre-reflective, pre-theoretical, pre-linguistic knowledge' (van Manen and Li, 2002, p. 217).

Pathic knowledge is, as the word suggests, knowledge related to sympathy and empathy, i.e. it is a form of inter-subjective relationship between teacher and pupil. It is this kind of knowledge that helps teachers become attuned to pedagogical situations and the experiential dimensions of pupils. Pathic knowledge is embodied knowing, which in addition to providing a corporeal sense of ourselves, things and others, can be described in several forms:

- *Actional knowing*: knowledge expressed through personal styles of teaching, habits and kineasthetic memories.
- *Temporal knowing*: humans are temporal beings in the sense that the present now is a projection of past knowledge towards the future. Temporal knowing is expressed through intentions, inclinations and orientations.
- *Situational knowing*: all knowledge, including knowledge of ourselves is distributed and relational, residing to some extent in the world around us and the way we interact with it.
- *Relational knowing*: teachers' knowledge also resides in the relationships they form with others.

Van Manen and Li's (2002) elaboration of the pathic is based on phenomenology and is a form of practical knowledge. Whereas practical knowledge in the previous chapters has described the kind of knowledge embodied by pupils when they move, pathic, practical knowledge is held by teachers and takes on a different form. Pathic, practical knowledge is based on pupils' experiences in a given situation and the implications these experiences have for the pedagogical work of the teacher.

To the extent that van Manen does answer the question of *how*, it is not so much to explain how teachers can use phenomenological pedagogy. Instead, he describes what it consists of (i.e. its epistemology rather than its method). What van Manen does describe several times and in great detail is how teachers can develop pathic knowledge. In most of his published work, anecdotes, vignettes and short, life-world descriptions of pedagogical incidents (van Manen, 1990) play a crucial role. Van Manen believes that an effective method of developing pedagogical tact is to read and write phenomenological texts. It is only by absorbing language that is 'sensitive to the thoughtfulness required in contingent, moral, and relation situations' (van Manen, 2007, p. 21) and using that language to form teaching narratives that truly responsive pedagogical tact can be developed.

Here, there is also a link between van Manen's pedagogy and his methodological classic, *Researching Lived Experience: Human Science for an Action Sensitive Pedagogy* (van Manen, 1990). The author outlines a methodology of researching lived experience in order to generate human science knowledge that can inform pedagogy, or more generally, phenomenological practice (van Manen, 2007). The means by which this knowledge is generated are the same as those van Manen suggests are necessary for developing pedagogical tact in teachers: using personal experiences, being sensitive to language (for instance by tracing etymology and idiomatic expressions), interviewing or closely observing others, and attending to experiential descriptions in literature.

Phenomenological pedagogy for physical education?

Tinning (2010) briefly introduces phenomenological pedagogy in his book *Pedagogy and Human Movement*. He pays particular attention to phenomenological pedagogy's emphasis on the relationship between the pedagogue and the pupil, and how this relationship must be informed by ethical reflection. Without this kind of reflection, the pedagogue is reduced to an instructor who merely hands over prescriptions for practice. The way van Manen avoids the question of how to teach is indicative of his commitment to an ethically informed, non-technical teaching approach. If we think of the DEP-method of teaching as the traditional and most common style of teaching in physical education (Kirk, 2010; Tinning, 2010), then phenomenological pedagogy represents a useful supplement. Or perhaps even more than that, it can provide an alternative to technical, instructional teaching methods – a much needed framework for ethical considerations on the process of teaching physical education.

This is not to suggest that current physical education literature is devoid of ethical and moral reflection. One common argument used to justify physical education is its potential for developing moral character in pupils (Loland, 2006; Stolz, 2014). However, this line of thought has traditionally been more concerned with how sports and physical activity can strengthen the pupils' moral character than with ethical issues pertaining to the teaching and learning process *per se*. Furthermore, the critical-pedagogical perspective, which is advocated by Tinning (2010), among others, certainly has ethical commitments. Critical pedagogy insists on a reconstruction of physical education in order to make the subject more socially just and equitable. However, the way I understand it, the commitment of critical pedagogy is focused primarily on institutions, school systems, policies, and so on – in short, it maintains a macro perspective. Phenomenological pedagogy, on the other hand, concentrates on the micro interactions between teacher and pupils. This is not to say that critical pedagogy is not at all interested in the micro perspective. Indeed, proponents of critical pedagogy are greatly concerned with how individual, subjective experiences are shaped by socio-cultural contexts as well as the ethical implications this may have for teaching and learning in physical education. Yet, as Tinning (2010) argues, critical pedagogy's line of inquiry is different from that which is characteristic of the phenomenological perspective. They are set in different research paradigms, which, along with other differences, means that their commitment to ethical reflections on the micro-interaction of pedagogical encounters is built on different ontological and epistemological assumptions.[3]

However, phenomenological pedagogy's emphasis on the need for ethical reflection is not, in my judgment, its most significant contribution to physical education. Rather, it is the insistence on the pupils' lived experiences as the starting point for the teacher's work that is the primary contribution of phenomenological pedagogy. I would suggest that the work of van Manen offers an important argument for justifying the place of physical education in educational systems. Stolz (2014) recently called attention to major point in phenomenological pedagogy: 'we need to locate the body as a focal point in the production of lived experience, and also recognise the role corporeal movement and embodiment plays in learning, in, by, and through physical education' (p. 89).[4] Stolz also makes the connection between the work of van Manen and P. J. Arnold's education in movement, which – as shown in Chapter 2 – is thought of as a central work in defining the educational value of physical education. I will now expand upon this point to show how phenomenological pedagogy can contribute to movement literacy as a pedagogical model for physical education.

Phenomenological pedagogy and movement literacy

There is a clear analogy between phenomenological pedagogy and physical literacy as developed by Whitehead (2007). Not only do they both have their origin in the phenomenological tradition, but the notion of tact (see definition above) and the way Whitehead (2013) describes the teacher's relationship with her learners are quite similar:

> listening to the learners' voices demonstrates the teacher's real interest in the experiences of young people. Acting, as appropriate, on their views is a clear indication that the learners are seen as having a contribution to make to decisions relating to the learning/teaching in lessons.
>
> (p. 45)

However, when Whitehead goes on to talk about *how* and *what* to teach, her focus shifts towards a more psychological orientation: she refers to concepts like goal setting, self-perception, self-confidence and self-esteem. Haydn-Davies'

(2010) chapter on physical literacy, teaching and learning shares many of the same phenomenological sentiments that Whitehead presents in her work, but my overall impression is that both Whitehead and Haydn-Davies interpret the teaching/learning process mostly via psychological concepts. My question then is whether the phenomenological perspective underpinning physical literacy could become further strengthened by drawing attention to how phenomenology can inform the pedagogical work.

There is in principle nothing wrong with drawing on psychological theories of teaching and learning, and in the context of physical literacy it is not a very surprising choice, given physical literacy's commitment to 'motivation and confidence'. When Whitehead (2013) discusses the goals of physical literacy, she mentions 'the confident use of generic movement patterns … a curriculum that looks widely at movement competences' (p. 48). Even though she also refers to 'broad categories of movement experience' (ibid.), her focus is undoubtedly on the development of confidence or specific patterns of movement, as opposed to phenomenology's emphasis on the experience of movement. van Manen's work on phenomenological pedagogy and the promotion of embodied experience can broaden the utility of movement literacy as a pedagogical model for physical education.

Subjective and objective experiences of the body

The concept of experience is central to much – if not all – of the physical education literature dealing with phenomenology (see Chapter 2). Phenomenology provides conceptual tools to understand the embodied dimensions of human experience. If we want to have a proper understanding of the pupils we work with in physical education, we must include the experiential and embodied dimensions of their existence (Stolz, 2014). Phenomenology's contribution is a non-dualistic understanding of the human body. Any understanding of the body as primarily a bio-mechanical and physiological machine that can be exercised is overlooking a central aspect of our humanity. In this part of the chapter, I will therefore trace the modes of embodied experience from the prenoetic operations of the body-schema to objectifying self-distancing.

The body schema and the body object

Secondary literature on Merleau-Ponty makes frequent use of the notions 'lived body' and 'body-subject' (e.g. Hass, 2008; Matthews, 2004). As I understand it, lived body and body-subject are overlapping, but not synonymous. In order to explain this, I will draw upon another distinction central to the work of Merleau-Ponty, namely that between body schema and body image. As Gallagher (e.g. 2001; 2005) makes clear, these terms have a long history in various fields of study, such as philosophy and psychology, but neither their individual meaning nor the conceptual distinction between them are clear. It has therefore been advocated that the terms should be abandoned to history, but Gallagher (2005) argues that if properly clarified, the notions body schema and body image can be helpful in explicating the role of embodiment in the structure of consciousness.

Merleau-Ponty (2002) takes up the body schema in his investigation of the spatiality of the body. He describes it initially as a

> compendium of our bodily experience … supposed to register for me the positional changes of parts of my body for each movement of them … a total awareness of my posture in the intersensory world, a 'form' in the sense used by Gestalt psychology.
>
> (pp. 113–114)

The body schema, in this interpretation, is a system that registers body movements and body postures as gestalts, that is, as figures standing out on an undifferentiated background. In *The Structure of Behavior*, Merleau-Ponty (1963) drew on the work of gestalt psychologists in order to lay the foundation for his phenomenological analysis of perception (see Chapter 3 above), but he also criticized the gestalt psychologists for being entrenched in physiology and lacking an understanding of being-in-the-world. '"figure and ground" has a meaning only in the perceived world', he wrote. 'It is there that we learn what it is to be a figure and what it is to be a ground. The perceived would be explicable only by the perceived itself, and not by physiological processes' (p. 92). Therefore, if the body schema is to be understood as a gestalt 'this occurs in virtue of [the body] being polarized by its tasks, of its *existence towards* them … the body [schema[5]] is finally a way of stating that my body is in the world' (Merleau-Ponty, 2002, p. 115, italics in original).

In this interpretation, the body schema does its work 'before we know it' (Gallagher, 2005, p. 5), and is thus a structure that structures our experiences of the body in action. It pragmatically takes account of objects in the environment, incorporating them into its structure and thus blurring the limits between the body and environment. This does not mean that the body schema is purely reflexive, or reacting automatically. Gallagher takes care to point out that the body schema operates in a *close* to automatic way and that it is involved in goal-directed behaviour: 'motor action is not completely automatic; it is often part of a voluntary, intentional project' (p. 26), in which the body has a tendency to efface itself. The body schema thus supports intentional actions.

According to Gallagher (2005) the body image 'consists of a complex set of intentional states and dispositions – perceptions, beliefs, and attitudes – in which the intentional object is one's own body' (p. 25). It is to the extent that we attend to our own bodies that the body image comes into play. In the body image, the body appears as differentiated from the environment. Bodily features or specific parts of the body can be discriminated or isolated, such as the conscious registering of a limb's position. In this sense, the body image involves abstract representations of the body. That is, the body, or parts of the body, is consciously attended to as an object of perception. In other words, the difference between body schema and image is that with the body image 'one is consciously attending to body', whereas with the body schema one is 'marginally aware of the body' (Gallagher, 2005, p. 27). The body is more of a fully fledged object in the body image than it is in the body schema.

The term 'lived body' clearly points to the phenomenological ambition to give an account of the body *as we live it*. In Gallagher's interpretation, the body schema is a prenoetic structure of embodiment. The term prenoetic refers to the hidden aspects of our embodiment, or as Gallagher (2005) puts it: 'To ask about the prenoetic effects of embodiment is to ask about what happens behind the scenes of awareness, and about how the body anticipates and sets the stage for consciousness' (p. 2). What the distinction between body schema and body image makes clear is that there are aspects of purposive movements that are phenomenologically hidden: they are not accessible to subjective experience. The crucial difference between the lived body and the body-subject then, is that the body-subject incorporates the prenoetic operations of the body schema and the pre-reflective awareness of the body as it is lived. The lived body is not consciously aware of those aspects of the body-subject that are phenomenologically hidden, but it does have pre-reflective access to the outcome of the phenomenologically hidden operations of the body schema. In my reading, then, the body-subject refers to a broader range of experience than either the lived body or the body schema.

The distinction between body image and body schema is a conceptual one, which on the behavioural level is not so clear-cut: 'The dancer or the athlete who practices long and hard to make deliberate movements proficient so that movement is finally accomplished by the body without conscious reflection uses a consciousness of bodily movement to train body-schematic performance' (Gallagher, 2005, p. 35). Similarly, aspects of body image, such as my sense of how my body looks, can shape my perceptions of the world *before I know it*. That is, the body image can itself function in a prenoetic way. The latter issue I will return to later, in the context of queer phenomenology (Ahmed, 2006). For now, it suffices to note that Slatman (2014), referring to Iris Young (see Chapter 8), claims that

> Young's analysis of gendered embodiment makes clear that adapting to (and internalizing) dominant gender norms can have a literally inhibiting effect on motor capacity [...] Inhibition or enforcement of one's I can is produced by social differences, which, in turn, are produced by one's body's visible manifestation.
>
> (p. 554)

The issue concerning how both the body image and body schema are involved in learning movement raises several questions that are relevant to phenomenology and pedagogy in physical education, about the relationship between subjective, pre-reflective experience and the role of more objective forms of reflection in learning and developing movement capabilities. In order to pursue such questions, I will next examine Drew Leder's (1992) essay 'A Tale of Two Bodies'.

A tale of two bodies: Relevant for physical education?

The history of physical education is linked to the Swedish system of Ling gymnastics, which was originally developed for medical purposes (Kirk, 2010; Tinning, 2010). Presently, physical education in schools is touted for its effectiveness as a type of preventive medicine. The argument is that more physical education leads to more physical activity defined in physiological terms (see note 1, chapter 1) and hopefully, or so the argument goes, this in turn will lead to both short and long-term health benefits. In this section, I will draw on Drew Leder's (1992) essay 'A Tale of Two Bodies: The Cartesian Corpse and the Lived Body', in order to highlight the contribution of phenomenology to understanding the subjective nature of embodiment. Leder's critique is directed at medicine, but I ask whether and how his claims could be relevant to physical education.

Leder begins by examining Cartesianism, a doctrine of philosophy based on the work of René Descartes. Descartes divided the body and the mind into two separate entities, *res extensa* and *res cogitas.* The body belonged to *res extensa*, the extended substance, which is part of the natural world and as such, governed by the mechanical forces of nature. The mind, on the other hand, was thought of as *res cogitas*, which is the definitional mark of human beings: I think therefore I am.

Leder claims that modern medicine is at its heart a Cartesian project. More specifically, a central point for Leder is that 'Cartesian thought is profoundly shaped by the figure of the dead body. This body … provides a tool for securing knowledge; and finally, it rests at the heart of the mechanist world-view and its associated projects of mastery' (p. 21). Since illness is expressed in a body that belongs to the extended, material world (*res extensa*), Cartesianism suggests that the mechanical causes of the illness could be exposed through dissections of dead bodies.[6] Thus, Leder argues that the corpse – the dead body – has epistemological primacy in medicine.

It is not only in the context of finding the causes of illnesses that the dead body holds primacy in medicine. According to Leder, 'given the vision of embodiment which underlies our disease categories and diagnostic methods, it is not surprising that the process often culminates in mechanistic forms of treatment' (p. 22). In therapies based on this paradigm, the body is understood via a machine-model: its different parts are observed as though they are unrelated to each other, yet nevertheless mechanically connected, similarly to, say, the parts of an engine in a car. The separated parts can be manipulated and acted upon in isolation from the other parts.

Being a medical doctor, however, Leder does not fail to praise the success and benefits of modern medicine, but his critique is that the body-as-machine model of medicine has hampered the medical establishment's ability to acknowledge the importance of patients' subjective experiences of illness.[7]

Starting with an evocative description of his first visit to the anatomy lab, Pronger (1995) explores how knowledge of anatomy, obtained via dissections and other images of dead bodies, shapes the attitudes of future physical education teachers. Pronger's concern is how the implicit lessons of anatomy go beyond the seemingly innocent knowledge of the various names and functions of different parts of the body. More specifically, through anatomy courses, physical education teachers learn about the body as an object, which can (or even should) be scrutinized with a scientific gaze, as though it were an instrument.

> implicit in the pedagogy of anatomy is a technological attitude toward the body; the bridge between functionality and usefulness being easy to traverse once the body has been rendered a functional object.
>
> (Pronger, 1995, p. 436)

Pronger is careful to point out that neither the implicit nor the explicit lessons of anatomy in and of themselves create the technological attitude towards the body as an object in physical education teacher education. Rather, Pronger claims that these lessons, together with other natural scientific subjects in their education, merely confirm the student's preconception of the body as a technological object. This preconception, already shaped and formed during their own sporting or fitness practices as well as other socio-cultural experiences, is endorsed by their education. In other words, viewing the body as an object, which is mechanically manipulable, becomes invested with a sense of power.

However, Pronger (1995) argues that every student 'has a subjective, experiential understanding of the body that is very unlike the objective, mechanistic, technological approach of gross anatomy' (p. 440). A similar point is made by Sigmund Loland (1992), who has examined the mechanics and meaning of alpine skiing. Loland distinguishes between an analytical (mechanics, natural science) and a holistic (lived experience, existential) approach to understanding sport technique. Whereas Pronger (1995) takes a critical view of the analytical approach, Loland (1992) argues for a more pluralistic position. Noting the incommensurability of the two approaches, and the improbability of combining them into a single integrative paradigm, Loland argues that epistemological pluralism is necessary.The alternative, choosing one instead of the other, would lead to the loss of valuable forms of knowledge.

Pronger (1995) and Loland (1992) have different aims in their respective articles: Pronger's concern is to uncover and criticize knowledge assumptions that are taken for granted, but nonetheless have great impact on physical education students. Loland, on the other hand, is investigating how we can get a broader view of the knowledge and skills involved in alpine skiing and, by implication, sports in general. What their respective analyses bring out, however, are two different worldviews, or should I say, two different views on the moving body. They both point out that the moving body is always an experiencing body, even when it is examined using an analytical, mechanical approach. The very same point is made by Leder (1992) about patients who are exposed to the objectifying gaze of medicine: 'The anatomy and physiology of the lived body are always intertwined with the body's intentionality in ways that undermine facile claims of priority' (p. 29).

Leder made a further, important clarification when he wrote that the lived body is not a purely subject-body, it is, as argued by Merleau-Ponty (2002; 1968), both subject and object, perceiver and perceived. Even when the body is objectified, it is a different sort of object than other objects in the world. An object, according to Merleau-Ponty (2002), can be separated into its different parts. In the mechanical world view, there are only external and mechanical relations between these parts, and between the object itself and the world. However, the body as object is different from other objects in the sense that it is 'an object which does not leave me' (2002, p. 103). Whereas other objects in the world possess the potential to be absent, our body precludes such a possibility. The body can only become an object like other objects when it is dead, comatose or in other situations when the subject has no experiential access to herself.

This, then, is the tale of two bodies, both in medicine and physical education: one body objectified through a third-person, technological gaze from the outside and one body, lived as a subjective experience from the first-person perspective. It is important to recognize that even when the moving body is objectified, this experience of objectification is still a subjective experience. The moving body will never become wholly objectified – as if it were a dead body – by the moving subject. It may be objectified through bio-mechanical analysis that can be used, for instance, to enhance the technique of the moving subject. However, going from the objectifying analysis to the enhanced performance necessitates the involvement of the moving subject. Thus, there is a space in which the body as objectified and the body as subjectively experienced are co-dependent.

Bodily objectification and self-distancing

Leder (1992) draws attention to the German language distinction between *Leib* and *Körper*, where the former is the living, sensing body and the latter is the dead, purely physical body. In the context of medicine, Slatman (2014) has used this distinction to draw attention to the 'double ontology' of the body, i.e. that the body is always both visible and invisible; seer and seen; perceiver and perceived (Merleau-Ponty, 1968).

Slatman analyses Husserl's exposition of the *Leib–Körper* distinction found in *Ideen zur einer Phänomenologie und phänomenologischen Philosophie*. For Husserl, *Leib* is the zero-point for movement and orientation, the Here and Now of our existence. As such, *Leib* is an almost disembodied experience, since it does not entail the body as an object. Although Slatman (2014) points out that the *Leib* is a non-thing, it should not be regarded as disembodied, since it is essentially the here and now of the body. *Körper*, on the other hand, appears as an extended thing in space and is comparable to other things in the world. The *Körper*-experience is so commonplace that it is sometimes referred to as the apparent truth of Cartesian dualism (Leder, 1990). However, as Leder (1992), Pronger (1995) and Loland (1992) pointed out, this tale of the two bodies is not actually a tale of two separate bodies, and Slatman makes this clear by stating that the *Leib*-experience:

> seems to appeal directly to the notion of *'erleben'* and thus to 'lived experience'; it is the *Leib* that Merleau-Ponty calls 'lived body' (*corps vécu*). The German concept *Erlebnis* indeed refers to the subjective, lived dimension of the process of experiencing. This aspect of experience, however, is not restricted to non-intentional experiences, i.e. experiences that have no intentional object (such as pain). This means that the experience of one's own body as *Körper* (or intentional thing) also involves an *Erlebnis.*
>
> (p. 552)

On the basis of this, Slatman concludes that it is 'misleading to reserve the term 'lived experience' to the *Leib* experience only' (p. 553).

Slatman's analysis is relevant because she points out the problem with a unilateral critique of the 'body as object ontology'. In other words, we can find in the work of Leder (1990; 1992) and other philosophers of medicine, such as Toombs (1992; 2001), a critique of medical practices that objectify the patient's body. In the context of physical education, many have made a similar critique of healthism[8] and its objectification of the body (see e.g. Tinning, 2010). Slatman's (2014) contribution is to show that the problem is not connected to the 'body as object ontology' (p. 556). Rather, the problem lies in the instrumental view of medicine and healthism in which the body as object is taken to be an individual entity, and thereby separated from its social context.

Analyzing further the unity of subjectivity and thinghood in bodily experiences, Ingerslev (2013) also draws on Husserl's exposition of the body as *Leib* and *Körper*. Ingerslev points out that *Leibkörper* 'refers to the way that the body is experienced by itself … a peculiar kind of bodily awareness' (p. 164). This means that the body is experienced as an object by the body as subject. This is the also a fundamental element in Merleau-Ponty's non-dualistic ontology, where the body is at the same time object and subject, and any analysis separating the two into pure subject or pure object is merely an analytical derivation (Dillon, 1997; Merleau-Ponty, 1968).

Ingerslev (2013) proposes the idea of self-distancing, explaining that

> bodily self-consciousness consists in a reflective stance where you conceive of your body as a physical thing, an object in the world as well as

> the subject of bodily experiences. If it were not for this basic distance where you are aware of more than one aspect of how the body appears to you, basic everyday bodily self-consciousness would not be possible … The body is not 'just another thing', nor is it pure feeling or pure subjectivity. We attend to the body as a feeling thing.
>
> (p. 167)

The reflective stance Ingerslev is talking about does not in principle require that the lived body is interrupted in its habitual flow. That is, she argues against those who hold that the body is experienced as a subject when everything is going well and as an object when the project that the body is involved in breaks down. Put differently: in the context of health and illness it is sometimes argued that the body disappears from attention when we are engaged in projects in the world – we simply forget about our bodies. It is only when the project breaks down, for instance if the football player stumbles and falls or someone reading becomes aware of a headache, that the body is noticed as an object. Leder (1990) can be interpreted as a proponent of this view. The notion of self-distancing does not deny that such experiences take place, but Ingerslev (2013), on the other hand, argues that while such experiences can occur, self-distancing comes in degrees so that it is possible to have an objectifying experience of the body while being engaged in worldly projects.

The necessity of bodily objectification

At this point, I would like to return to the concept of physical literacy as developed by Whitehead (2007), and in particular her discussion of the body as object in relation to propositional knowledge. I would argue that the point Ingerslev (2013) made that the concept of the lived body entails objectification of the body through self-distancing can help to highlight how bodily objectifications can be enabling and productive, but also potentially problematic and oppressive.

Like Pronger (1995), Whitehead (2007) points out that objectification of the body through, for example, discourse about health and fitness is so commonplace that it is 'hard for people to appreciate that there is more to the body than just a machine to be managed' (p. 293). Continuing from this, Whitehead goes on to state that '*sadly*, it is a fact that we can and do objectify our embodiment' (ibid., italics added). She then takes up two issues involving objectification of the body which are essential to her account of physical literacy, namely health and skill acquisition. With the prevalent focus on health in contemporary society and the demand for pupils to learn skills in physical education, physical literacy must incorporate practices that involve bodily objectifications. Thus, the following was added to the working definition of physical literacy:

> The individual has the ability to identify and articulate the essential qualities that influence the effectiveness of his/her own movement performance, and has an understanding of the principles of embodied health, with respect to basic aspects such as exercise, sleep and nutrition.
>
> (p. 294)

By using the word 'sadly' above, Whitehead is suggesting that all body-objectification is to some extent problematic or undesirable. As the preceding discussion about bodily objectification showed, objectifying the body is not in and of itself problematic (or sad). It is an ontological, human condition and it is – as Whitehead rightly points out – a necessity in skill learning.

Importantly, Ingerslev (2013) points out that I can experience my body as an object 'in a not yet normative way' (p. 177). I would assume that it is the normativity involved in the health and skill acquisition discourses that Whitehead sees as problematic. These discourses are replete with an understanding of the body as a machine-like entity, and it seems justified to call the situation sad when such discourses overshadow the lived experience of the body to the extent that the only language that can possibly be used about the body is the language of normative bodily objectification. Another way of seeing it, as Slatman (2014) argued, is that the problem is not so much that one considers the body as an object. Rather, *the problem is the instrumentalism that considers the bodily object as an individual entity separate from the subject's experience as well as the social context.* I would agree with Slatman (2014) and Ingerslev (2013), and argue that bodily objectification can be productive for learning and understanding concepts such as how poise is a qualitatively felt experience (see Chapter 4). Thus, for the purpose of developing a phenomenological pedagogy for physical education (movement literacy), the next chapter will outline and discuss literature of a more pragmatic inclination that makes lived, bodily objectifications possible.

Notes

1 Clearly, this kind of 'orientation' is related to the *phenomenological attitude*. However, I prefer the term *being oriented* to avoid confusion with the phenomenological attitude as proposed by Husserl. I make this distinction in order to clarify one of the differences between philosophical phenomenology, in particular the philosophy developed in the early works of Husserl (a phenomenological attitude in the strict, methodological sense), and phenomenological pedagogy (phenomenological orientation).

2 In his later work (e.g. van Manen, 2007), van Manen has begun to use the notion *phenomenological practice*, which in many respects covers the same topics as phenomenological pedagogy. However, unlike pedagogy, practice is not limited to relationships between adults and children. It is a more general practice that also incorporates the caring professions, such as nursing.

3 Similarly, there is of course a strong connection between the ethics of teaching and the way sports, play and games are taught in order to strengthen moral character.

Positing that participation in sports automatically develops moral character is a very tenuous argument given all the apparent moral problems on display by professional athletes on an daily basis. Thus, the *way* sports are taught is critical to the potential development of moral character (Stolz, 2014).

4 I would point out that van Manen's interest in embodied, lived experience is developed further in the work of Maureen Connolly (1995; 2002; 2008).

5 The English translation of *Phenomenology of Perception* in the 1962 and 2002 editions adds to the confusion between body schema and body image, because the French *schema corporel* (i.e. body schema) was translated as body image.

6 One could add to this that modern technology, from the stethoscope to the fMRI, allows inspection of living bodies, but the ultimate purpose of revealing mechanisms and their faults is the same.

7 Leder (1990; 1992) uses the term dis-ease to signify the lived experience of illness, that is, an experience of a loss of the ease which under normal circumstances charachterizes our way of dealing with the world.

8 Tinning (2010, p. 116) refers to healthism as an ideology which 'is premised on the assumption that [physical education] contributes to better health because exercise = fitness = health'.

References

Ahmed, S. (2006). *Queer phenomenology: Orientations, objects, others.* London: Duke University Press.

Connolly, M. (1995). Phenomenology, physical education, and special populations. *Human Studies*, 18, 25–40.

Connolly, M. (2008). The remarkable logic of autism: developing and describing an embedded curriculum based in semiotic phenomenology. *Sport, Ethics and Philosophy*, 2(2), 234–256.

Connolly, M. and Craig, T. (2002). Stressed embodiment: doing phenomenology in the wild. *Human Studies*, 25, 451–462. Dillon, M. C. (1997). *Merleau-Ponty's ontology* (2nd edn). Evanston, IL: Northwestern University Press.

Gallagher, S. (2001). Dimensions of embodiment: body image and body schema in medical contexts. In S. K. Toombs (ed.), *Handbook of phenomenology and medicine* (pp. 147–176). Dordrecht: Kluwer.

Gallagher, S. (2005). *How the body shapes the mind.* Oxford: Clarendon Press.

Hass, L. (2008). *Merleau-Ponty's philosophy.* Bloomington: Indiana University Press.

Haydn-Davies, D. (2010). Physical literacy and learning and teaching approaches. In M. Whitehead (ed.), *Physical literacy: Throughout the lifecourse* (pp. 165–174). London: Routledge.

Ingerslev, L. R. (2013). My body as an object: self-distance and social experience. *Phenomenology and the Cognitive Sciences*, 12(1), 163–178.

Kirk, D. (2010). *Physical education futures.* London: Routledge.

Kirk, D. (2013). Educational value and models-based practice in physical education. *Educational Philosophy and Theory*, 45(9), 973–986.

Leder, D. (1990). *The absent body.* Chicago: University of Chicago Press.

Leder, D. (1992). A tale of two bodies: the Cartesian corpse and the lived body. In D. Leder (ed.), *The body in medical thought and practice* (pp. 17–36). Dordrecht: Kluwer.

Loland, S. (1992). The mechanics and meaning of alpine skiing: methodological and epistemological notes on the study of sport technique. *Journal of the Philosophy of Sport*, 19, 55–77.

Loland, S. (2006). Morality, medicine, and meaning: toward an integrated justification of physical education. *Quest*, 58(1), 60–70.

Martinkova, I. and Parry, J. (2011). An introduction to the phenomenological study of sport. *Sport, Ethics and Philosophy*, 5(3), 185–201.

Matthews, E. (2004). Merleau-Ponty's body-subject and psychiatry. *International Review of Psychiatry*, 16(3), 190–198.

Merleau-Ponty, M. (1963). *The structure of behavior*. Pittsburg, PA: Duquesne University Press.

Merleau-Ponty, M. (1968). *The visible and the invisible*. Evanston, IL: Northwestern University Press.

Merleau-Ponty, M. (2002). *Phenomenology of perception*. London: Routledge.

Priest, S. (1998). *Merleau-Ponty*. London: Routledge.

Pronger, B. (1995). Rendering the body: the implicit lessons of gross anatomy. *Quest*, 47, 427–446.

Slatman, J. (2014). Multiple dimensions of embodiment in medical practices. *Medicine, Health Care and Philosophy*, 17(4), 549–557.

Standal, Ø. F. (2008). Celebrating the insecure practitioner: a critique of evidence-based practice in adapted physical activity. *Sport, Ethics and Philosophy*, 2(2), 200–215.

Stolz, S. (2014). *The philosophy of physical education: A new perspective*. London: Routledge.

Tinning, R. (2010). *Pedagogy and human movement: Theory, practice, research*. London: Routledge.

Toombs, S. K. (1992). *The meaning of illness: A phenomenological account of the different perspectives of physician and patient*. Dordrecht: Kluwer.

Toombs, S. K. (2001). Reflections on bodily change: the lived experience of disability. In S. K. Toombs (ed.), *Handbook of phenomenology and medicine* (pp. 247–261). Dordrecht: Kluwer.

van Manen, M. (1977). Linking ways of knowing with ways of being practical. *Curriculum Inquiry*, 6(3), 205–228.

van Manen, M. (1978). An experiment in educational theorizing: the Utrecht school. *Interchange*, 10(1), 48–66.

van Manen, M. (1982). Phenomenological pedagogy. *Curriculum Inquiry*, 12(3), 283–299.

van Manen, M. (1990). *Researching lived experience: Human science for an action sensitive pedagogy*. Ontario, Canada: SUNY Press.

van Manen, M. (1993). *Pedagogisk takt* [*The tact of teaching: The meaning of pedagogical thoughtfulness*]. Bergen, Norway: Caspar Forlag.

van Manen, M. (1996). Phenomenological pedagogy and the question of meaning. In D. Vandenberg (ed.), *Phenomenology and educational discourse* (pp. 39–64). Durban, South Africa: Heinemann Higher and Further Education.

van Manen, M. (2007). Phenomenology of practice. *Phenomenology and Practice*, 1(1), 11–30.

van Manen, M. (2014). *Phenomenology of practice: Meaning-giving methods in phenomenological research and writing*. Walnut Creek, CA: Left Coast Press. van Manen, M. and Li, S. (2002). The pathic principle of pedagogical language. *!Lost Data*, 18(2), 215–224.

Whitehead, M. (2007). Physical literacy: philosophical considerations in relation to developing a sense of self, universality and propositional knowledge. *Sport, Ethics and Philosophy*, 1(3), 281–298.
Whitehead, M. (2013). What is physical literacy and how does it impact on physical education? In S. Capel and M. Whitehead (eds), *Debates in physical education teaching*. London: Routledge.
Zahavi, D. (2003). *Husserl's phenomenology*. Stanford, CA: Stanford University Press.

7 Experiencing the body as object

In this chapter I will work further on the idea that the body can and should be objectified for educational reasons in physical education. For this purpose, I draw on pragmatism. Admittedly, this is a change of perspective when it comes to philosophy. The reason for this change of focus is the critique I proposed towards van Manen's phenomenological pedagogy. While it makes a significant contribution by highlighting how pupils' lived experiences can and should be a starting point for teachers' pedagogical work, phenomenological pedagogy does not have much to say about how pupils' own lived experiences can be brought to self-reflective awareness. Taking the place of the body seriously in physical education implies that we must be attending to and reflecting on the body as it appears to us in movement experience. It is for that purpose I propose that pragmatism can be helpful. A problem with the change of focus from phenomenology to pragmatism is that questions can be raised about the coherence of the two philosophical traditions. However, I argue that despite their basis in different traditions, they also share some key similarities.

Pragmatism and phenomenology

Pragmatism originated in America after the Civil War through the works of Oliver Wendell Holmes, Charles Saunders Peirce, William James and John Dewey (Menand, 2001). More specifically, pragmatism – as a name for a set of philosophical ideas – was coined by William James with a specific reference to Peirce (Bernstein, 2010). Notwithstanding the differences between the founders of pragmatism, Menand (2001, pp. xi–xii) argues that they had a common 'attitude towards ideas' which stressed that ideas are social rather than individual, that the development of ideas is dependent on the interaction between individuals and their environment, and that the survival of ideas – mirroring the perspective of Darwinism that arose at the same time – depends on the adaptability of the ideas.

A full overview of pragmatism, both the classical and the more contemporary thinkers – such as Richard Rorty and Hilary Putnam – is beyond the scope of this book. I will instead highlight how pragmatism shares 'deep similarities' (Bernstein, 2010, p. 17) with phenomenology. Interestingly, Bernstein argues that the similarities between them are not the result of a direct influence. There is little evidence to suggest that phenomenologists such as Husserl and Heidegger engaged deeply with the work of pragmatism, or that the pragmatists studied the work of the phenomenologists. Rather, Bernstein holds that the two philosophical directions were motivated by a *felt difficulty*. Discussing Dewey, Heidegger and Wittgenstein, Bernstein suggests that

> each of them detects that something is profoundly wrong with Cartesianism, and each of them seeks to rethink a more adequate way of understanding our forms of life and our being-in-the-world. They are critical of what Dewey called the 'spectator theory of knowledge' and shift our attention to know-how, to how we engage in the world and social practices ... we witness a similar dialectic at work in their thinking, a dialectic that starts with the same problematic and thinks through its radical consequences.
> (Bernstein, 2010, pp. 19–20)

A concrete illustration of the similarities between pragmatism and phenomenology can be given by referring back to Merleau-Ponty's critique of the behaviourists' account of learning (see Chapter 3) and juxtapose it with Dewey's deconstructive analysis of the reflex arc. In a paper called 'The Reflex Arc Concept in Psychology', Dewey (1896) criticized how the stimulus–response system explains behaviour. Beginning by pointing out the dualism inherent in operating with the twin notions stimulus and response, Dewey goes on to argue that a stimulus such as 'sound' is not passively received. Instead, sound must be understood as the active process of hearing. In addition, hearing always takes place within a context, so that hearing the same sound is a different experience when the sound is heard while reading a book, when one is out hunting, or when one is performing an experiment: 'in each case, the noise has a very different psychical value; it is a different experience' (p. 361).

The theory of the reflex arc takes sensation, idea and movement to be discrete steps in a linear process, 'a patchwork of disjointed parts, a mechanical conjunction of unallied process' (p. 358). For the purpose of his argument, Dewey proposes using the term 'coordination' for 'the psychical organism of which sensation, idea and movement are the chief organs' (p. 358). Similar to Merleau-Ponty, who argued that the situation must be taken as a whole and that stimuli are always integrated into structural processes that play a regulating role, Dewey argued that the stimulus and the motor response are not distinct existences. For Dewey, they are, rather, always within a coordination and their significance and meaning arise because, and only because, they play a part in either maintaining or reconstituting a coordination. In a similar vein, Merleau-Ponty argued that stimulus and response are only meaningful when understood as part of structural processes (and recall here that structure means gestalt) in which a relation of meaning between the situation and the response is established.

The point I am emphasising here is that the felt difficulty which both Merleau-Ponty and Dewey encountered was the problem of dualistic and mechanistic thinking. They both saw that the human body does not passively await external stimuli. Rather, the body, or as Dewey called it, the body–mind matrix, must be attuned to a situation in order to perceive stimulations as cues for action. While Merleau-Ponty sought to carve out a third way between intellectualism and empiricism, Dewey tried to

> expose a tacit hierarchy in the terms in which people conventionally think about [problems]. We think that a response follows a stimulus; Dewey taught that there is a stimulus only because there already is a response. [...] We think we know in order to do; Dewey taught that doing is why there is knowing.
>
> (Menand, 2001, p. 330)

However, pointing out such similarities only goes some way in showing that there are deep similarities between phenomenology and pragmatism. It must also be remembered that there are differences between pragmatists and phenomenologists. My approach in the following is to trade on a couple of such differences and in that process I hope to find a more complete understanding of the role of embodied experiences in physical education than phenomenology alone can provide.

Somaesthetics

Is it possible to think of physical education as a body discipline[1] 'designed to improve our somatic experience and performance' (Shusterman, 2012, p. 13)? Even though the philosopher Richard Shusterman is not directly concerned with physical education, his work on somaesthetics has recurrent references to the learning of sport skills, to physical activities and body-based practices such as body building, golf, yoga and the martial arts.[2] His work, I submit, is relevant for physical education, because it is helpful to think with when we are considering how we can think about the body as an instrument in a way that avoids the pitfalls of instrumental rationality. Stated differently, Shusterman's work is relevant for physical education because he has developed a way of turning explicit attention to the body while at the same time respecting the subjectively lived experiences of the body.

Shusterman defines somaesthetics as concerning

> the body as a locus of sensory-aesthetic appreciation (aesthesis) and creative self-fashioning ... it aims to enrich not only our abstract, discursive knowledge of the body but also our lived somatic experience and performance; it seeks to enhance the understanding, efficacy, and beauty of our movements and improve the environments to which our

movements contribute and from which they draw their energies and significance.

(2012, p. 27)

With the use of the word 'soma' for body, Shusterman intends to avoid a purely biological interpretation of body, and at the same time he wants to capture the dual meaning of body as *Körper* (the body as a physical object) and *Leib* (the body as a subjectively lived experience). Splicing soma and aesthetics, Shusterman aims to give the body, both as object and subject, careful aesthetic attention. Drawing on Dewey, Shusterman highlights that aesthetics is not only about the experience of art, but has as its core issues perception, consciousness and feeling. Thus, somaesthetics has as one of its aims to 'increase our powers of awareness, focus, and feeling through better mastery of their somatic source' (Shusterman, 2012, p. 3).

Somaesthetics is divided into three branches: analytic, pragmatic and practical. Analytic somaesthetics is the theoretical and descriptive part of somaesthetics. Originally, this branch was philosophical, drawing on philosophy of mind, phenomenology (in particular phenomenology of the body) and pragmatist philosophy. Analytic somaesthetics also includes more interdisciplinary work, drawing on biology, cognitive science and physiology. Finally, it engages with the social sciences, for instance in cultural analysis showing how perception and bodily norms are constructed and shaped by social forces.[3]

Pragmatic somaesthetics is the critical and comparative study of methods proposed to improve the use of the body. Shusterman is pointing here to methods designed to enhance not only performance, but also the experience of the body. Pragmatic somaesthetics can be divided into holistic and atomistic methods as well as self-directed and other-directed practices. Whereas holistic methods are practices directed at the 'person as an integrated whole' (p. 43), atomistic methods are concerned with specific body parts and surfaces such as body building or plastic surgery. The distinction between self- and other-directed practices concerns whether the practitioner is working for oneself or for others. A further distinction in pragmatic somaesthetics is between practices that are oriented towards external appearance or inner experience, that is, representational and experiential dimensions. In terms of inner experiences, Shusterman notes that the aim of such practices is to feel better in the dual sense of that notion: feeling more satisfied and becoming more attentive towards one's own feelings.

While pragmatic somaesthetics is a comparative analysis of body practices, Shusterman proposes a third form of somaesthetics called 'practical somaesthetics', which is the actual practice of 'engaging in programs of disciplined, reflective, corporeal practice aimed at somatic self-improvement (whether representational, experiential, or performative)' (p. 45). Systematically performing, and not only reading and writing about bodily practices is a neglected area in academic work on the body. Indeed, a central tenet in Shusterman's entire work is that living a philosophical life involves knowing oneself. The credo *know thyself*, inscribed at Apollo's temple in Delphi, must – according to Shusterman – be taken to also involve knowing oneself as a bodily being (Shusterman, 2000).

Shusterman's critique of the body as a silent background

As discussed earlier (Chapters 4 and 5), it is a commonly held view that the performance of embodied, practical knowledge requires that the body retreat into the background of attention. Shusterman acknowledges the importance of the body as background for the performance of both everyday habits as well as sport skills. In other words, he is in general agreement with the view that the body as a powerful background presence is a means to reach other ends. However, Shusterman also points out that sometimes it is beneficial to turn attention towards the means rather than the end. By foregrounding the body, Shusterman's intention is to improve our understanding of the body and improve its performance. Therefore, presenting Shusterman's critique of Merleau-Ponty is a way of showing how somaesthetics and its pragmatic orientation is a useful supplement (or perhaps even critical corrective) to the phenomenological perspective.

According to Shusterman (2005), Merleau-Ponty furnishes a strong and problematic distinction between tacit, non-representational learning of bodily habits, and learning by relying on cognitive representations of one's movements (see Chapter 3 for an examination of Merleau-Ponty's account of learning). Shusterman (2005) maintains that there are problems with Merleau-Ponty's account of acquisitions of habit. First, we may acquire bad habits just as well as good and useful ones. Since this form of learning takes place *before we know it*, there is no guarantee that the habits learned this way are good and useful rather than bad and detrimental. Second, once bad habits have been acquired, there is no sure way to correct them. Sedimented habits cannot be used to this end because it is these habits that are wrong in the first place. In addition, the spontaneous learning of new habits is not a solution because it is this process that went wrong in the first place when bad habits were acquired.[4]

Shusterman maintains that Merleau-Ponty ignores the way that we can intervene in learning through paying conscious, representational attention, for instance, to movements and body postures.

> In advocating the *unreflective lived body* in opposition to the *abstract representation of scientific explanation*, Merleau-Ponty creates a polarization of 'lived experience' versus 'representations' that neglects the fruitful option of 'lived corporeal reflection', that is, concrete but representational and reflective body consciousness.
>
> (p. 165, italics added)

The lived, corporeal reflection that Shusterman is pointing out is a learning process in between the positions of learning as (i) a completely tacit, unreflective process, and (ii) a propositional, mentalistic process. The lived corporeal reflection is representational, but still situated between (i) and (ii). In addition, Shusterman holds that Merleau-Ponty cannot provide an explanation of learning other than as mindless acquisition of habits.

In my judgement, Shusterman provides an important critique of Merleau-Ponty and the phenomenology of skill acquisition, but before I continue to present his alternative, I would also like to show where I disagree with Shusterman's critique of Merleau-Ponty. The binary opposition between (i) and (ii) is equivalent to the distinction between body schema and body image. As I have argued several places earlier in this book, Merleau-Ponty not only wanted to avoid dualism, but also the opposite alternative, namely monism. His solution to the problem of dualism was found in the notion of *gestalt*, where both dichotomous terms are mutually co-present. In this context, the gestalt can be thought of as incorporating both the body image and the body schema. The co-presence of body schema/image would, in the case of learning through observation and imitation, for instance, imply that we can have an awareness of others and learn from them without retreating from the lived world in order to observe and analyse what they are doing. Instead of either forming explicit representations of one's own body in learning (i.e. body image) or working with a non-representational intentionality (i.e. body schema), the body schema/image gestalt fluctuates so that there can be various degrees, shapes, and forms of background and foreground presences, depending on the situation and the task at hand.

Indeed, the distinction between the pre-reflective and the reflective is not clear-cut and ordered in the sense that the former belongs to the realm of the unconscious and the latter to the conscious. Rather, they are mutually conditioned and interwoven. What I take this to mean is that Merleau-Ponty's view is that the gestalt of body schema/image is general enough to subsume a lived corporeal reflection without fully objectifying one's own body.[5] However, based on Shusterman's critique one could argue that there are certain, important holes in Merleau-Ponty's phenomenology of embodied learning. By pointing out a 'somatic attention deficit' in the work of Merleau-Ponty, Shusterman is highlighting a one-sidedness towards the unreflective and the tacit, not only in Merleau-Ponty, but in many other theorists of the body as background (see Shusterman, 2012, chapter 2).

On a more apologetic note, I would say that these omissions in Merleau-Ponty are not devastating to his project, but have in themselves been the opportunity for Merleau-Ponty's critics to further deepen our understanding of living, human embodiment. Hass (2008), for instance, concludes that 'if theorists have been able to demand and carry out treatment of these features of embodiment [that Merleau-Ponty has overlooked], it is to some extent because Merleau-Ponty, following Nietzsche, brought our carnal lives to philosophical significance in the first place' (p. 98). Therefore, Shusterman gives us cause to think about how the body can be represented in reflection. As argued in the previous chapter, much of the work on phenomenology of physical education celebrates the pre-reflective, lived experience of the body in movement and is critical of third-person forms of objectification of the human body. Following Slatman (2014), I argue that there is a need to abandon the criticism of the body as object ontology. If this assertion is correct, then following Shusterman, there are good reasons to find ways of promoting a lived, corporeal reflection that foregrounds the body.

Somaesthetic attention

A main source of inspiration for somaesthetics is the pragmatist philosophy briefly introduced earlier in this chapter. In particular, Shusterman draws on the work of William James and John Dewey. In this section, I explain how the work of William James is made relevant, but also corrected by Shusterman.[6] Briefly stated, Shusterman argues that James has made a significant contribution to pragmatic somaesthetics, but that he also, quite surprisingly – given his pragmatist orientation – did not elaborate the practical consequences of his theory to any sufficient degree.

The theory that Shusterman is referring to comes primarily from James' work in psychology, in particular 'his scattered but insightful remarks about what we could call somaesthetics introspection, the examination of one's own bodily feelings' (Shusterman, 2008, p. 158). James pointed out how difficult introspective examinations of our bodily feelings are, and explained this with consciousness' tendency to be attentive to change. Since consciousness has evolved to help us survive in a constantly changing world, it is remarkably difficult to stay attentive to an object that does not change. For instance, try to concentrate on the simple movement of breathing, exhaling and inhaling through the nose. For those of us untrained in meditative breathing, it does not take long before our mind starts to wander to other issues than the breathing. A second point raised by James and which bears relevance to somaesthetics is that consciousness evolved to serve our interests. Therefore, we need continued interest to stay attentive to an object.

Based on the two key principles of change and interest, James suggested some practical ideas in order to make introspection more effective. These ideas for heightening our attentiveness towards the body can be exemplified with a 'body scan' (see Shusterman, 2012, chapter 5). The body scan is a common technique deployed by many different body–mind disciplines and 'involves systematically scanning or surveying one's own body, not by regarding or touching it from the outside but instead by introspectively, proprioceptively feeling ourselves as we rest motionless, typically on our backs with our eyes closed' (2012, p. 115). The following is a brief excerpt from a body scan performed seated, as described by Shusterman (2012, pp. 115–117):

> Starting with your left foot, notice how your heel makes contact with the floor. Does most of the weight go to the center of the heel or to the right

> or left of the heel? We do not want to change anything or to judge how it should be; we simply want to feel where the heel contacts the floor.

The body scan then continues to examine other parts of the body, as well as both the right and the left side respectively. Shusterman (2012) elaborates six strategies[7] of introspection involved in the body scan:

1. In order to sustain attention towards a body part as an object, *asking questions* (e.g., how does the right heel make contact with the floor? How does it compare to the left?) helps to direct attention to different aspects and qualities of the somatic object.
2. In the body scan, *division into parts* gives a more precise bodily introspection. By transitioning from one body part to the next, the division into parts also helps provide a sense of change.
3. *Contrast of feelings*: While attending to one body part, questions can help to stimulate discriminations in how we feel that body part. Here, Shusterman distinguishes between existential and differential contrasts. The former concerns whether or not a feeling is present, for instance whether some parts of the hand that is lying on the table actually is in contact with the table. The latter is a comparison of the nature or quality of existing feelings: When standing up, which foot carries the most weight?
4. *Associative interest*: This implies cultivating the awareness of the recognition that a bodily feeling is a key to something we care about, for instance how a certain 'feeling in the body scan has had the capacity to induce muscular readjustment' (p. 121).
5. *Avoiding distracting interests*: Given that consciousness is attracted to change, one must take measures to avoid competing interests. Hence, the body scan is performed with the eyes closed or half-closed.
6. If we want to heighten or sharpen our attention of a feeling of a body part, it is possible to prepare oneself – *pre-perception* – by conceptualizing and imaging where and how the feeling will be felt.

The body scan and other introspective techniques that aim to heighten our awareness of bodily feelings are conducted with little or no movement. On the basis of this, I would expect questions to be raised over its relevance for physical education. Keeping pupils active during lessons is considered an ideal (see Chapter 1 above), and phenomenologically inspired researchers such as P. J. Arnold (1979), argue for education in *movement*. Stillness and closed eyes therefore seems to be in conflict with a core value in physical education. In contrast to this, I would like to advance two arguments in favour of the relevance of the somaesthetic practice of introspection such as the body scan. First, if one aim of physical education is to contribute to an holistic education of pupils, including knowledge of themselves as embodied beings,[8] then it appears that the capacity of *feeling better* in the sense of becoming more perceptive towards one's own bodily feelings and perception is necessary. As Shusterman (2008) argues, in movement our interest is first and foremost directed towards the goal of our movement, such as throwing the basketball into the hoop. In this process, the feelings of joints and muscles that are detected in a body scan, are absorbed as signs of the limb's movement and therefore ignored or not noticed. Slowing down, and even lying still, is therefore crucial in the form of somaesthetic practice discussed here.

The first argument could be disregarded if one adamantly holds on to the view that lying still is antithetical to what physical education is all about. However, a second argument could be constructed claiming that the embodied knowledge gained through a body scan is valuable also for the learning of movement skills. This argument would claim that somaesthetic awareness is a skill that can be learned and perfected by exercises in introspection. For instance, through 'focused awareness, we can learn to feel when we are contracting our muscles more than is necessary and in places that conflict with the efficient execution of the movements desired' (Shusterman, 2008, p. 166). In other words, the lessons learned through the body scan are valuable in relation to learning new skills as well as improving skills and habits that have gone awry. The somaesthetic practice of introspection enables pupils to get to know themselves as bodily beings in a manner that is crucial and beneficial for the learning and development of skills.

Somaesthetic reflection

If questioning the value of introspection is an argument against practices such as the body scan or other means for heightening pupils' bodily feelings, then it must be noted that this is also precisely the point at which Shusterman launches his critique of William James. Although contributing strongly with his studies of consciousness and introspection, James was also convinced that one should leave as much as possible to the spontaneity and automatism of habits. Paying attention to bodily feelings would only distract people in their practical enterprises. The body, according to James' normative account, should be a background presence. Another reason for James' reluctance to recommend introspective practice was that he, following Immanuel Kant, feared that it would lead to hypochondria, depression and ultimately the madhouse. It is, according to James, no better moral training than paying attention to what we do and express rather than how it feels. This is also Shusterman's critique of James:

> James's unfeeling insistence on vigorous dorsal contraction and stiff upright posture is thus a sure prescription for the kind of back pain he indeed suffered throughout his life, just as it is surely an expression of his puritan ethics more than a product of clinical research. If 'action and feeling go together' (GR,[9] 100), as James shrewdly remarked, they *both* need our careful attention for optimal functioning.
>
> (Shusterman, 2008, p. 169, italics in original)

There is thus a one-sidedness in James' work on somaesthetic introspection that Shusterman believes must be corrected, and for that purpose he turns to the work of James' follower, John Dewey. Shusterman (2008) notes that through practical experiences with the Alexander technique,[10] Dewey had pragmatic evidence for the value of directing somatic reflections towards the body in order to improve its use. Whereas James thought that people should trust and nurture spontaneity, Dewey was more inclined to doubt James' seemingly blind trust in the usefulness of habits. In this sense, Dewey was much more favourable to the idea of bringing the body into reflective awareness.

The relevance of Dewey's position on somatic introspection is relevant to the argument made at the end of the previous section, namely that heightened awareness of bodily feelings is relevant to physical education because it promotes the learning of bodily skills. Since 'we cannot reliably change our actions if we do not really know what we are doing', bringing the body into critical, conscious attention helps us 'reconstruct or refine it so that one can actually do with one's body what one really intends to do' (Shusterman, 2012, pp. 63–64). This is important in relation to acquisition of skills, because skills can always be further honed and perfected and they need to be adapted to new situations, environments and technologies. Expressed in another manner, embodied learning is always an unfinished process.

Shusterman further makes the point that the foregrounding of – and reflection on – bodily feelings is an intermediary phase, because in the ordinary course of events, either in our everyday lives or in specific movement situations, bodily feelings should return to the background, thus allowing us to focus on other issues. Therefore, when Shusterman argues that some of the elements of the bodily background can sometimes usefully be foregrounded, he does not insist that all spontaneity should be avoided. Neither does it imply that one should seek full transparency of one's actions and feelings. Analysing Peirce's critique of Cartesianism, Bernstein (2010) notes that 'all knowledge has a foundation in the sense that there are tacitly held beliefs which we don't doubt and that we take to be the bedrock of truth' (p. 34). Quoting Wilfred Sellars, Bernstein makes the point that pragmatism is a self-correcting enterprise where any claim can be put in jeopardy, *but not all at once*. Similarly, Shusterman (2012) argues that the somatic background, which he criticized Merleau-Ponty for being entrenched in, can be usefully foregrounded in learning, developing or correcting bodily skills. The background of bodily skills forms a bedrock of our embodied knowledge that always entails the possibility of being foregrounded, although not every part at the same time. That is, full transparency about embodied knowledge is not possible. This would not only be 'unachievable, but not worth achieving in practice; on most occasions, our focus is best directed elsewhere, to the world in which we must act' (Shusterman, 2012, p. 65).

Dewey always insisted on overcoming dualisms. The dualism that has been at work in these sections is that between mindlessness and mindfulness. Whereas advocates of the bodily background, such as Hubert Dreyfus, emphasize 'mindless coping' (e.g. Dreyfus, 2007), one can get the impression that somaesthetics, particularly though practices such as the body scan, prioritizes mindfulness.[11] Dewey's point, however, would be to challenge any claims about a dualism between mindlessness and mindfulness. Discussing this point with reference to Dewey's understanding of the relationship between habit and will, Shusterman (2008) shows how Dewey not only challenged this dualism, but that he also turned the relationship between habit and will upside down. A will to do something always involves some form of embodied idea as to how this doing is performed and felt. 'The act must come before the thought, and a habit before an ability to evoke the thought at will' (Dewey's *Middle Work* 14, pp. 25–26, quoted in Shusterman, 2008, pp. 195–196). In order to fully appreciate what this means, we must turn to Dewey's theory of reflective experience and discuss its relevance for (physical) education.

Dewey's ideas of reflective thinking

Knowledge in physical education is of a practical kind (e.g. Carr, 1981. See also Chapter 3). It could therefore be easy to jump to the conclusion that in physical education *we learn by doing*. Learning by doing is a cornerstone of Dewey's theory of education (Dewey, 1910; 1938), but it would be a gross misrepresentation of his ideas to suggest that merely doing is enough to satisfy his idea of learning by doing. Following up on the themes introduced in the review of Shusterman's work, this section explores Dewey's concept of reflective experience and then discusses what it is that can make physical education experiences educational.

Reflective thinking

In *How We Think*, Dewey (1910) pointed out that there are different forms of thinking, ranging from idle thought to a more systematic and analytical form that he conceived as reflective thinking. Rodgers (2002) argues that there are four criteria which characterize Dewey's conception of reflective thinking. First, reflection is a meaning-making process. Meaning-making is what moves the learner from one experience to the next with a deeper understanding of the experience and its relation to other experiences and relevant facts. Second, reflection is structured and systematic. Dewey defined it as the 'active, persistent, and careful consideration of any belief or supposed form of knowledge in the light of the grounds that support it, and the further conclusions to which it tends' (Dewey, 1910, p. 6). Third, reflection must take place in interaction with a community; and fourth, reflection requires an attitude that values growth of both oneself and others.

Reflective thinking takes place in a series of different steps or phases with a certain systematic approach to thinking about one's experiences. The process leads the subject of experience from a pre-reflective, problematic situation towards a post-reflective situation in which the initial problem is satisfied. As Rodgers (2002) points out, Dewey was unclear about the precise numbers of steps, for instance outlining first two then five phases in *How We Think*, and later, five slightly different phases in *Democracy and Education*. The five steps from *Democracy and Education* are:

> (i) perplexity, confusion, doubt, due to the fact that one is implicated in an incomplete situation whose full character is not yet determined; (ii) a conjectural anticipation – a tentative interpretation of the given elements, attributing to them a tendency to effect certain consequences; (iii) a careful survey examination, inspection, exploration, analysis of all attainable considerations which will define and clarify the problem in hand; (iv) a consequent elaboration of the tentative hypothesis to make it more precise and more consistent, because squaring with a wider range of facts; (v) taking one stand upon the projected hypothesis as a plan of action which is applied to the existing state of affairs: doing something overtly to bring about the anticipated result, and thereby testing the hypothesis.
>
> (Dewey, 1916, pp. 114–115)

Step (i) is the pre-reflective experience of being in a situation where one's habits of action in similar situations are not adequate for the specific situation at hand. There is a problematic situation in which the subject is not certain about how to go on. According to Quay (2013) there are two forms of experiences that can follow from (i), which are differentiated by the proportion of reflection found in them. One possibility is the trial and error kind, where the anticipation described in (ii) leads directly to action (v). This kind of reflective thinking is typically used when confronting simple, basic problems. However, in order to know not only *that* some action is connected to a specific outcome, but also *how* they are connected, the more reflective kind of experience must be engaged in.

The subject who confronts a problematic situation must be able to describe the features of the situation. At this point, Dewey (1910) stresses the importance of not jumping to conclusions or making hasty interpretations. Rather, through a careful description of the situation, the subject can be lead forward to the next step, which is the forming of hypothesis about what could have been done otherwise. Steps (iii) and (iv) can therefore be considered as reflective thinking *per se*. However, just as learning by doing is not only about doing, so reflective thinking is not solely concerned with thinking. Reflective thinking is conditioned by practical experiences (step i) and incomplete unless its consequences are tested in action (step iv). Inquiry, then, is a process of noticing, describing and analysing perplexing experiences, imagining other possible ways of handling the given situation, and finally testing the consequences obtained from the analytical phase in actual practice. There is a cyclical continuity between experience and reflection, and as such these two aspects of inquiry cannot be entirely separated from one another (Rodgers, 2002).

Educational experiences

There is a close connection between thinking, experimenting and experiencing: 'What is unequivocally clear is that for Dewey the human subjects under scrutiny need themselves to be conceived of as experimenting' (Tiles, 2010, p. 104). When considering the Greek word for experience, *empeiria*, we can come to see the intimate relation between having an experience and doing experimentations, since the verb *peiraô* means to attempt or undertake.

Therefore, Dewey's conception of education was intimately related to experience: 'education is a development within, by, and for experience' (Dewey, 1938, p. 28). In his educational philosophy, Dewey sought to reconstruct the concept of experience. First of all, on Dewey's account, the subject of experience is not to be seen as a passive receiver of information. In addition, Dewey argued that parts of human experience take place subconsciously, so that contrary to the (at that time, at least) commonly held belief that experience had to be confined to consciousness, Dewey claimed that experience is not confined to modes of consciousness (Tiles, 2010). Experience therefore,

> is not appropriately conceived as one-way traffic from somewhere (the physical environment, or an 'external world' about which we can only conjecture), but as an interaction between a creature and its environment … The subject of experience is not a passive recipient of information; it is an active creature adapting its routines, modifying its habits, reconfiguring its dispositions, and it is the effect on its routines, habits or dispositions that determines what parts of the given the animal has taken (deliberately or otherwise) to constitute its experience.
>
> (Tiles, 2010, pp. 102–103)

Experiences have both an active and a passive part (Dewey, 1938). On the passive side, experience is something the subject undergoes in the sense that what happens is to some extent beyond the control of the subject. On the active part, the subject actively takes or grasps the experience. This active process is what Dewey referred to as inquiry or reflective thinking.

Dewey distinguished two central criteria for educational experiences, namely continuity and interaction. Continuity means that every experience takes up something from previous experiences and in turn modifies the quality of later experiences. This means that we can only make sense of our current experience in light of previous ones. In educational terms, a consequence of the principle of continuity is that education should be defined as the 'reconstruction or reorganization of experience which adds to the meaning of experience, and which increases ability to direct the course of subsequent experience' (Dewey, 1916, p. 61).

Not all experiences are educative. The subject of experience must, as a consequence of experiencing, develop physically, intellectually or morally, but truly educative experiences are directed towards growth. That is, experiences and their reconstruction and reorganization must be directed towards a desirable end, the value of which 'can be judged only on the grounds of what it moves toward and into' (Dewey, 1938, p. 38).

The principle of interaction implies that in experience a transaction between an individual and the environment takes place. This is referred to as an interaction between the objective conditions that constitute the environment and the internal conditions of the subject, understood as the needs, desires, purposes and capacities of the individual. In their interaction, these two aspects form a situation (Dewey, 1938). The duty of the educator, Dewey observes, is to 'determine that environment which will interact with the existing capacities and needs of those taught to create a worth-while experience' (Dewey, 1938, p. 45). This means that it is the obligation of the teacher to construct an environment by manipulating the objective conditions so that the learner can have experiences which match his or her capacities and desires. Failure to construct such an environment, both in terms of adaptation of the material and the 'total social set-up of the situation' (ibid.), leads to miseducative experiences.

Contributions to movement literacy as a pedagogical model

Surprisingly little is written about John Dewey and the other pragmatists' relevance to physical education. However, as Kirk (2010) and Ennis (2006) point out, Dewey's reconstruction of education in a child-centred direction was picked up by some early physical educationalists from before the First World War and up to the 1950s and 1960s. These educationalists sought to rethink physical education in a manner that created a more enriching atmosphere where education of the whole child was a central objective. Recently, Quennerstedt and associates (Quennerstedt et al., 2011; Quennerstedt, 2013) have utilized Dewey's notion of transaction as an analytical tool to study learning in physical education.

Reflective thinking is crucial to Dewey's educational philosophy. But what is the relevance of this kind of thinking to a subject that is said to be body-based? (Stolz, 2014). An objection to any kind of relevance is that the maxim of reflective thinking *stop and think* seems antithetical to physical education. This objection is a variation of the objection that was discussed earlier in this chapter concerning the body scan. That is, in a subject which (or so the argument goes) is all about keeping the pupils busy and active, there is no place for lying still. Similarly, why should pupils stop and think if the subject is all about being active? More specifically related to reflection, the question is: If reflective thinking is the 'careful survey, examination, inspection, exploration, analysis of all attainable considerations which will define and clarify the problem in hand … [and] a consequent elaboration of the tentative hypothesis to make it more precise and more consistent' (Dewey, 1916, p. 114) then does not this lead to a pedagogy that emphasizes a disembodied, analytical perspective on movement, skills and physical activity? In other words, does not reflective thinking promote a spectator theory of knowledge to physical education, a subject which – taking the phenomenological tradition as a source of 'inspiration' – should promote pre-reflectively lived experiences of oneself as a moving subject?

Here, it may be said that I am merely erecting a straw man because there are very few who would be holding the arguments I have been presenting. If that is the case (but I am not entirely convinced that, in fact, it is the case), then at the very least this straw man can serve a pedagogical function because it can help bring more clarity to what Dewey meant by reflective thinking. First of all, as should be clear from my presentation of reflective thinking above, thinking for Dewey is not an isolated process that takes place outside of action and experience. Thinking is not a retreat from the problematic situation it tries to solve. Thinking and acting are both parts of an experiential arc that starts from a problematic situation and returns to transform the situation (Johnson, 2010). This means that we have to understand thinking as a habit rather than as a disembodied, logical form of reasoning. According to Johnson (2010):

> Dewey honors his principle of continuity by arguing that thinking is a naturally evolving process of experience that occurs only for certain complex animals, under certain very specific bodily conditions. Thinking operates through the recruitment of sensory-motor and other bodily processes. Following William James and C. S. Peirce, Dewey crafts a non-dualistic, body-based theory of human cognition, a view … remarkably consonant with so-called 'embodied cognition' views in contemporary cognitive neuroscience.
>
> (p. 129)

Thus, it is, neither in Dewey's philosophy nor in contemporary neuroscience for that matter, the case that thinking can stand outside of embodied experience. Thinking is itself an embodied experience and the object of reflective thinking (i.e. what we think about) arises from pre-reflective experience.

If that is the case, then what are the contributions from Dewey and the other pragmatists to physical education pedagogy? Bearing in mind the purpose of this book, I want to conclude this chapter by furthering the development of movement literacy as a pedagogical model in physical education that I began in Chapter 5. Before going on that, I must very briefly recap the development of movement literacy I have been proposing hitherto.

1 I have argued that physical literacy as developed by Margaret Whitehead is in need of a stronger philosophical grounding (or perhaps a more precise and philosophically adequate grounding) and that the definition of physical literacy has gradually expanded, and become too encompassing. At the very least it has become less distinct as a pedagogical model for physical education. Based on these interpretations, as well as a recent observation

from Kirk (2013) that physical literacy is a philosophy in search of pedagogy, I have set out to develop a model specifically for physical education that takes its starting point from phenomenological philosophy. I have chosen to call this model *movement literacy.* My intention has been to both honour the important work of Whitehead, but at the same time distinguish my development from recent development of physical literacy by Whitehead and colleagues (e.g. Whitehead, 2010).

2 As described in Chapter 5, movement literacy has two central learning outcomes, namely to move with poise and to be perceptive in reading and writing the environment. Based on phenomenological philosophy, poise must be understood as a qualitatively felt experience. Whereas reading the environment was argued to be the capacity to search for and identify opportunities for movement, writing the environment is an expression for the moving subject's capacity for shaping the environment in order to create opportunities for movement.

3 Based on varied sources ranging from the phenomenological philosopher Martin Heidegger to recent developments in motor learning suggesting a non-linear pedagogy, I proposed in Chapter 5 some teaching strategies that are in alignment with the learning outcomes of movement literacy. With the aid of the work of John Dewey and Richard Shusterman, I am now in a position to continue the development of movement literacy as a pedagogical model in physical education.

The learning outcome of moving with poise, which is the qualitatively felt experience of moving, can be further developed by applying Shusterman's somaesthetics. In this regard, movement literacy could draw inspiration from what Shusterman sees as holistic methods aimed at inner experiences:

> the focus on aesthesis concerns the soma's perceptual acuity and inner experience, where cultivation of improved aesthesis means 'feeling better' both in the sense of enjoying better feelings but also in the sense of perceiving what we experience more accurately and clearly.
>
> (Shusterman, 2012, p. 111)

Developing the capacity for 'feeling better' is therefore important in movement literacy, but it is important to make note of the distinction between the two ways of feeling better. The first is the straightforward meaning where one can enjoy better feelings in relation to movement. The second sense implies that one more accurately perceive one's own experiences. The latter point is crucial because it means that one is able to move beyond rather simplistic descriptions of experience such as *positive* movement experience. In other words, one can become better at describing in more detail what it is like to move.

The presentation in this chapter creates a ground for arguing that attention to and reflection on bodily sensations and feelings are conducive to vital learning experiences in physical education. The body scan (see Shusterman, 2012, chapter 5) illustrates how focussed attention on parts of the body can make us more aware of sensations, feelings, or tensions. In addition, the body scan can help develop a language for bodily feelings. It is worth pointing out that the idea of developing a language for such bodily feelings does not imply a privileging of linguistic thought. Shusterman states that we must recognize that 'language can improve our perceptions of how we feel', but that it can also be 'a distracting obstacle when the range of language is assumed to exhaust the entire range of experience' (2012, p. 121).

Shusterman also argues that the methods of somaesthetics can help improve skills. Experiencing the body as an object enables skill learning by helping the moving subject to become more aware of how she performs her movements. More precisely, it is not the end product of the performance she becomes aware of, but the way her body moves through space in order to complete the performance: What does it feel like to move? By becoming more aware, the moving subject can more easily improve her existing habits, develop new ones and repair faulty ones.

If the dominant way of teaching skills or techniques in physical education is through demonstration, explanation and practice (Tinning, 2010), then with the perspective on skill acquisition advanced through somaesthetics,[12] the pedagogy needs to change. Instead of an instrumental approach where drills of supposedly correct movements reinforced by a teacher are the main ingredient, the alternative pedagogy would connect the present movement experience with future ones through reflective thinking. This conforms with Dewey's definition of education (Dewey, 1916, p. 61) as a process of reconstruction or reorganization of experience which has as its purpose to add meaning to the experiences in order to increase the ability to direct the course of ensuing experiences. Indeed, there is a clear parallel between Dewey's critique of traditional education, which he saw as being centred on the 'acquisition of isolated skills and techniques by drill' (Dewey, 1938, p. 19) and Kirk's (2010) critique of physical education-as-sport-technique. Dewey's development of progressive education, where the acquisition of skills is a means for attaining ends that make 'direct vital appeal' (ibid.), serves as a good starting point for a different form of physical education than the traditional approach described by Kirk (2010).

Applied to skills learning, I would suggest that this requires a pedagogical approach where the pupils first of all must have a presence to their own experiences. The doing of activities must not be a matter of mindless, but rather mindful, doing. Next, pupils must be enabled to describe these experiences. For that reason, a language for bodily experience is absolutely necessary.[13] Finally pupils must be provided with the opportunity to analyse their experiences and try out new ways of solving movement problems through experiment.

It is worth noticing that on Dewey's account, movement experiences would not have any intrinsic meaning or value in themselves because everything depends on the quality of the experiences (Dewey, 1938). Movement experiences should prepare the pupils for further experiences; in short, help pupils develop the capacity for feeling better. As such, this ties in with Dewey's first principle of education – continuity. Taking the principle of continuity seriously, movement literacy – and indeed physical education in general – must have a different pedagogical approach when compared to a presentation of the subject matter that emphasizes 'short taught "blocks" of a limited range of physical activities, particularly team games' (Bailey et al., 2009, p. 8). Rather, there must be both progression and increasing depth in the learning experiences.

Earlier in this chapter I asked whether it is possible to think of physical education as a body discipline 'designed to improve our somatic experience and performance' (Shusterman, 2012, p. 13). In order to respect the non-negotiable feature of movement literacy to avoid comparing pupils to an external norm, some comments are in order: Developing skills must be done in such a way that it is always the personal development of the individual pupil which is in focus. Assessments of development must therefore be ipsative (self-referential) rather than norm- or criterion-based. This means that although any skill can be developed in a linear fashion towards an ideal that is bio-mechanically more efficient or economical, it is the individual's personal development which remains in focus.

Interaction is the second principle of Dewey's philosophy of education, and implies the interplay between the pupil and the environment; or, in Dewey's terms, the interaction between the internal and objective conditions. This interaction forms the educational situation. In terms of movement literacy as a pedagogical model, I want to draw attention to the relevance interaction has for the proposed learning outcome 'to read and write the movement environment'. The pragmatist philosophy I have been drawing on in this chapter holds that meaning does not reside in the environment, as if meaning was already to there to be read. Neither is it something ascribed, imposed on the environment by the moving agent. It is precisely in the interaction between objective conditions[14] and personal needs, desires, purposes and capacities that an environment emerges. The active part of experience, the grasping of meaning is, as far as I can see, to write the environment, because the active grasping introduces something new, personal and individual to the environment. Shusterman (2012) also underscores the point of actively contributing to the movement environment when, in defining somaesthetics, he claims that 'it seeks to enhance the understanding, efficacy, and beauty of our movements and *improve the environments to which our movements contribute* and from which they draw their energies' (p. 26). This point was already made in Chapter 5 with resources from phenomenology. The addition which is made here is to put it into educational terms: it means that in order for movement experiences to become educative, the teacher must create learning environments that interact with the internal conditions of the learner to produce a worthwhile experience.

Movement literacy as I have developed here requires a phenomenological pedagogy. The work of van Manen (e.g. 1993; 1982; 2007) underscores the importance of the qualities of the intersubjective relations between teachers and pupils. The teaching strategies of movement literacy must begin with acknowledging and working from the experiences of the individual pupils as these experiences are expressed and communicated in the present situation. The outcome of my discussion in the two previous chapters has therefore been to give substance to how the experiences of the pupils should play a central role in the teaching of movement literacy. My contribution to phenomenological pedagogy applied to physical education has been to highlight the importance of making these experiences the object of reflection for the pupils. In this way, pupils do not only (or primarily) learn to master different skills, but they will come to learn something about themselves as moving subjects.

Notes

1 It is relevant here to note the different meanings of word *discipline*. On the one hand it can mean a branch of learning or academic discipline. Physical education can be considered an academic discipline, or at least we could say that there is an academic study of physical education that draws upon a variety of academic disciplines. Discipline is also a corporeal form of exercise, such as the discipline needed to take part in training regimes or even show up for one's football training or yoga practice. Discipline has also a somewhat negative connotation through application of the work of Foucault where, for instance, sporting activities and fitness practices exert a certain discipline on people. This usage has a negative ring to it because this form of discipline is thought to make people less free, i.e. the discipline involved in this form of bio-power allows only certain, quite narrow subject-positions to be taken.

2 There are scattered references to Shusterman's somaesthetics in the physical education literature (e.g. Brown, 2013; Nyberg and Larsson, 2014), but to my knowledge his work has not been systematically elaborated on in this context.

3 Shusterman is eclectic in this regard, arguing that the value of historical and socio-cultural analysis offered by Foucault and Bourdieu for instance, does not preclude analysis of a more universalist bent such as the phenomenology of Merleau-Ponty (Shusterman, 2000).

4 'But what if our habits are flawed, as they often are? To act spontaneously will simply reinforce these bad habits and the damage they cause. We cannot correct these bad habits without inhibiting their free flow, nor can we learn improved bodily habits without paying attention to the different somatic feelings that these new ways of using one's body involve' (Shusterman, 2008, p. 169).

5 Hass (2008) makes the claim that 'Merleau-Ponty is really a cognitivist' (p. 84). This claim is surprising because we have learned, for instance through the work of Dreyfus (cf. 2002), that Merleau-Ponty's work represents a challenge to – and even a rejection of – classical cognitivism. Hass (2008), however, makes the very important qualification 'that cognition [must] be understood as thoroughly embodied and situated' (p. 84). For Merleau-Ponty, consciousness is not a positing consciousness (as is the alternative of learning through forming propositional representations that subsequently are acted upon). Rather, this consciousness 'infuses the body from the get-go. As I live and breathe, act and flow through my day, I am not a machine with a ghost attached to the pineal gland. Instead, I am a living-conscious body' (ibid.).

6 The references to William James' work in this section are all taken from Shusterman's writings (2008; 2012).

7 In Shusterman (2008), seven strategies are outlined. The seventh comprises linguistic tags or descriptions that can be used to name certain vague feelings. In Shusterman (2012), naming and putting into language is not a separate point, but is nevertheless 'crucial even to those disciplines of body consciousness that regard the range and meaning of our feelings as going well beyond the limits of language' (p. 121).

8 This is the crucial argument in favour of including physical education in the school curriculum against the educational theory proposed by Hirst and Peters, and it is in terms of arguments such as this that phenomenology is thought to be relevant for research in physical education (e.g. Stolz, 2014).

9 This refers to James' essay 'The Gospel of Relaxation' reproduced in *Talks to Teachers*.

10 The Alexander technique was developed by an Australian actor, Frederick M. Alexander, who suffered from problems with his voice and throat. By studying himself in the mirror, he came to see that his habitual posture when declaiming constrained his breath, and he also noted how his sensory awareness of his postures and movements was highly inaccurate. He also observed the same in others, and thus constructed a technique to increase somaesthetic awareness. His technique also involves inhibition of habitual movements and a conscious focus on the desired actions.

11 Hence the title *Body Consciousness: A Philosophy of Mindfulness and Somaesthetics* (Shusterman, 2008).

12 'learning of intelligent somatic self-use is not a matter of blind drill in mechanical techniques but requires a careful cultivation of somatic awareness' (Shusterman, 2012, p. 37).

13 I would here suggest that this languaging of embodied experience is not commonly done in physical education, either because such experiences are overlooked or because the idea of tacit knowledge is so strong that this kind of knowing has been silenced. As Collins (2010) pointed out, 'a heavy diet of examples of tacit knowledge that turns on the abilities of the body' has made the problem of tacit knowledge more difficult than it should be.

14 Objective conditions 'includes what is done by the educator and the way in which it is done, not only words spoken but the tone of voice in which they are spoken. It includes equipment, books, apparatus, toys, games played. It includes the material with which an individual interacts, and, most important of all, the total set-up of the situations in which the person is engaged' Dewey (1938, p. 45).

References

Arnold, P. J. (1979). *Meaning in movement, sport and physical education*. London: Heinemann.

Bailey, R., Armour, K., Kirk, D., Jess, M. and Pickup, I. (2009). The educational benefits claimed for physical education and school sport: an academic review. *Research Papers in Education*, 24(1), 1–27.

Bernstein, R. J. (2010). *The pragmatic turn*. New York: Polity Press.

Brown, T. D. (2013). A vision lost? (Re) articulating an Arnoldian conception of education 'in' movement in physical education. *Sport, Education and Society*, 18(1), 21–37.

Carr, D. (1981). Knowledge in practice. *American Philosophical Quarterly*, 18(1), 53–61.

Collins, H. (2010). *Tacit and explicit knowledge.* Chicago: University of Chicago Press.

Dewey, J. (1896). The reflex arc concept in psychology. *The Psychological Review*, III(4), 357–370.

Dewey, J. (1910). *How we think.* New York: D. C. Heath & Co.

Dewey, J. (1916). *Democracy and education.* Middlesex: The Echo Library.

Dewey, J. (1938). *Experience and education.* New York: Kappa Delta Pi.

Dreyfus, H. L. (2002). Intelligence without representation: Merleau-Ponty's critique of mental representation. *Phenomenology and the Cognitive Sciences*, 1, 367–383.

Dreyfus, H. L. (2007). The return of the myth of the mental. *Inquiry*, 50(4), 352–365.

Ennis, C. D. (2006). Curriculum: forming and reshaping the vision of physical education in a high need, low demand world of schools. *Quest*, 58(1), 41–59.

Hass, L. (2008). *Merleau-Ponty's philosophy.* Bloomington: Indiana University Press.

Johnson, M. (2010). Cognitive science and Dewey's theory of mind, thought, and language. In M. Cochran (ed.), *The Cambridge companion to Dewey* (pp. 123–144). Cambridge: Cambridge University Press.

Kirk, D. (2010). *Physical education futures.* London: Routledge.

Kirk, D. (2013). Educational value and models-based practice in physical education. *Educational Philosophy and Theory*, 45(9), 973–986.

Menand, L. (2001). *The metaphysical club.* London: Macmillan.

Nyberg, G. and Larsson, H. (2014). Exploring 'what' to learn in physical education. *Physical Education and Sport Pedagogy*, 19, 123–135.

Quay, J. (2013). *Education, experience and existence.* Abingdon: Routledge.

Quennerstedt, M. (2013). Practical epistemologies in physical education practice. *Sport, Education and Society*, 18(3), 311–333.

Quennerstedt, M., Öhman, J. and Öhman, M. (2011). Investigating learning in physical education: a transactional approach. *Sport, Education and Society*, 16(2), 159–177.

Rodgers, C. (2002). Defining reflection: another look at John Dewey and reflective thinking. *Teachers College Record*, 104(4), 842–866.

Shusterman, R. (2000). *Pragmatist aesthetics: Living beauty, rethinking art* (2nd edn). Oxford: Rowman & Littlefield.

Shusterman, R. (2005). The silent limping body of philosophy. In T. Carman and M. B. N. Hansen (eds), *The Cambridge companion to Merleau-Ponty* (pp. 151–180). Cambridge: Cambridge University Press.

Shusterman, R. (2008). *Body consciousness: A philosophy of mindfulness and somaesthetics.* New York: Cambridge University Press.

Shusterman, R. (2012). *Thinking through the body: Essays in somaesthetics.* Cambridge: Cambridge University Press.

Slatman, J. (2014). Multiple dimensions of embodiment in medical practices. *Medicine, Health Care and Philosophy*, 17(4), 549–557. Online first, 1–9.

Stolz, S. (2014). *The philosophy of physical education: A new perspective.* London: Routledge.

Tiles, J. E. (2010). The primacy of practice in Dewey's experimental empiricism. In M. Cochran (ed.), *The Cambridge companion to Dewey* (pp. 101–122). Cambridge: Cambridge University Press.

Tinning, R. (2010). *Pedagogy and human movement: Theory, practice, research.* London: Routledge.

van Manen, M. (1982). Phenomenological pedagogy. *Curriculum Inquiry*, 12(3), 283–299.

van Manen, M. (1993). *Pedagogisk takt* [*The tact of teaching: The meaning of pedagogical thoughtfulness*]. Bergen, Norway: Caspar Forlag.
van Manen, M. (2007). Phenomenology of practice. *Phenomenology and Practice*, 1(1), 11–30.
Whitehead, M. (2010). The concept of physical literacy. In M. Whitehead (ed.), *Physical literacy: Throughout the lifecourse* (pp. 10–20). London: Routledge.

8 Inclusion and difference

A phenomenological perspective

As a response to exclusionary educational practices as well as a growing trend towards pluralism in society, inclusion has become a significant factor in education debates, so also in the area of physical education (e.g. Dagkas and Armour, 2013; Goodwin and Watkinson, 2000). The premise of the next two chapters is that physical education – and therefore by implication any pedagogical model for physical education – must deal adequately with the challenges of inclusion.

The issue of inclusion is important to a discussion of movement literacy as a pedagogical model for physical education for several reasons. First of all, physical literacy as developed by Whitehead has from its start emphasized the importance of understanding literacy in relation to each individual's 'endowment'. However, as noted earlier, the physical literacy literature has exhibited some difficulty with the role of endowment, for example when it is assumed that pupils who are labelled obese have lower levels of physical literacy (Gately, 2010). This indicates the need for further work on how literacy in movement contexts can deal with individual differences.

Second, the phenomenological foundation of movement literacy and in particular the phenomenology of the body are often criticized for being essentialist and for being too general and incapable of addressing questions crucial to inclusion, namely, questions of power and how individual experiences are shaped by social contexts. As Shusterman (2012, p. 5) puts it:

> The definite article in [philosophy of the body] suggests a dangerous essentialism or uniformity about our embodiment, as if we are dealing with only one single thing – 'the body' – rather than doing justice to the diversity of our bodies (in terms of gender, age, and ethnicity, for example) and the different ways of experiencing them.

Larsson and Quennerstedt (2012) levelled a similar criticism against Whitehead's work, arguing that all phenomenological approaches, including physical literacy, are problematic due to their commitment to monism,[1] and that 'understanding movement as universal leads to the same tendency of decontextualizing movements as do conventional dualist perspectives, like those underpinning motor development testing' (p. 294). Part of this chapter is devoted to rebutting this assertion by showing that phenomenology is indeed capable of understanding movement and difference, and that it is erroneous to say that all forms of phenomenology decontextualize movements. To the contrary, as I will argue, phenomenology provides theoretical resources that can be extremely useful for analysing movement experiences and inclusion in physical education.

A third reason for connecting movement literacy and inclusion is the concept of capability. Whitehead (2010) invokes this concept with reference to Martha Nussbaum's list of essential capabilities (see Chapter 9). Physical literacy, Whitehead observes, 'does not fit neatly into' Nussbaum's theory, but there are 'a number of key features in [Nussbaum's] description of capabilities that lead to the categorization of physical literacy as a capability' (p. 18). My concern is not so much whether or not physical literacy should be categorized as a capability. Rather, from my perspective, it is how Nussbaum uses her capabilities approach to outline a theory of social justice, that makes it a useful tool for understanding inclusion as an ethical dimension in physical education. Most importantly in this context, her theory can help specify what a pedagogical model, such as one for physical education, must include to be minimally just.

This chapter will deal with the first two of these three reasons. By outlining a phenomenological approach to inclusion and difference, I hope to lay the foundation for a discussion of the normative decisions that teachers must make when they attempt to establish an inclusive physical education curriculum.

Inclusion and difference

As societies, schools and physical education classes become more heterogeneous, the topic of inclusion has become increasingly important. This section will explore the concept of inclusion and its relationship to individual differences in physical education. Establishing a physical education programme that is truly inclusive – both in its curriculum and in everyday pedagogical practice – is an ethical challenge. Ensuring social justice in physical education requires respecting and celebrating individual differences, as well as a fair and equitable distribution of its benefits.

Inclusion: a complex concept

As Kirk (2010) has pointed out, contemporary physical education reproduces rather than challenges social inequalities in areas such as gender, disability, social class and ethnicity. The history of physical education (and schools in general) is replete with exclusionary practices (Reid, 2003). These practices have been documented by many researchers (e.g. Goodwin and Watkinson, 2000; Goodwin and Fitzgerald, 2009; Svendby and Dowling, 2013). With respect to pupils who experience disability, efforts to counter exclusion have traditionally taken the form of mainstreaming or integration, i.e. placing these pupils in the same school environment as every other child (Reid, 2003). Similarly, girls and boys now participate in physical education classes together, whereas formerly they were taught separately, with different curricula (in some societies, this is still the case) (Penney, 2002).

Over the past two decades, inclusion has emerged as a progressive alternative to integration (Vislie, 2003). Although these two terms are sometimes used interchangeably, the differences in their meaning are particularly significant in the case of special needs education. Integration, as Vislie (2003) points out, is an effort to counter segregation and exclusion. It has three distinct foci: securing the right to education, ensuring that this education takes place in the local school rather than in special facilities, and including special needs pupils in mainstream classes. Inclusion is more comprehensive. As proclaimed in the Salamanca Declaration on Special Needs Education (UNESCO, 1994), inclusion is a process that pertains to all pupils as individuals rather than to individual pupils or specific groups of pupils. Finally, inclusion should be seen as a continuing effort to make curricula and school cultures flexible, open and accepting of difference.

Integration was primarily concerned with efforts to counteract the segregation and exclusion of pupils who experience disability. Inclusion has a broader meaning. As Ainscow and Cesar (2006) have pointed out, the assumption that inclusion is about pupils who experience disability and/or have been assessed as having special needs 'has been questioned, since, in attempting to increase the participation of students, it focuses on a "disabled" or "special needs" part of them and ignores all the other ways in which participation for any student may be impeded or enhanced' (p. 233). Inclusion, in contrast, can be defined as a response to the needs and interests of pupils from a variety of groups who are at risk of being excluded. Although this way of understanding inclusion suggests that some common processes may underlie the experiences of members of different groups who experience exclusion, it perpetuates what we might call 'group thinking', i.e. the idea that any commonalities among individuals who are designated as members of a group constitute their dominant identity. This perspective ignores the differences that surely exist among individuals assigned to any such group. In response, some scholars have advocated understanding inclusion as a comprehensive way of thinking about schools and education for all, which would entail viewing each pupil as an individual rather than as a member of a specific group (Ainscow and Cesar, 2006).

This disagreement is evident in recent literature on physical education and sports. In their book *Inclusion and Exclusion Through Youth Sport*, Macdonald and colleagues (Macdonald et al., 2012, p. 21) warn that thinking about inclusion in terms of groups is problematic: 'those who are not included [...] are positioned as a "problem" [...] this approach serves to reproduce a bio-politically predetermined group membership where the classification of "the group" [...] is spurious and potentially limiting'. In other words, 'group thinking' is problematic because it positions individuals in groups that may not be relevant to their lived experiences. In addition, being positioned in a specific group may even have negative consequences for the individual members, for instance due to stigmatization and stereotyping. However, on the very same page the authors note that many chapters in their book 'will outline the experiences of those individuals and groups who have been excluded' (ibid.). At first glance, warning against the problems inherent in categorizing individuals by group and then presenting chapters in which individuals are discussed in terms of their group membership is contradictory. However, I would argue that the authors' approach reflects a paradox in inclusion: Individual differences must always be seen in relation to what they differ from. In the process of identifying either yourself or others as being different, you are also taking on (or ascribing) an identity of being similar to others with the same identity and different from those who do not share it.

Inclusion is thus a complex concept which is under debate, where some see inclusion as a being about responding to groups of pupils who are at risk of being excluded and others who see inclusion as a more radical and transformative approach. As such, there is a potential conflict between inclusion as a general process of relevance to all pupils and the need for additional educational efforts that some pupils may need or benefit from.

Difference and equity

As the previous section indicates, the relationship between inclusion and difference is important and complex. Both terms can be interpreted in different ways, partly depending on the writer's theoretical standpoint. Discussing the implications of difference in physical education, Flintoff and Fitzgerald (2012) observe that 'how differences are conceived and which differences get noted, and why some, and not others, are viewed as significant or relevant, and by whom, are all important questions for those wishing to *make* a difference in education' (p. 16). They go on to identify three theoretical 'waves' commonly applied in analysing difference: categorical, relational and postmodern/post-structural research.

Categorical research identifies categories of difference, such as gender, ethnicity, disability or social class and highlights differences between individuals belonging to different categories. This approach is useful in identifying potential inequalities between different categories (e.g. differences in participation in sports between men and women). Usually, it is not concerned with distinguishing differences within a particular group. In other words, this approach is not particularly well suited to discerning how individuals grouped into a particular category differ from each other.

Relational research examines how differences within and between groups vary historically and culturally. It seeks to 'understand how inequalities are produced and reproduced through everyday practices and institutions across different contexts' (p. 20). Thus, this theoretical perspective introduces the notion of power and how physical education is linked to structures of inequality in the wider society.

Finally, postmodern/post-structural research asks questions about the very relevance of binary categories (boy/girl, disabled/non-disabled), asserting that such categories are static and not sufficiently capable of explaining how identities and subjectivities are shifting and unstable. This theoretical wave sees individual experiences as shaped by power and socio-cultural resources that are highly complex and shifting. In the field of research on physical education, Flintoff and Fitzgerald note (2012, p. 27), the many versions of 'post-theorizing … [are] interested in exploring how young people are differently positioned in relation to gender, "race", class, sexuality, disability or religion to benefit from particular truths within PE, sport and health'.

Both theorizing and research on the role of difference in physical education grapple with issues of equity and social justice; how current (and envisioned) practice is (or is not) contributing to a fair distribution of benefits and outcomes of participation and learning. As noted by Penney (2002), equity in physical education means that difference must not be construed as a deficit or a lack of something. Rather, equity demands that differences are not only recognized and respected, they are seen as a resource and an enrichment that can facilitate valuable learning experiences for all pupils (Esser-Noethlich, 2011).

As mentioned in the introduction to this chapter, phenomenology is often considered to be incapable of dealing with difference and social justice. At least, this seems to be the perception in the physical education literature (e.g. Larsson and Quennerstedt, 2012). In a review of Stolz's (2014) book on the philosophy of physical education, which takes a phenomenological approach, Pringle (2014) argues that

> as a critical sociologist, I am not sold on *Merleau-Ponty's phenomenological and seemingly 'asocial' or individualistic approach* [as detailed by Stolz] for understanding how humans construct meaning … Stolz, in my subjective view, *tends to neglect the influence of the social and the workings of power in understanding how humans negotiate embodied experiences.*
>
> (pp. 280–281, italics added)

Even though Pringle specifies that he is criticizing Stolz's approach to phenomenology, rather than phenomenology *per se*, given the frequency of this type of criticism, it is incumbent upon researchers using a phenomenological approach to explain why this criticism does not apply to their work. In other words, we need to show that phenomenology is indeed capable of working with 'the influence of the social and the workings of power.' This is particularly important in the context of the topics dealt with this chapter, and inspires the following discussion of queer phenomenology.

Queering phenomenology

Recent developments in phenomenology provide ample evidence of its interest in and capacity for understanding how social structures shape embodied experiences. Two excellent examples are the scholars Iris Marion Young – in particular her classic essay, 'Throwing Like a Girl' (Young, 1998a) – and Sara Ahmed, who has produced seminal work on queer phenomenology and inclusion (Ahmed, 2006; Ahmed, 2012).

Throwing like a girl

The essay 'Throwing Like a Girl' was first published in 1980.[2] In this essay, Young observes that when girls throw, they generally do not make full use of the body's spatial and lateral potential. She points out that this is a general feature of feminine comportment,[3] in which movements

> have in common first that the whole body is not put into fluid and directed motion, but rather, in swinging and hitting, for example, the motion is concentrated in one body part; and second that the woman's motion tends not to reach, extend, lean, stretch, and follow through in the direction of her intention.
>
> (p. 263)

Referring to Simone de Beauvoir's existential, phenomenological work, Young argues that femininity in movement is not caused by biology, anatomy or physiology, but by 'structures and conditions that delimit the typical situation of being a woman in a particular society' (p. 261).

On the basis of her analysis, Young delineates three modalities of feminine movement, namely ambiguous transcendence, inhibited intentionality and discontinuous unity. In the case of throwing, ambiguous transcendence is represented by the lack of whole-body involvement in the throwing motion. According to Merleau-Ponty, the lived body is characterized by its transcendence, i.e. its capacities for projecting out from the body's immanence toward the world. Young, in contrast, observes that when parts of the body are not engaged in the act of throwing, they remain rooted in immanence, thus making the body's transcendence ambiguous. She also argues that by not making full use of the body's potential for movement, 'feminine bodily existence is an inhibited intentionality, which simultaneously reaches towards a projected end with an "I can" and withholds its full bodily commitment to that end in a self-imposed "I cannot"' (p. 265). As elaborated in Chapter 3, embodied learning consists of the experience of a harmony between what the mover seeks to achieve and her performance.[4] Inhibited intentionality breaks this intimate relationship between aim and act. In her discussion of discontinuous unity, Young posits two dimensions. One of these dimensions is the discontinuous unity with oneself, in the sense that while some parts of the body transcend to achieve the aim of the movement, other parts remain immobile and immanent. The other is a discontinuous unity between the body's capacities and the possibilities that exist in the movement environment.

While all three modalities are illustrated by the body's movement, Young also takes care to show the spatial dimensions of these experiences. The ambiguous transcendence of the body simultaneously implies that it does not use all of the space available for movement. In the context of movement literacy's aim of taking full advantage of the body's capacity to read and write the movement environment, Young's approach would suggest that the objective should be to encourage pupils to make fuller use of the space they already inhabit for movement. In other words, physical education should promote a form of critical movement literacy (Wright and Burrows, 2006) that enables pupils to understand the environment which is available to them critically, as well as make to use of it. In addition, they should become capable of expanding their own possibilities by writing (creating) a movement environment that is friendlier and more inclusive of their own movement needs and interests.

Young (1998a) goes on to elaborate on discontinuity:

> [A] distinction between space that is 'yonder' and not linked with my own body possibilities and the enclosed space that is 'here,' which I inhabit with my bodily possibilities, is an expression of the discontinuity between aim and capacity to realize the aim that I have articulated.
>
> (p. 268)

In this sense, the experience of discontinuous space is remarkably similar to Toombs' (2001, p. 249) description of the experience of living with a motor disability: 'Locomotion opens up space, allowing one freely to change position and move towards objects in the world. Loss of mobility anchors one in the Here, engendering a heightened sense of distance between oneself and surrounding things.' The parallels between female and disabled movement experiences was also noted by Young (1998a), who asserted that 'women in sexist society are physically handicapped … physically inhibited, confined, positioned and objectified' (p. 269). Even though we have to take care to avoid conflating analogous experiences, it seems evident that the processes of oppression and exclusion that women and people with disabilities experience in movement contexts have strong structural similarities. In both cases, it can be argued that a lack of opportunities and acquisition of specific habits hinders the full exploitation of one's movement potential.

Although 'Throwing Like a Girl' was informed by Merleau-Ponty's account of embodiment and movement, Young (1998b) notes that he could be criticized for not examining whether and how bodies that are differently gendered express differing subjectivities. In developing her concept of 'gendered modalities of the general categories of body experience and spatiality Merleau-Ponty theorizes' (Young, 1998b, p. 287), she draws on Simone de

Beauvoir's existential, phenomenological framework. This enables her to show how phenomenology can indeed take difference, social structures and power issues into account. Young (2005) goes on to caution that 'after reading Lacan, Foucault, Derrida, Kristeva, Deleuze, Irigaray, and Bourdieu, we cannot be so innocent as to believe that phenomenology can discover a 'pure' embodied experience prior to ideology and science' (p. 8). That noted, she argues that existential phenomenology offers an excellent framework for a theory of embodied subjectivity that can (and should) be sensitive to difference. Such a phenomenology would complement post-structural and postmodern theories, rather than duplicate them.

Several earlier chapters in this book have offered a more or less explicit critique of what I would call total subjectification of the body, i.e. the idea that the body can be understood as a pure subject. For example, although an important and valid critique is often levelled against physical education practices that objectify the body in instrumental ways, this criticism may lead to its opposite: an over-emphasis on the subjective aspects of embodiment. My argument about the necessity of bodily objectifications (Chapters 6 and 7) and the intimate relationship between the body as a knowledge object and the embodied, knowing subject in practical knowledge, is consistent with Young's (1998a) point that 'for feminine existence the body is frequently both subject and object for itself at the same time and in reference to the same act' (p. 266). Although Young's point is slightly different, in the sense that it offers a perspective on bodily objectifications (for instance, how women in movement experience are objects of the gaze of others) that I have not explored so far, her contributions certainly support the argument that phenomenology can be a valuable tool for understanding difference and diversity in physical education. The next part of this section will develop this point further through a discussion of Sara Ahmed's work on queer phenomenology and its relevance to inclusive physical education.

Queer phenomenology and inclusive physical education

Queer phenomenology is a termed coined by Sara Ahmed (2006). To understand her argument, we can begin by looking at the meaning of the word queer. Etymologically, it means twisted or crossed, and Ahmed states that one way of using the word is to signify specific non-normative sexual practices 'seen as odd, bent, twisted' (p. 161). The second traditional way that the term queer has been used, according to Ahmed, is to describe what is oblique; in other words, something that deviates from the line. (Interestingly, the same meanings exist in Norwegian: queer as in sexual orientation is commonly denoted as *skeiv*, which is also the word used for an oblique angle. Tellingly, in geometry the oblique angle deviates from the normal line.) One of Ahmed's central points concerning queer phenomenology is that bodies are oriented and straightened by taking up time and space. She makes a connection between the basic phenomenological idea that consciousness is always oriented and the concept of sexual orientation[5]:

> The question of orientation becomes, then, a question not only about how we 'find our way, but how we come to feel at home' [...] . Familiarity is shaped by the 'feel' of space or by how spaces 'impress' upon bodies. This familiarity is an effect of inhabitance; we are not simply in the familiar, but rather the familiar is shaped by actions that reach out towards objects that are already within reach.
>
> (p. 7)

For Ahmed, becoming oriented is a process of making the unknown known through the unfolding of bodies in a space. Certain spaces allow some bodies to extend, while other bodies may not be extended in the same way, or at all. This is consistent with Young's point that feminine movement fails to take full advantage of the potentialities of either the body or the space around it.

Ahmed's analysis of 'doing things' is relevant to inclusive physical education. In physical education, we are constantly doing things in the sense that taking part in its actions, activities and practices involves objects that we manipulate and play with. Drawing on Heidegger's concept of equipmentality, Ahmed notes that 'what makes an object "itself" is what it allows us to do, and that "doing" takes the object out of itself and makes it "point" towards something, whether that something is an action or other objects' (p. 46). In other words, the objects used in physical education, such as balls, bean bags, volleyball nets, gymnastics apparatus and so forth, are defined by their use. When they are used in the context of physical education, they become pedagogical objects.

Ahmed argues that the use of objects does not extend to all bodies equally: 'An object tends towards some bodies more than others, depending on the "tendencies" of bodies' (s. 51). And what happens, she asks, when pedagogical objects fail to do the work they were intended to? For instance, when the jump box is too high for some pupils to surmount, the box as a pedagogical object fails to extend those pupils who are not able to jump over it. Ahmed understands these failures to be 'about the loss of capacity to perform an action for which the object was intended' (p. 49), and argues that they are not caused by properties of the object in itself or the subject working with the object. Rather, she asserts, the failure occurs in the relationship or interplay between objects and subjects; it is a failure to extend bodies: 'It would be the failure of subjects and objects to work together. The failure would be the failure of the object to enable the action with which it is identified' (p. 50).

One of the useful concepts that Ahmed develops is the 'straightening device', which I understand as a process of straightening what is queer or oblique so that it follows the 'normal' or straight line. Social expectations are one example of a straightening device, hetero-normativity is another. I would suggest that physical education has incorporated a number of straightening devices. One vivid historical example is Ling gymnastics, which was also known as line gymnastics: Pupils were placed in a straight line and their bodies were disciplined through following the teacher's instructions precisely, like a chorus line. Similar, contemporary examples include aerobics or other fitness activities in which participants are also lined up and expected to move in sync, again following the instructions of the trainer exactly. Yet another example is sports techniques that specify a (bio-mechanical) movement pattern and correct deviations from the normative ideal. In all these examples, the condition for bodies to be extended in space is that they follow the supposedly correct, straight line. Bodies that fail to, or refuse to, stay in that line are regarded as queer or deviant. Straightening devices in physical education, then, are educational processes based on normative ideas of how a particular movement or activity should be performed. These ideas are put into practice through teaching and the pedagogical use of certain objects. In this sense, straightening devices are potential producers of exclusion.

In discussing colour, Ahmed shows what happens when queer moments arise, for example when coloured bodies are present in rooms filled with whiteness. The presence of such bodies disrupts the line: 'The proximity of such *bodies out of place* can work to make things seem "out of line", and can hence even work to "queer" space; people "blink" and do "double turns" when they encounter such bodies' (s. 161). Queer moments in which bodies of difference are suddenly noticed arise frequently in physical education, as is evident from a large body of research documenting the experiences of girls, pupils who experience disability, pupils from certain ethnic or religious minorities, and pupils who openly express a commitment to queer sexual practices. This research indicates that pupils who experience having a body 'out of place' are either sidelined (excluded) or exposed to straightening devices designed to bring them back to the norm, the straight line. In this context, I believe it is important to note that failure of achieving what one aims for does not necessarily constitute a queer moment. If the notion of a queer moment is going to be meaningful, there must be a certain repetition or habituality in these experiences. Ahmed is not so much concerned about avoiding[6] such queer moments as she is in inquiring into what happens when queer moments arise and how we should meet queer moments.

Critical movement literacy

Earlier in this chapter, I made a passing reference to the concept of critical movement literacy, citing an article by Jan Wright and Lisette Burrows (2006) in which they discussed Evans' (2004) concept of ability. Wright and Burrows (2006) noted that Whitehead's use of the concept literacy is promising, but added this caveat:

> What [physical literacy] doesn't have is any reference to the social and cultural contexts in which we learn and use movement; it does not acknowledge how particular repertoires of being, including movement, are socially constructed in relation to gender, class, race and how

> particular forms of movement have relevance for particular social and cultural contexts.
>
> (p. 279)

Wright and Burrows went on to argue that there is need for a *critical* literacy. Using the analogy of reading and writing, they assert that just as people must also be able to recognize the socially structured nature of language and the texts they read and write, a critical movement literacy would require understanding how movements and movement cultures are social products that enable and disable different participants.

Now that I have shown how the phenomenology underpinning movement literacy can meet the criteria that Wright and Burrows set in their critique of Whitehead's work, I will outline what critical movement literacy would involve from a phenomenological perspective. Before doing so, I should caution that my arguments rely on an understanding of the term 'critical' that may differ from the meaning attached to it by critical sociologists/pedagogues. My use of the term is informed by recent work in feminist phenomenology and it highlights the importance of the reconstruction of experience that Dewey (1938) advocated in his educational philosophy.

Sara Ahmed stresses the relationship between inhabitance and difference: In movement contexts, she notes, some bodies have more potential for being extended than others. Their experience is one of inhabitance, of being oriented. Ahmed (2006) discusses this concept in relation to whiteness:

> White bodies do not have to face their whiteness; they are not orientated 'toward' it, and this 'not' is what allows whiteness to cohere, as that which bodies are orientated around. By not having to encounter being white as an obstacle, *given that whiteness is 'in line' with what is already given, bodies that pass as white move easily, and this motility is extended by what they move toward.* The white body in this way expands; objects, tools, instruments, and even 'others' allow that body to inhabit space by extending that body and what it can reach. Whiteness becomes habitual in the sense that white bodies extend their reach by incorporating objects that are within reach. To make this point simply: what is 'within reach' also 'extends the reach' of such bodies.
>
> (p. 132, italics added)

It would be possible to substitute 'male', 'heterosexual' or 'non-disabled' for 'white' and Ahmed's argument would still be essentially valid[7]: Norms and expectations allow certain bodies to move with ease, while others have the experience of continuously noticing themselves and how they deviate from these norms and expectations.

The concept of poise, as developed by Samuel Todes (2001), implies that one goal in movement literacy is to enable the moving subject to make the movement environment 'habit-able' (Todes, 2001, p. 65). The contribution of queer phenomenology is to show that pedagogical practices designed to develop poise must build in attention to difference and, specifically, must structure movement environments so that they are responsive and adaptive to a wide range of movers. I would like to point out that even if physical education were to become a much more inclusive learning environment than it presently appears to be, exclusion and the experience of queer moments will still occur. It is unlikely that there will be such a thing as a barrier-free utopia (Shakespeare, 2006). One of the virtues of critical movement literacy is that it accepts this, and suggests ways of understanding how teachers and pupils should respond to queer moments and make the spaces of physical education habit-able.

This raises the important question: What can (and should) teachers do when queer moments arise? Here, van Manen's (1993) conception of tact as the ability to *see* that a situation calls for sensitivity and an ethically correct *pedagogical response* is instructive. Seeing the situation correctly, it must be noted, is not a neutral process of unbiased observation. Perceptual norms govern what we see and what we miss. Critical movement literacy requires that teachers are alert to queer moments and to how straightening devices produce them. This demands that teachers be sensitive to what Ahmed (2006) refers to as a phenomenology of being stopped: how does it feel to be stopped, in the sense of not being able (habit-able) to express oneself in a specific movement situation? From this perspective, critical movement literacy and, indeed, physical education in general, faces a particular challenge when teachers come from a motor elite, as is often the case, and who have never experienced any problems with movement. Like whiteness, as described above by Ahmed, being *severely able-bodied* may make it difficult for teachers to fully appreciate what pupils experience in being stopped. This is a challenge that physical education teacher education will need to meet as classrooms become more inclusive.

The second part of van Manen's concept – responding with the ethically right pedagogical act – is also a normative issue. In inclusive physical education, the normative guideline would be to choose the pedagogical alternative that is most effective in enabling pupils to experience the environment of movement as habitable. This is a topic that I will return to in the next chapter.

Phenomenological pedagogy could be criticized for placing too much emphasis on the teacher's understanding of pupil experiences. The perspective of critical movement literacy in particular calls for a greater focus on pupils' understanding of their own experiences. This was discussed in Chapter 7, along with suggestions for how pupils' own embodied experience of movement can be elucidated. Here, I will suggest three ways that self-reflection can promote critical movement literacy. First, as Young (1998a) has noted, 'girls and women are not given the opportunity to use their full bodily capacities in free and open engagement with the world, nor are they encouraged as much as boys to develop specific bodily skills' (pp. 269–270). Similarly, Fitzgerald's (2005) research indicates that pupils who experience disability have little opportunity to display and express their abilities because these abilities are not recognized. Critical movement literacy could respond to this problem by enabling pupils to become fully cognizant of these absences in their experiences and facilitate ways of redeeming this unfortunate situation.

Second, as Young (1998a) notes, girls acquire habits of timidity[8]: their inhabitance is hindered by their adoption of certain forms of movement. In this situation, the role of critical movement literacy should be to help pupils become aware of how what they already know (i.e. their present habits) potentially prevents them from experiencing a freer and more open engagement with their movement environment.

Third, it is important to notice and reflect on the kinds of situations in which pupils' possibilities for inhabitance are limited or prevented by certain normative conventions about how a movement environment should be inhabited. Put differently, this means that pupils should be encouraged to reflect on how straightening devices produce queer moments. In this regard, it's important to recognize that deviating from the straight line is not necessarily a unwanted situation. In a study of the experiences of pupils identifying as lesbians or gays, Walseth and Hæhre (2014) show that some of their participants found positive opportunities in a physical education environment which they experienced as strongly hetero-normative. One opportunity was the potential for queering. That is, by being openly gay and at the same time displaying strength and masculinity, one of the male participants used physical education to contradict stereotypical prejudices of gay men as weak or effeminate. In this case, it is those who harbour stereotypes who might experience the situation as queer. Conversely, a girl in the study who described herself as 'butch' (i.e. having a somewhat masculine identity) used physical education as an opportunity to express herself, rather than conform to normative expectations of how a girl should behave. Thus, the straightening device of hetero-normativity allowed this girl to express her queer identity.

These three points represent experiences that can be a source of learning. They also imply that the pedagogy of Dewey and Shusterman, as outlined in Chapter 7, provides a helpful approach in developing a critical movement literacy. Ultimately, however, to succeed in replacing traditional pedagogies with an approach that is both more inclusive and more effective, critical movement literacy must meet this challenge: It is not sufficient for us to notice our experiences and then critically reflect on how movement and movement contexts are socially constructed in oppressive ways; these reflections must also lead to a new form of doing, to the creation of new habits.

As a final comment, I want to point out how this way of thinking about critical movement literacy relates to inclusion. Ahmed's book *On Being Included* (2012) explores the experiences of diversity workers (i.e. administrators whose task is to promote diversity) at academic institutions. In her conclusion, she reflects on the relationship between knowledge and transformation. Contrasting her views with traditional approaches (e.g. Marx and Freire), Ahmed argues that 'rather than suggesting that knowledge leads (or should lead) to transformation, I offer a reversal that in my view preserves the point or aim of the argument: transformation, as a form of practical labor, leads to knowledge' (p. 173). In other words, situations in which we confront obstacles that prevent us from advancing in the direction we were going or compel us to stop can generate insight. Becoming aware of queer moments and experiences of exclusion provides both teachers and pupils with opportunities to generate knowledge about inclusion and the processes that might have generated these moments.

Notes

1 As noted earlier, although Whitehead identifies herself as a monist, it is manifestly incorrect to assume that this is true of all phenomenologists. Merleau-Ponty, for instance, developed an ontology that was non-dualistic rather than monist.

2 In a reflection on 'Throwing Like a Girl' written almost twenty years after its publication, Young (1998b) commented that even though the social contexts in which girls move had changed dramatically, the essay was neither outdated nor irrelevant: '[A]lthough there is something dated about the way the essay expresses its feminist sentiments, […] many teachers and students have told me that they continue to read the essay and find exciting the discussion it generates' (p. 10).

3 'Not only is there a typical style of throwing like a girl, but there is a more or less typical style of running like a girl, climbing like a girl, swinging like a girl, hitting like a girl' (Young, 1998a, p. 263).

4 Here, Young quotes Merleau-Ponty (2002, p. 167): 'to understand a movement is to experience the harmony between what we aim at and what is given, between the intention and the performance'.

5 At the risk of belaboring this point, it is instructive to see how Ahmed, like Young, sees phenomenology as a useful approach, rather than an obstacle to understanding difference: 'Phenomenology can offer a resource for queer studies as it emphasizes the importance of lived experience, the intentionality of consciousness, the significance of nearness or what is ready-to-hand, and the role of repeated and habitual actions in shaping bodies and worlds' (Ahmed, 2006, p. 2). My contention is that researchers in the field of physical education who claim that phenomenology does not and cannot incorporate an understanding of difference and social forces do not have a thorough understanding of phenomenology's theoretical capacities. My objective is to attempt to trouble those taken for granted viewpoints so that even critical sociologists can think critically about their assumptions concerning phenomenology.

6 It might be impossible to avoid the fact that exclusion takes place in society in general and physical education more specifically. Indeed, the whole idea of inclusion would be logically meaningless without the existence of exclusion (Hansen, 2012). This does of course not mean that one should accept exclusion or other processes that assimilate pupils into ethically deplorable practices, but it seems evident that as long as difference is a condition for pedagogical work in physical education, queer moments will arise.

7 It becomes more complicated if the white body is also female and disabled. This underscores the importance of considering individual differences rather than group membership.

8 E.g. 'subtle habits of feminine bodily comportment – walking like a girl, tilting her head like a girl, standing and sitting like a girl, gesturing like a girl, and so on. The girl learns actively to hamper her movements' (Young, 1998a, p. 270).

References

Ahmed, S. (2006). *Queer phenomenology: Orientations, objects, others.* London: Duke University Press.

Ahmed, S. (2012). *On being included: Racism and diversity in institutional life.* Durham, NC: Duke University Press.

Ainscow, M. and Cesar, M. (2006). Inclusive education ten years after Salamanca: setting the agenda. *European Journal of Physical Education*, 21(3), 231–238.

Dagkas, S. and Armour, K. (2013). *Inclusion and exclusion through youth sport.* Abingdon: Routledge.

Dewey, J. (1938). *Experience and education.* New York: Kappa Delt Pi.

Esser-Noethlich, M. (2011). Sensitivity towards strangeness (sts): development of a concept-based measuring instrument in the context of intercultural movement education. Ph.D. dissertation. Oslo: Norwegian Shool of Sport Sciences.

Evans, J. (2004). Making a difference? Education and 'ability' in physical education. *European Physical Education Review*, 10(1), 95–108.

Fitzgerald, H. (2005). Still feeling like a spare piece of luggage? Embodied experiences of (dis)ability in physical education and school sport. *Physical Education and Sport Pedagogy*, 10(1), 41–59.

Flintoff, A. and Fitzgerald, H. (2012). Theorizing difference and (in)equality in physical education, youth sport and health. In F. Dowling, H. Fitzgerald and A. Flintoff (eds), *Equity and difference in physical education, youth sport and health: A narrative approach* (pp. 11–36). London: Routledge.

Gately, P. (2010). Physical literacy and obesity. In M. Whitehead (ed.), *Physical literacy: Throughout the lifecourse* (pp. 83–99). London: Routledge.

Goodwin, D. L. and Watkinson, E. J. (2000). Inclusive physical education from the perspective of students with physical disabilities. *Adapted Physical Activity Quarterly*, 17, 144–160.

Goodwin, D. and Fitzgerald, H. (2009). The voices of students with disabilities: are they informing inclusive physical education practice?In H. Fitzgerald (ed.), *Disability and youth sport* (pp. 53–75). London: Routledge.

Hansen, J. H. (2012). Limits to inclusion. *International Journal of Inclusive Education*, 16(1), 89–98.

Kirk, D. (2010). *Physical education futures.* London: Routledge.

Larsson, H. and Quennerstedt, M. (2012). Understanding movement: a sociocultural approach to exploring moving humans. *Quest*, 64(4), 283–298.

Macdonald, D., Pang, B., Knez, L., Nelson, A. and Mccuaige, L. (2012). The will for inclusion: bothering the inclusion/exclusion discourses of sport. In S. Dagkas and K. Armour (eds), *Inclusion and exclusion through youth sport* (pp. 9–23). London: Routledge.

Merleau-Ponty, M. (2002). *Phenomenology of perception.* London: Routledge.

Penney, D. (2002). Equality, equity and inclusion in physical education and school sport. In A. Laker (ed.), *The sociology of sport and physical education* (pp. 110–128). London: RouledgeFalmer.

Pringle, R. (2014). The philosophy of physical education: a new perspective. *Sport, Education and Society*, 20(2), 279–282.

Reid, G. (2003). Moving towards inclusion. In R. D. Steadward, G. Wheeler and E. Watkinson (eds), *Adapted physical activity* (pp. 131–147). Edmonton, Canada: University of Alberta Press.

Shakespeare, T. (2006). *Disability rights and wrongs.* London: Routledge.

Shusterman, R. (2012). *Thinking through the body: Essays in somaesthetics.* Cambridge: Cambridge University Press.

Stolz, S. (2014). *The philosophy of physical education: A new perspective.* London: Routledge.

Svendby, E. B. and Dowling, F. (2013). Negotiating the discursive spaces of inclusive education: narratives of experience from contemporary physical education. *Scandinavian Journal of Disability Research*, 15(4), 361–378.

Tinning, R. (2010). *Pedagogy and human movement: Theory, practice, research.* London: Routledge.

Todes, S. (2001). *Body and world.* Cambridge, MA: MIT Press.

Toombs, S. K. (2001). Reflections on bodily change: the lived experience of disability. In S. K. Toombs (ed.), *Handbook of phenomenology and medicine* (pp. 247–261). Dordrecht: Kluwer.

UNESCO (1994). *The Salamanca statement and framework for action on special needs education*Geneva: UNESCO.

van Manen, M. (1993). *Pedagogisk takt* [*The tact of teaching: The meaning of pedagogical thoughtfulness*]. Bergen, Norway: Caspar Forlag.

Vislie, L. (2003). From integration to inclusion: focusing global trends and changes in the western European societies. *European Journal of Special Needs Education*, 18(1), 17–35.

Walseth, K. and Hæhre, H. (2014). Heteronormativitet i kroppsøvingsfaget [Heteronormativity in physical education]. *Tidsskrift for Ungdomsforskning*, 14(2), 28–51.

Whitehead, M. (2010). The concept of physical literacy. In M. Whitehead (ed.), *Physical literacy: Throughout the lifecourse* (pp. 10–20). London: Routledge.

Wright, J. and Burrows, L. (2006). Re-conceiving ability in physical education: a social analysis. *Sport, Education and Society*, 11(3), 275–291.

Young, I. (1998a). Throwing like a girl. In D. Welton (ed.), *Body and flesh: A philosophical reader* (pp. 259–273). Oxford: Blackwell.

Young, I. M. (1998b). 'Throwing like a girl': twenty years later. In D. Welton (ed.), *Body and flesh: A philosophical reader* (pp. 286–290). Oxford: Blackwell.

Young, I. (2005). *On female body experience: 'Throwing like a girl' and other essays.* Oxford: Oxford University Press.

9 Abilities and capabilities

Normative questions

The previous chapter ended with a discussion of the possibilities of critical movement literacy. It invited reflection around what pupils can do – if they are allowed – to include themselves in movement practices. I find that much of the writing and research on inclusive physical education is concerned with the importance of pupils *being included*. I fully acknowledge that in the educational system, where inclusion is a matter of policy, curriculum formulations, and other structures, it is very meaningful and important to investigate and debate those structures and efforts that others are producing in order to include all pupils. It is also clearly an obligation for teachers to work to include pupils of all abilities in physical education. Nothing less can be expected. But I also believe it is important to pay attention to what pupils can do to include themselves. In other words, that they can become active participants in their own inclusion. However, it is of utmost importance to stress that this assertion does not imply that pupils have a responsibility to assimilate themselves, i.e. that they have to work on themselves in ways they find undesirable to fit into ready-made movement practices. This is why previous discussions about the learning outcome of movement literacy have brought out the distinction between reading and writing the movement environment. As such, including oneself means that to some extent one creates conditions for one's own way of moving (Bjorbækmo and Engelsrud, 2011). This also means that we have to understand inclusion 'not solely as a matter of access or acts of accomplishment or completion but as an on-going process, something that has to be routinely and continually achieved' (Evans, 2014, p. 322).

Earlier in the book, I was concerned with practical knowledge which was defined as purposive and as having a form of rationality, which is distinct from the rationality of theoretical knowledge. In addition, practical knowledge can be intersubjectively validated and confirmed via the demonstration of a reasonable degree of success (see the three conditions outlined by Carr, 1981). In terms of inclusion and equity, the latter condition introduces a form of normativity that may be problematic: What kind of norms and standards of excellence are imposed to determine the degree of success? If, as Penney (2002, p. 118) notes: 'From an equity perspective, no one set of values or behaviours should be regarded as superior to others, or as 'the norm' against which others are measured or judged', then the idea conveyed in the definition of practical knowledge (Carr, 1981) appears problematic in the perspective of inclusion and equity.

It is, however, difficult to see that any pedagogical project of learning can avoid being normative: the very idea of learning (just like socialization or development) has a telos (Lave, 1996); it moves towards a change, something new that the pupil presently is not. Thus, if we want physical education to be a subject for learning, then it is important to discuss the norms that are employed in the teaching process. To begin to address this challenge, I draw upon the work of John Evans (2004) about abilities.

Abilities and difference

Evans (2004) launched a debate about how the notion of ability is and should be understood in physical education. He held that ability is mainly considered as equivalent to talent, that is, as an individual, static entity that pupils have more or less of. Evans, however, wanted to get beyond this notion of ability and questioned 'what "abilities" are recognized, valued, nurtured and accepted, while others are rejected by whom, where and why in schools?' (p. 104). By asking questions like these, Evans attempted to move attention away from ability as an individual characteristic towards an understanding of ability as something constructed in social situations. In other words, ability should more appropriately be seen as an outcome of a socio-cultural process where it is not possible to say what ability is 'without reference to a person's gender, age, ethnicity, "disability" and the values prevailing within and across particular fields' (p. 101). Thus, how ability is understood depends on processes of valuation and recognition. As such, it becomes important to question which (and whose) abilities are valued and recognized in physical education and what consequences such recognition has for pedagogical practice.

In his paper, Evans drew on the work of Pierre Bourdieu and in particular the concepts of habitus, capital and field. Without going into detail about this theoretical perspective, the main point made by Evans is that habitus is formed and moulded through socialization and education, and is influenced by categories of difference such as social class, gender, ethnicity and disability. These categories are differences that in the field of school physical education become important forms of differentiation, because the prevailing values in the field of physical education reward certain forms of abilities and devalue others. Evans notes that this process of valuation is socially constructed and shaped through the education of physical education teachers, through curricula, the practice of physical education and how the subject is perceived by teachers, parents, pupils and the wider society. Ability is therefore always an expression of both individual differences and the particular processes of valuation and recognition taking place in the field of physical education. Following from this, we can begin to understand that certain forms of ability traditionally are more likely to be cashed in and exchanged for praise, high grades and status.

Consequently, other abilities become the subject of either ignorance, seen as deficits that must be fixed, or as forms of behaviour that lead to exclusion.

Evans' article spurred a great deal of empirical research that can be used to further illustrate his perspective on ability. Fitzgerald (2005) investigated how pupils with disabilities experience physical education. She found that the participants experienced that the subject emphasized traditional team games and sports and thus promoted a typical masculine ideal. Despite being active in sports like boccia, the pupils in Fitzgerald's study experienced that the skills they had acquired were not recognized by their teachers. Drawing on the perspective of Evans' (2004) understanding of ability, Fitzgerald (2005) suggested that the teachers seemed to have a normative conception of ability where different forms of sporting skills are ranked against each other. In this process, the teachers conveyed a message, either explicitly or implicitly, whereby they told the pupils how they should behave and what kind of sports they should excel at in order to gain status. On this basis, Fitzgerald advocated an expansion of how ability is understood so that ability can mean something more than a rather narrow conception of (sporting) performance.

The same structures were also found in different studies on ability in relation to gender, social class and ethnicity (Wright and Burrows, 2006). There is a certain norm for what kinds of ability are valued, and pupils who have skills that are different from the norm are more or less devalued. Thus, it appears that certain categories of difference are especially important in relation to whether physical education is experienced as an inclusive setting. It is important to note that these normative and potentially damaging ways of considering ability are not only a result of teachers' actions. Hay and Macdonald (2009) pointed out that it is not sufficient that teachers change the ways by which they consider abilities and confer recognition. Pupils themselves must also change how they recognize and evaluate different skills and abilities. Unless this happens, 'the apparent rigid ability constraints of students may well be perpetuated through their own misperception and ignorance' (p. 17). If this is not learned then it appears that pupils can come to degrade their own as well as others' abilities. In relation to the discussion of critical movement literacy in the previous chapter, this points towards an important aspect of inclusion. Being included or excluded sounds like passive processes, something that just happens to pupils. The aim of critical movement literacy should not only be to understand how and why one experiences being excluded, but it must also involve the active process of including oneself and one's peers.

Drawing on the earlier work of Evans (2004), Evans and Penney (2008) studied two different curricula from the UK, one from the 1950s and the second from 1990s. This study is interesting because it shows how curricula express and shape what is understood as ability. In the first plan (*Movement and Growing* from 1952), the emphasis is on creativity, spontaneity and taking risks. Furthermore, this curriculum accepts that differences in ability are fine and that such differences are normal and not something one should necessarily fix. Instead, the curriculum underlines that each individual pupil has a bodily potential which can be developed and that 'teachers are encouraged to guard against making premature and enduring judgements about a child's physical development and potential' (p. 39). As a contrast to this curriculum, Evans and Penney argue that the plan from the 1990s (the *National Curriculum for Physical Education*) targets and standardizes abilities that should be prioritized in the subject. The plan also emphasizes how pupils should be observed and evaluated. This way of organizing physical education creates a clear contrast to the first curriculum. The most recent curriculum refers to ranking pupils in a hierarchy which is vertically organized. This means that ability is something you have more or less of in relation to an external and supposedly objective standard or norm. In contrast, the earlier curriculum creates a horizontal organization of ability where ability is something you have and that can be developed from where you are, here and now. In the vertical organization, 'difference' is an expression of a lack of something, a condition that should be fixed, whereas difference in the horizontal organization is not assessed in relation to a hierarchy determining good and poor qualities. While the horizontal organization emphasizes competence, the vertical organization emphasizes performance.[1]

Figure 9.1 illustrates the points put forth by Evans and Penney (2008) as well as the other literature just referenced. It suggests that there are two ways of valuating difference in physical education.

I would also suggest that an inclusive teaching practice in physical education is one that leans towards the horizontal recognition of difference. This is an approach where differences are recognized and valued, and where difference is not regarded as lack of something that must be fixed by the teacher's pedagogical intervention. An inclusive physical education pedagogy takes the approach of valuing personal development rather than performance in relation to some external, general standard. As I see it, inclusive physical education has social

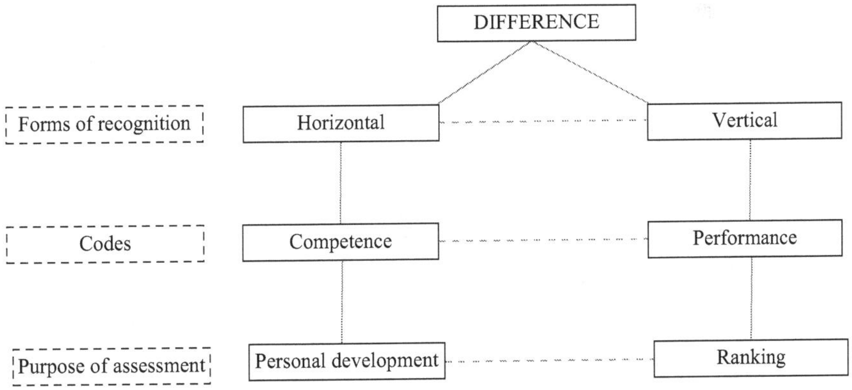

Figure 9.1 This figure proposes a relationship between two forms of recognition of difference and how they are related to codes of performance or competence and purposes of assessment.

justice as both a goal and a process. It aims at full and equal participation as well as equitable distribution of resources and learning opportunities.

Movement literacy, abilities and assessment

The perspective presented so far in this chapter provides a necessary addition to the pedagogical model for physical education that I am outlining in this book. In keeping with the perspectives on difference and ability described so far, I would argue that how learning outcomes are aligned with teaching strategies and choice of subject matter is of crucial importance for inclusive movement literacy. As I pointed out in Chapter 5, teaching strategies should promote pupils' choice and the construction of learning spaces that allow for different ways of solving the same movement task, and that allow pupils to utilize different options for progression at their own tempo. This requires using teaching strategies that are adaptive and that can meet the interests and needs of a wide variety of learners. Thus, avoiding a one-size-fits-all approach to teaching and learning is necessary in order to create inclusive learning spaces. In terms of subject matter, I argued in Chapter 5 that the most important choice is not so much what kinds of activity are taught, but rather how these activities are practised pedagogically. Bearing the figure above in mind, I would argue that the practices chosen for the movement literacy model should emphasize collaboration over competition, and personal development over ranking, i.e. emphasize a pedagogical approach that leans towards the horizontal recognition of differences.

Throughout her work, Margaret Whitehead has stressed the importance of seeing physical literacy in relation to the endowment of the individual. Responding to questions about the norms or standards for physical literacy and charges about motor elitism in physical literacy, Whitehead (2010a, p. 48) has continually stressed that physical literacy 'needs to be understood in the context of the individual's endowment, particularly in respect of their unique embodied dimension'. Whitehead has therefore stated that one must think in terms of a 'physical literacy journey' that every individual is undertaking, rather than seeing it as one uniform goal for all to reach. Endowment is, just like ability, susceptible to being interpreted as an individual characteristic, a static congenital disposition belonging to the individual. However, with reference to Evans' work (Evans, 2004; Evans and Penney, 2008), it is clear that endowment must be understood as the outcome of a socio-cultural process where differences are de/valued.[2] Vickerman and DePauw have discussed physical literacy and inclusion of individuals with disabilities (2010a) and diversity issues more generally (2010b). They stress that although diversity and difference should be considered an enrichment to any learning environment, it is often thought of in terms of being a problem. Further, Vickerman and DePauw clearly state that solutions to exclusionary practices are complex and difficult to specify in advance. Drawing inspiration from the work of Whitehead (2001; 2007; 2010) and Vickerman and DePauw

(2010a; 2010b), I pick up one pedagogical issue that in relation to the discussion of ability is of crucial importance, namely assessment.

Seen from the perspective of the ability literature (e.g. Evans, 2004; Fitzgerald, 2005), assessment and grading are ways of recognizing and valuing difference. One might think that when it comes to assessment, it is impossible to get away from the vertical recognition in Figure 1. Some pupils have better skills than others and it would be unfair if these pupils do not get better grades than the less skilled pupils. As such, assessment is way of ranking pupils in relation to each other. However, while there is no doubt that grading represents a vertical recognition of ability (some will get the highest grade; others will get lower grades),[3] it is also important to note that assessment must not be reduced to grading. Grades are an expression of assessment, but summative assessment, for which a grade can be one form of expression, is not the only form of assessment available.

While physical education teachers have traditionally made use of objective tests of motor skills and fitness, recent work has aimed to promote alternative forms of assessment that have more of an educational focus. Even though traditional tests of motor skills and fitness can be used to promote learning, they are more commonly used for accountability issues and for the purpose of ranking pupils (Lòpez-Pastor et al., 2012). Assessment for learning is one of the alternative approaches to assessment discussed in the physical education literature (Leirhaug and MacPhail, 2015) where the aim is to use assessment in order to promote learning. It is important to note that there are considerable differences in the definitions of the various forms of assessment in education. Formative assessment is sometimes used as a synonym to assessment *for* learning, and summative assessment as a synonym for assessment *of* learning. This, however, is not entirely correct (Bennett, 2011; Wiliam, 2011). Wiliam (2011) points out that

> the distinctions between assessment for learning and assessment of learning on the one hand, and between formative and summative assessment on the other are different in kind. The former distinction relates to the purpose for which assessment is carried out, while the second relates to the function it actually serves.
>
> (p. 10)

Although acknowledging the importance of properly understanding assessment practices in physical education, these distinctions are, for the purpose of the discussion I am taking up here, of lesser importance. I am interested in how assessment for learning can be used as a part of inclusive teaching and learning processes that 'respond to student learning in order to enhance that learning during the learning' (Cowie and Bell, 1999, p. 32, as quoted in Wiliam, 2011, p. 9). That is, I want to emphasize that in movement literacy teaching strategies must help pupils to become aware of and reflect on their own learning process for the purpose of learning better. As I understand it, assessment for learning is process-oriented in the sense that it aims to engage the learners in their own learning process. In addition, with its process focus, it is also inclined to emphasize progression rather than failure. These points suggest that utilizing assessment for learning in movement literacy may put more emphasis on personal development than on performance.

That said, if the teacher wants to focus on personal development, the assessment practice must be in constructive alignment (Biggs, 1996) with the goal or learning objectives that are emphasized in the pedagogical model and the teaching strategies employed to reach those objectives. In terms of using assessment for the purpose of facilitating inclusion in movement literacy, it is therefore necessary to be aware of what the end goal is. That is, in order to support an equitable and inclusive pedagogical practice in movement literacy, assessment must be used in such a way that it also dovetails with the goals of movement literacy.

The ideas put forth here about assessment practice in movement literacy are provisional and theoretical. I therefore suggest that this is an area that requires further research and theoretical development. Thus, I am agreement with Leirhaug and MacPhail (2015), who state that further exploration is needed in order to understand how assessment for learning can support the idea of physical education as a practical and embodied subject. Despite this, I would suggest that one point regarding assessment practices that have an educational focus and which develop pupils' self-reflection about the activities and practices they take part in should be added to the non-negotiable features of movement literacy:

- Emphasize forms of assessment that stimulate the individual in learning to become self-reflective about his/her progress in the learning process, as well as about the learning process itself.

Capabilities: norm for a socially just pedagogical model

The research and thinking done around abilities asks normative questions, such as: What should physical education be like? How is the subject best organized in order to secure equal opportunities for all pupils? In most – if not all – pedagogical situations teachers have choices to make. These choices have an impact on the pedagogical practice and on the inclusiveness of this practice. In the figure presented above, I suggest that in order for physical education in general – and the pedagogical model movement literacy more specifically – to be inclusive for pupils with a variety of differences, pedagogical practice must lean towards the horizontal recognition of difference. This interpretation of the figure can be seen as a norm that can help guide teachers in their choices about content, teaching methods, forms of assessment and so on.

The figure is provisional and open for further specification; one means of connecting the discussions about abilities with a stronger ethical norm can be the capabilities approach, developed by, among others, Amartya Sen and

Martha Nussbaum (2006; 2011). While Sen has been concerned mostly with economics and development, Nussbaum has been interested in philosophical, political and juridical questions. To some extent their works overlap, but in some important ways they also depart from each other. It is fair to say that Sen's work has paved the way for Nussbaum's development of the capabilities approach. Apart from the etymological similarities (cap/ability) and the already mentioned fact that Whitehead (2010b) considers physical literacy as a capability, the capabilities approach can be seen as a framework that is able to ethically guide and assess actions in inclusive physical education[4] (Silva and Howe, 2012).

Nussbaum's capabilities aproach: background

The idea of a capabilities approach was originally developed as an alternative way to make comparisons of nations' development. It sought to replace gross domestic product (GDP) as a measurement of how well nations fare in relation to development and quality of life for their citizens. This new paradigm is sometimes referred to 'the "human development" approach, and also the "capability approach" or "capabilities approach"' (Nussbaum, 2011, p. x). Two of the problems with the GDP approach to development are that it aggregates across lives and across components of lives. This means that even if a lot of people are doing well, the poorest people in a country may be unjustly suffering. Similarly, inhabitants in a country can, on average, be satisfied with their lives, but may be lacking some fundamental entitlements (e.g. having a job and being well fed, but lacking the opportunity to vote). Consequently, the capabilities approach takes the individual as the unit of analysis and asks about what people are actually able to do and to be.

Capabilities are the answers to the question: *What are people able to do and to be?* (Nussbaum 2011). It is important to note that capabilities do not reside in the person, but are created in an interplay between the individual and the environment in which she lives. Nussbaum (2011) therefore makes a distinction between internal capabilities which are fluid and dynamic states of a person, and combined capabilities which are 'the totality of the opportunities she has for choice and action in her specific political, social, and economic situation' (p. 21). In terms of internal capabilities, Nussbaum is in line with the perspective on abilities that has been outlined earlier (Evans, 2004): they are not innate and fixed, but changeable and dynamic. Also, there is no sharp distinction between internal and combined capabilities. In other words, people can have internal capabilities that are not possible for them to realize because of restrictions imposed by the environment.

Another important concept is functioning, which is the active realization of capabilities. To bring out the distinction between functioning and capability, Nussbaum gives an example of two persons where one is starving and the other is fasting. Their functioning is the same in terms of nutrition, but they have different capabilities because the person fasting has a choice that the person starving does not have. In other words, capabilities are the opportunities or freedoms to choose functioning. This is an important point because Nussbaum argues that it is capabilities rather than functioning which is the appropriate political goal.[5] To take an example from physical education: If the curriculum states that pupils shall understand that physical activity is important for good health (as is the case in the Norwegian curriculum), Nussbaum would argue that it is the capability rather than the functioning to engage in physical activity that should be promoted. 'There is a huge moral difference between a policy that promotes health and one that promotes health capabilities – the latter, not the former, honors the person's lifestyle choices' (Nussbaum, 2011, p. 26). In other words, quality physical education should expand pupils' capabilities for choosing whether and how to engage in physical activity, but this requires developing both the functioning and the capacity to make choices.

The list of capabilities

One of the issues where Nussbaum and Sen disagree is whether one should specify the basic capabilities. Nussbaum has developed a list of ten basic capabilities that are 'central to life with dignity. These ten capabilities are supposed to be general goals that can be further specified by the society in question, as it works on the account of fundamental entitlements it wishes to endorse' (Nussbaum, 2003, p. 40). All ten capabilities, Nussbaum argues, are part of a minimal account of social justice and important for each and every citizen:

> A society that does not guarantee these to all its citizens, at some appropriate threshold level, falls short of being a fully just society … a society that neglects one of [the capabilities] to promote others has shortchanged its citizens, and there is a failure of justice in the shortchanging.
>
> (ibid.)

Nussbaum's list of fundamental capabilities includes the following:

1. *Life.* Being able to live to the end of a human life of normal length; not dying prematurely, or before one's life is so reduced as to be not worth living.
2. *Bodily health.* Being able to have good health, including reproductive health; to be adequately nourished; to have adequate shelter.
3. *Bodily integrity.* Being able to move freely from place to place; to be secure against violent assault, including sexual assault and domestic violence; having opportunities for sexual satisfaction and for choice in matters of reproduction.
4. *Senses, imagination, and thought.* Being able to use the senses, to imagine, think, and reason – and to do these things in a 'truly human' way, a way

informed and cultivated by an adequate education, including, but by no means limited to, literacy and basic mathematical and scientific training. Being able to use imagination and thought in connection with experiencing and producing works and events of one's own choice, religious, literary, musical, and so forth. Being able to use one's mind in ways protected by guarantees of freedom of expression with respect to both political and artistic speech, and freedom of religious exercise. Being able to have pleasurable experiences and to avoid non-beneficial pain.

5 *Emotions.* Being able to have attachments to things and people outside ourselves; to love those who love and care for us, to grieve at their absence; in general, to love, to grieve, to experience longing, gratitude, and justified anger. Not having one's emotional development blighted by fear and anxiety. (Supporting this capability means supporting forms of human association that can be shown to be crucial in their development.)

6 *Practical reason.* Being able to form a conception of the good and to engage in critical reflection about the planning of one's life. (This entails protection for the liberty of conscience and religious observance.)

7 *Affiliation.*

  a Being able to live with and toward others, to recognize and show concern for other human beings, to engage in various forms of social interaction; to be able to imagine the situation of another. (Protecting this capability means protecting institutions that constitute and nourish such forms of affiliation, and also protecting the freedom of assembly and political speech.)

  b Having the social bases of self-respect and non-humiliation; being able to be treated as a dignified being whose worth is equal to that of others. This entails provisions of nondiscrimination on the basis of race, sex, sexual orientation, ethnicity, caste, religion, national origin.

8 *Other species.* Being able to live with concern for and in relation to animals, plants, and the world of nature.

9 *Play.* Being able to laugh, to play, to enjoy recreational activities.

10 *Control over one's environment.*

  a *Political.* Being able to participate effectively in political choices that govern one's life; having the right of political participation, protection of free speech and association.

  b *Material.* Being able to hold property (both land and movable goods), and having property rights on an equal basis with others; having the right to seek employment on an equal basis with others; having the freedom from unwarranted search and seizure. In work, being able to work as a human being, exercising practical reason, and entering into meaningful relationships of mutual recognition with other workers.

(Nussbaum, 2006, pp. 76–78)

As any philosophical position, the list is open for criticism and rebuttal. Therefore, Nussbaum does not make a final proposal, but clearly states that the list is open to future adjustments. Neither is the list made up from a purely theoretical vantage point, but is based on Nussbaum's cross-cultural discussions with activists and scholars working with human development.[6] Thus, the list is made to be sensitive to cultural differences. Nussbaum (2006) acknowledges that the list is 'specified in a somewhat abstract and general way' (p. 78), which is done to allow for culturally relevant specification 'by citizens and their legislatures and courts' (p. 79). As mentioned, the fundamental entitlements on the list are capabilities rather than functioning. This is done to ensure pluralism and some measure of freedom of choice. Having the capability to vote is necessary, but in Nussbaum's view it should be a capability because it must be up to the individual to choose whether to vote or not. Equally, the list should be acceptable from different religious viewpoints, and therefore it 'seeks an agreement for practical political purposes and deliberately avoids commitment to deep divisive issues about God, the soul, the limits of human knowledge and so on, that divide people along the lines of doctrine' (Nussbaum, 2011, p. 109). This is done to ensure equal respect for citizens regardless of religion or non-religion.

Capabilities and inclusive physical education

Nussbaum's discussions about capabilities are framed within the issue of social justice. The ten capabilities specify what a minimally just society must ensure for its citizens. Social justice, for Nussbaum (2003, p. 47) is 'a profoundly normative concept, and its role is typically critical: we work out an account of what is just, and we then use it to find reality deficient in various ways'. But even if social justice should be an issue for both teachers and researchers of physical education, one might wonder about the relevance of physical education in the realization of the ten capabilities. Many of the issues involved in the list are beyond what physical education can reasonably claim to contribute to. Indeed, one can be highly sceptical of the sometimes far-fetched benefits that are touted by physical education advocates when it comes to the values and benefits of the subject:

> Throughout history there has been a tendency to make extravagant claims for the benefits and outcomes of PESS [Physical Education and School Sports]. A recent UN resolution, 58/5 (United Nations 2003), for example, proclaimed 2005 the International Year for Sport and Physical Education 'as a means to promote education, health, development and peace'. Yet if peace does, or does not, break out across the world as a result of the 2005 efforts, it seems unlikely that PESS will be deemed responsible.
>
> (Bailey et al., 2009, p. 17)

There is, however, one item on Nussbaum's list that immediately looks like an area where physical education can contribute, namely play. This is not the place to go into an analysis of play and its meaning and place in physical education (see Stolz, 2014 for further discussion). Nevertheless, since play is an integral component of physical education, it can be argued that physical education can have a role in the expansion of human flourishing and well-being. With regard to play, Nussbaum (2011) argues that play 'is not merely instrumental but partly constitutive of a worthwhile human life' (p. 36). Even though Nussbaum puts considerable emphasis on the joyous aspect of play, Bloodworth et al. (2012) hold that it is not those aspects of the capability which are most important. Rather, they emphasize that when play is seen as a capability, this should 'encouraging the provision of facilities for physical activities as well as other games for those of a range of ages' (p. 508). What both Nussbaum (2006; 2011) and Bloodworth et al. (2012) point out is that the play capability should not be reduced to an activity pursued merely because of the joyous experiences it might provide. That would be a too shallow and hedonistic reason for pursuing play both within and beyond physical education (Bloodworth et al., 2012). This is not to say that enjoyment is not a good thing, but the more crucial point with play is that it must be pursued in such a way that it helps expand other capabilities as well, such as, for instance, the capacities for imagination and the senses (item 4) or affiliation with others (item 7). More importantly, a socially just physical education should provide opportunities for play for all pupils. The strength of the capabilities approach is to say that if physical education aims to achieve its potential contribution to human flourishing and well-being, the play capability must be developed among all pupils.

Play thus seems to be one of the capabilities where physical education really can have a crucial role in the expansion of a specific capability. However, rather than arguing that physical education can be instrumental in the realization of the list of capabilities, it is equally important to understand how the capabilities approach can be applied for the purpose of discussing inclusive physical education; that is, how the capabilities approach can provide standards or norms for a socially just provision of physical education. I will, therefore, discuss three ways that the capabilities approach can be of guidance for physical education.

First, Bloodworth et al. (2012) consider the capability of senses, imagination and thought and state that

> not all forms of physical activity will instantiate the demands of this capability. While skipping and step-aerobics may contribute to well-being on biomedical and subjectivist accounts they cannot develop this capability owing to the thinness of their cognitive repertoire. ... Physical activities certainly represent one way in which the whole person can be understood as expressing oneself, as in dance, tai chi or yoga, for example.
>
> (p. 506)

As the authors point out, this is not to say that everything that goes on in physical education must fulfil this value and contribute to the expansion of this particular capability.[7] However, one must say that this capability asks questions about what kinds of activities and practices pupils are introduced to in physical education. Are pupils, as Nussbaum's (2006) description of this capability states, educated to become 'able to use imagination and thought in connection with experiencing and producing works and events of one's own choice' (p. 76)? Equally importantly, however, is it that when learning outcomes or educational objectives in physical education aim (implicitly or explicitly) to stimulate senses, imagination and thought, the capabilities approach requires that all pupils have equal opportunity to reach this goal. Failure to do so would be an issue of injustice.

Second, let us consider the bodily integrity capability. The body plays an important part in physical education, for instance in the sense that I have developed here in this book: the knowledge objects are embodied by the knowing subjects. This means that in the process of learning practical knowledge, the pupils will also come to learn something about themselves as embodied beings. A case to be considered in relation to bodily integrity and inclusion is that of pupils who are labelled overweight or obese. On the one hand, physical education is considered as a useful intervention in tackling the so-called obesity epidemic.[8]Gard (2004), in his critique of the idea of the obesity epidemic, states that 'physical educators have responded to the recent avalanche of popular and academic interest in obesity by claiming special expertise in the area of weight control' (p. 69). On the other hand, Gard also warns against the harmful consequences that the focus on obesity and weight loss can have for those pupils who are the targets in the war on fat. Summarizing the latter viewpoints, Cale and Harris (2013) state that the policies that uncritically accept physical education's contribution to the public health agenda 'increasingly bear features of a "performative" culture celebrating comparison, measurement, assessment and accountability' (p. 440). In other words, Cale and Harris (2013) imply that the public health concern of reducing obesity through physical education leads to what I have earlier in this chapter called a vertical recognition of difference. In line with this perspective, other researchers have pointed out that physical education is a place where pupils who are labelled obese are met with prejudices and stereotyping that stigmatize them as lazy, weak-willed and incompetent (Rugseth, 2011; Sykes, 2011). Thus, there are substantial grounds for asking whether the practice of physical education violates the bodily integrity of those pupils.

Drawing on the capabilities approach, one can say that a minimal requirement for physical education is that pupils should not be in a worse situation when it comes to their bodily integrity because of how the subject is taught:

> We surely can't expect children to want to change into kit, reveal their bodies and take their place in physical activity or sport in public if they have been routinely told that their bodies are not the right size, shape or

> weight. We should no more 'exclude' or pathologise a child in PE for being 'the wrong' shape or weight than for being the 'wrong' 'ability', ethnicity, gender or class.
>
> (Evans, 2014, p. 329)

A positive reformulation of this point would be that in terms of inclusive physical education, teachers must consider their primary task to be that of adapting their teaching so that pupils with all sorts of bodies can take part in the subject without the risk of being told that their bodies are deviant (Cale and Harris, 2011). While Cale and Harris (2011, pp. 446–448) propose lists of both general and activity-related recommendations for physical education, Gard (2004) also draws attention to the need for teachers to think critically about 'the kinds of relationships being fostered between children, their bodies and physical activity' (p. 76).

The third point I want to make in relation to the capabilities approach concerns the exclusion of pupils with disabilities from physical education. This is related to the discussion of bodily integrity in two ways. First, research has documented experiences of exclusion among pupils with disabilities and shown that exclusion can be seen as a form of violation of bodily integrity leading to humiliation and social isolation (Fitzpatrick and Watkinson, 2003; Goodwin and Watkinson, 2000). Second, discussing exclusion and inclusion of pupils with disabilities in relation to what has already been said about pupils who are labelled overweight or obese demonstrates that much can be gained from thinking about individual differences rather than in terms of groups.

Nussbaum (2006) is particularly interested in disability because disability, together with trans-national justice and animal rights, is an unresolved problem for social justice. Her aim in *Frontiers of Justice* is to show that the capabilities approach offers superior insights on these matters as compared to social contract theories of, for instance, John Rawls. The details of and background for Nussbaum's discussion of Rawls and the social contract theory tradition need not worry us here. Of more relevance is that the capabilities approach reminds us that any argument along the lines of 'inclusion of pupils with disabilities can restrict the learning opportunities of the other pupils' is inappropriate in terms of social justice. My own experience as an educator of future physical education teachers is that this sort of argument comes up every year in my course. As such it seems to be a strongly held prejudice that the interests of pupils with disabilities are at odds with the interests of the other pupils. Apart from my own experiences, Block and Obrusnikova also report that 'one argument against inclusion is that there is a fear that students with disabilities will somehow diminish from or significantly alter the program for children without disabilities' (Block and Obrusnikova, 2007, p. 109). The capabilities approach helps challenge such viewpoints in two ways. First, it insists that the basic entitlements are entitlements for each and every child. Even if it were true that inclusion of pupils with disabilities is to the detriment of students without disabilities, the problem would then be the educational practice and not inclusion per se. Second, Nussbaum challenges the idea inherent in the viewpoint that there are pupils with disabilities on the one side, and then there are the rest on the other. Nussbaum (2006, pp. 190–191) talks about 'the continuity between so-called normal people and people with impairments. … Instead of segmenting off people with impairments, as if they belonged to a different (and lower) kind, we insist on their equal entitlement to the wherewithal of good lives'. Furthermore:

> It would be progress if we could acknowledge that there really is no such thing as 'the normal child': instead, there are *children*, with varying capabilities and varying impediments, all of whom need individualized attention as their capabilities are developed.
>
> (p. 210)

The danger of seeing pupils with disabilities as a homogeneous group which has needs and interests that are 'so special' that they are different from the rest not only robs these children of their individuality, it also serves to mask the considerable differences that exist among the so-called normal populations.[9] As Silva and Howe point out, the capabilities approach 'demands individual differentiation as the basis for adaptation and denies categorical approaches based for instance on types of impairment' (Silva and Howe, 2012, p. 38).

Difference is an ontological condition for teaching physical education. Indeed, it might be the case that thinking in terms of inclusion is not a harm but a benefit for most – if not all – pupils, since it highlights their individuality. This means that leaning more towards the horizontal recognition of difference as suggested in Figure 1 would be supported by the capabilities approach and also supportive of inclusion. Moving towards a more inclusive physical education may involve curtailing the benefits of some of those pupils who are thriving in an environment where it is the horizontal recognition of difference that is prominent. But, according to the capabilities approach, the freedom of some may legitimately be limited if that is what is needed to support those that are under-privileged.[10]

The purpose of my presentation of the capabilities approach has been to elaborate on norms that can help guide inclusive physical education. My reasoning has been that because teachers face situations of pedagogical choice there is a need for some kind of standard that can tell whether alternative A, B, or C is the most appropriate. The capabilities approach gives some guidance to such choice situations: In comparing the alternatives, which alternative is best suited to be adaptive and inclusive for the widest variety of individual differences? The capabilities approach and the list of the ten capabilities do not in and of themselves provide ready-made answers to pedagogical choice, but as I have tried to illustrate here, they provide teachers with resources to think with, when they think about inclusive physical education.

Concluding comments on inclusion

The aim of this and the previous chapter has been to discuss inclusion as an ethical dimension of physical education from a phenomenological perspective. Contrary to what seems to be the taken for granted view in the physical education literature, I have shown that phenomenology indeed can deal with issues of individual differences and power, and how this may be done. With the help of Sara Ahmed's (2006) queer phenomenology, I suggested that in the context of physical education straightening devices are educational processes based on normative ideas about how movement practices should be performed. These ideas are enacted in practice through teaching and the use of pedagogical objects, and are potential producers of exclusion and queer moments. Drawing on the capabilities approach as developed by Nussbaum (2006; 2011), and the discussions of abilities instantiated by Evans (2004), I have outlined and discussed norms for physical education that can be used to create a more equitable and just pedagogical practice. The norms call upon the teacher to make choices that expand the capabilities of all pupils.

Inclusion, as I have discussed it here, has pertained to physical education. As Evans (2014) reminds us, it is important to highlight the *education* part of physical education. 'Education is the key to inclusion; indeed, it seems odd to have to be reminded of this, but inclusion without education is like having a car but no fuel; knowing the desired destination but having no means of getting there' (p. 323). That is, mere integration, or inclusion without learning, democracy, participation or fellowship (Haug, 2010), is close to meaningless. Inclusion must mean that pupils learn.

One important aspect of the capabilities approach can further illustrate the importance of learning and education for inclusion in physical education. The individual's experience is important for the way the capabilities are described by Nussbaum (note the use of words like 'to experience', 'to enjoy' or 'to use the senses'). However, Nussbaum (2011) also notes that 'the capabilities approach is not based upon subjective preferences' (p. 80). What this means is that people, and in particular those who live under oppressive circumstances, may exhibit 'adaptive preferences'. That is, they might be adjusting preferences to what they think they can do or to what they believe society tells them to do. This is exemplified in Young's (1998) 'Throwing Like a Girl', where she claimed that girls either shun certain forms of physical activity because they think it is not appropriate for them, or they acquire certain bodily habits that inhibit them in movement contexts. In a different, but very much related way, Bloodworth et al. (2012) criticize hedonistic and subjectivist accounts of well-being, where 'the efficacy of judgments of well-being properly rests under the dominion of the individual' (p. 499). Objectivist theories, like the capability approach, would in contrast 'hold that certain values or goods are central to an agent's well-being regardless of his or her attitude toward them' (ibid.). This means that there might be situations in which an individual experiences enjoyment, well-being or being included when in fact there are reasons to distrust this experience. One might even suggest that phenomenology's interest in subjective experience is at odds with this point in the capabilities approach.

To this (hypothetical) objection to the contribution from phenomenology, I would say that there are two issues discussed in this book that make phenomenology relevant to the application of the capabilities approach to inclusive physical education. The first is phenomenological pedagogy's insistence on the importance of the teacher's sensitivity to the pupils' lived experience. This sensitivity also involves understanding if and when pupils' experiences are the results of adaptive preferences, and consequently helping pupils understand that their experiences are generated from normative and possibly unjust conditions. Second, and relatedly, Shusterman's (2008; 2012) notion of feeling better is helpful. The point is not that pupils should feel better in the hedonistic sense, but rather that they are enabled to experience more accurately their moving bodies. This can involve experiencing one's own adaptive preferences, bringing them to reflective awareness and working to change them. Weiss (2015) discusses Iris Young's 'Throwing Like a Girl' and notes that to change one's restricted movement habits has

> the strange consequence that seeking to move more 'naturally' by not restricting one's movements to comply with accepted feminine norms, usually occurs through a most 'unnatural' process, namely through conscious reflection upon habitual gendered patterns of motor behavior that need to be unlearned in order to be replaced with more fluid and expansive styles of comportment that maximize one's bodily capabilities.
>
> (p. 83)

In other words, what Weiss is suggesting here is something akin to the Deweyan idea of reflective thinking as a process that both begins and ends in practical doing. Feeling better, then, somewhat paradoxically involves experiencing more accurately the results of oppressive conditions.

In conclusion, straightening devices can also, I suggest, be producers of inclusion. While queer moments involve a sense of feeling out of place, it is also the case that 'bodies that experience being out of place might need to be orientated, to find a place where they feel comfortable and safe in the world' (Ahmed, 2006, p. 158). This is central to the notion of finding one's own way of moving: In order for *a* specific way of moving to become *my* way of moving, then repetition and becoming straightened to that specific norm of moving is necessary.

Notes

1 This distinction between competence and performance is something that Evans developed together with Brian Davies (Evans and Davies, 2004), drawing on the work of Bernstein. It expresses how 'codes' of competence and performance are enacted in curricula and pedagogical practice: 'Each has a social logic, that is to say, an implicit model of communication, interaction and the subject' (p. 209).

2 Disability is one such example. It is only in a now outdated medical model that disability is thought of as something residing solely in the individual. With the critique of the social model of disability and the development of a new medical model, disability is seen as an interplay between individual differences and the environment (e.g. Shakespeare, 2006).

3 It must also be noted that it is not necessarily the skills or the sport techniques that have to be assessed. One could imagine a physical education subject that is wholly theoretical and where it is the theoretical knowledge about sports and physical activity that were to be assessed. This, however, need not worry us here.

4 Silva and Howe (2012) discuss the capabilities approach of Amartya Sen and Martha Nussbaum in relation to the professional practice of adapted physical activity (APA). Adapted and inclusive physical education is one part of the domain of APA.

5 There are some exceptions to this, for instance children, according to Nussbaum (2006), should not have the opportunity to choose whether to get an education or not (i.e. she argues for functioning rather than capability in that case): 'Compulsory functioning is justified both by the child's cognitive immaturity and by the importance of such functioning in enabling adult capabilities' (p. 172). Nussbaum's starting point is that of political liberalism, and other starting points would yield different views on whether it is functioning or capability that should be promoted.

6 'Working with many activists over the years, and noticing what their experienced eyes notice as significant in the lives of women in their own societies, I have tried to educate my judgment accordingly, and continue to do so' (Nussbaum, 2011, p. 15).

7 If physical education is also about understanding sport, then it could be argued that learning about and experiencing the drudgery and repetitiveness of training is important (Bloodworth et al., 2012).

8 This assertion rests on the idea that there is a growing number of children (and adults) world-wide who are obese and that this leads to serious health problems and massive costs for societies. In such a situation, increased levels of physical activity are considered necessary. Further, the idea is that since the school is an arena where interventions to increase levels of physical activity can reach all children, physical education can serve as a battle ground in fighting obesity. This perspective has been challenged by questioning whether there is anything like an obesity epidemic, as well as questioning whether physical education should or even can be a contribution to a public health agenda (Gard, 2004).

9 Nussbaum (2006) talks about normal in scarecrows and sees 'normals' as 'people with average flaws and limitations. … Although a theoretical analysis may attempt to distinguish phases of a "normal" life from lifelong impairment, the distinction in real life is hard to draw, and is becoming harder all the time' (p. 101).

10 Discussing gender justice, Nussbaum (2011) argues that the many traditional male privileges must be curtailed, because 'no society that pursues equality or even an ample social minimum can avoid curtailing freedom in very many ways and what it ought to say is: those freedoms are not good, they are not part of a core group of entitlements required by the notion of social justice, and in many ways, indeed, they subvert those core entitlements' (p. 73).

References

Ahmed, S. (2006). *Queer phenomenology: Orientations, objects, others.* London: Duke University Press.

Bailey, R., Armour, K., Kirk, D., Jess, M. and Pickup, I. (2009). The educational benefits claimed for physical education and school sport: an academic review. *Research Papers in Education*, 24(1), 1–27.

Bennett, R. E. (2011). Formative assessment: a critical review. *Assessment in Education: Principles, Policy and Practice*, 18(1), 5–25.

Biggs, J. (1996). Enhancing teaching through constructive alignment. *Higher Education*, 32(3), 347–364.

Bjorbækmo, W. S. and Engelsrud, G. (2011). 'My own way of moving': movement improvisation in children's rehabilitation. *Phenomenology and Practice*, 5, 27–47.

Block, M. E. and Obrusnikova, I. (2007). Inclusion in physical education: a review of the literature from 1995–2005. *Adapted Physical Activity Quarterly*, 24(2), 103–124.

Bloodworth, A., McNamee, M. and Bailey, R. (2012). Sport, physical activity and well-being: an objectivist account. *Sport, Education and Society*, 17(4), 497–514.

Cale, L. and Harris, J. (2013). Every child (of every size) matters in physical education! Physical education's role in childhood obesity. *Sport, Education and Society*, 18(4), 433–452.

Carr, D. (1981). Knowledge in practice. *American Philosophical Quarterly*, 18(1), 53–61.

Evans, J. (2004). Making a difference? Education and 'ability' in physical education. *European Physical Education Review*, 10(1), 95–108.

Evans, J. (2014). Equity and inclusion in physical education PLC. *European Physical Education Review*, 20(3), 319–334.

Evans, J. and Davies, B. (2004). Endnote: the embodiment of consciousness: Bernstein, health and schooling. In J. Evans, B. Davies and J. Wright (eds), *Body knowledge and control: Studies in the sociology of physical education and health* (pp. 207–217). London: Routledge. Evans, J. and Penney, D. (2008). Levels on the playing field: the social construction of physical ability in the physical education curriculum. *Physical Education and Sport Pedagogy*, 13(1), 31–47.

Fitzgerald, H. (2005). Still feeling like a spare piece of luggage? Embodied experiences of (dis)ability in physical education and school sport. *Physical Education and Sport Pedagogy*, 10(1), 41–59.

Fitzpatrick, D. and Watkinson, E. (2003). The lived experience of physical awkwardness: adults' retrospective views. *Adapted Physical Activity Quarterly*, 20, 279–297.

Gard, M. (2004). An elephant in the room and a bridge too far, or physical activity and the 'obesity epidemic'. In J. Evans, B. Davies and J. Wright (eds), *Body knowledge and control: Studies in the sociology of physical education and health* (pp. 68–82). London: Routledge.

Goodwin, D. L. and Watkinson, E. J. (2000). Inclusive physical education from the perspective of students with physical disabilities. *Adapted Physical Activity Quarterly*, 17, 144–160.

Haug, P. (2010). Approaches to empirical research on inclusive education. *Scandinavian Journal of Disability Research*, 12(3), 199–209.

Hay, P. J. and Macdonald, D. (2009). Evidence for the social construction of ability in physical education. *Sport, Education and Society*, 15(1), 1–18.

Lave, J. (1996). Teaching, as learning, in practice. *Mind, Culture and Activitity*, 3(3), 149–164.

Leirhaug, P. E. and MacPhail, A. (2015). 'It's the other assessment that is the key': three Norwegian physical education teachers' engagement (or not) with assessment for learning. *Sport, Education and Society*, 21(1), 1–17.

Lòpez-Pastor, V. M., Kirk, D., Lorente-Catalàin, E., MacPhail, A. and Macdonald, D. (2012). Alternative assessment in physical education: a review of international literature. *Sport, Education and Society*, 18(1), 57–76.

Nussbaum, M. (2003). Capabilities as fundamental entitlements: Sen and social justice. *Feminist Economics*, 9(2–3), 33–59.

Nussbaum, M. C. (2006). *Frontiers of justice: Disability, nationality, species membership.* London: The Belknap Press of Harvard University Press.

Nussbaum, M. C. (2011). *Creating capabilities: The human development approach.* London: The Belknap Press of Harvard University Press.

Penney, D. (2002). Equality, equity and inclusion in physical education and school sport. In A. Laker (ed.), *The sociology of sport and physical education* (pp. 110–128). London: RouledgeFalmer.

Rugseth, G. (2011). *Overvekt som livserfaring: Et empirisk-teoretisk kunnskapsbidrag.* [*Obesity as life experience: An empirical-theoretical knowledge contribution*]. Oslo, Norway: University of Oslo.

Shakespeare, T. (2006). *Disability rights and wrongs.* London: Routledge.

Shusterman, R. (2008). *Body consciousness: A philosophy of mindfulness and somaesthetics.* New York: Cambridge University Press.

Shusterman, R. (2012). *Thinking through the body: Essays in somaesthetics.* Cambridge: Cambridge University Press.

Silva, C. F. and Howe, P. D. (2012). Difference, adapted physical activity and human development: potential contribution of capabilities approach. *Adapted Physical Activity Quarterly*, 29(1), 25–43.

Stolz, S. (2014). *The philosophy of physical education: A new perspective.* London: Routledge.

Sykes, H. (2011). *Queer bodies: Sexualities, genders and fatness in physical education.* New York: Peter Lang.

Vickerman, P. and DePauw, K. P. (2010a). Physical literacy and individuals with a disability. In M. Whitehead (ed.), *Physical literacy: Throughout the lifecourse* (pp. 130–141). London: Routledge.

Vickerman, P. and DePauw, K. P. (2010b). Physical literacy and issues of diversity. In M. Whitehead (ed.), *Physical literacy: Throughout the lifecourse* (pp. 142–164). London: Routledge.

Weiss, G. (2015). The normal, the natural and the normative: a Merleau-Pontian legacy to feminist theory, critical race theory and disability studies. *Continental Philosophy Review*, 48(1), 77–93.

Whitehead, M. (2001). The concept of physical literacy. *European Journal of Physical Education*, 6(2), 127–138.

Whitehead, M. (2007). Physical literacy: philosophical considerations in relation to developing a sense of self, universality and propositional knowledge. *Sports, Ethics and Philosophy*, 1(3), 281–298.

Whitehead, M. (2010). The concept of physical literacy. In M. Whitehead (ed.), *Physical literacy: Throughout the lifecourse* (pp. 10–20). London: Routledge.

Whitehead, M. (2010a). Physical literacy, physical competence and interaction with the environment. In M. Whitehead (ed.), *Physical literacy: Throughout the lifecourse* (pp. 44–55). London: Routledge.

Whitehead, M. (2010b). The concept of physical literacy. In M. Whitehead (ed.), *Physical literacy: Throughout the lifecourse* (pp. 10–20). London: Routledge.

Wiliam, D. (2011). What is assessment for learning? *Studies in Educational Evaluation*, 37(1), 3–14.

Wright, J. and Burrows, L. (2006). Re-conceiving ability in physical education: a social analysis. *Sport, Education and Society*, 11(3), 275–291.

Young, I. (1998). Throwing like a girl. In D. Welton (ed.), *Body and flesh: A philosophical reader* (pp. 259–273). Oxford: Blackwell.

10 Concluding comments

With this book, I have tried to develop the contribution of phenomenology to physical education. My intention has been to move beyond the mere celebration of the potential of phenomenology. Therefore, I have tried to show how a phenomenological perspective can elucidate the embodied learning of practical knowledge in physical education. More specifically, I have drawn on a conception of practical knowledge where the objects of practical knowledge are understood as actions, activities and practices that the knowing subject purposively engages in (Carr, 1981). Building on Svenaeus' (2009) supposition that phenomenology can be a theory for practical knowledge, I have investigated the work of Maurice Merleau-Ponty (2002; 1968; 1963), all the way from his first thesis, *Structure of Behavior*, via *Phenomenology of Perception* to his post-humously published *The Visible and the Invisible*. The non-dualistic ontology developed by Merleau-Ponty, his elaborations of the acquisition of motor habits and his critique of behaviouristic models of learning all show how the knowing subject as an embodied being is interconnected with the knowledge object. Far from being trivial, the idea that the knowledge objects are embodied has important consequences for pedagogy in physical education. In particular, it has great consequences when it is seen in conjunction with the requirements of inclusion: teaching and learning in physical education must be able to deal with bodily differences in ethically sensitive and pedagogically sound ways.

A pedagogical model founded on phenomenology

I have been inspired by Kirk's (2013; 2010) proposal for a models-based physical education:

> physical education is such a large, rich and complex field of practice that it can legitimately aspire to achieve a wide range of educational outcomes for school-age children and youth. In order to do this, however, it needs to take particular and different forms in contrast to its current and traditional 'one-size-fits-all', sport technique-based, multi-activity form.
>
> (Kirk, 2013, p. 974)

In this book I have begun to develop the model of *movement literacy*,[1] drawing inspiration from the work of Margaret Whitehead (2007; 2001; 2010). Movement literacy is based in phenomenology and is supported by pragmatist philosophy. I have attempted to see where phenomenology will take pedagogy in physical education if we stay oriented to its philosophy. This has meant that when Whitehead or others (Haydn-Davies, 2010) who have been working with physical literacy have drawn on other resources, such as psychological theories of learning, I have been interested in seeing where phenomenology can take us if we instead stay committed to that perspective.

A pedagogical model must specify its learning outcomes, how these outcomes are constructively aligned with teaching strategies and subject matter, and its non-negotiable features (Haerens et al., 2011). Taking as a starting point the work of Whitehead (2001), the learning outcomes of movement literacy are described as being capable of moving with poise and being perceptive in reading and writing the movement environment. In terms of subject matter, I have been concerned with showing that it is not so much a matter of specific activities, but more how the activities are practised. The learning outcomes and the subject matter come into alignment through a phenomenological pedagogy that starts from – and works with – the movement experiences of the pupils. Finally, I have suggested the following non-negotiable features:

1 Emphasize the qualitatively felt experience of moving, rather than a linear understanding of skill. Avoid normative ideals of performance where pupils are compared with each other or with norms.
2 Emphasize a teaching style that encourages exploration of each pupil's individual potential. Avoid demonstrations intended to convey a 'correct' way of moving that pupils should imitate.
3 Emphasize collaboration between pupils, as opposed to competition.
4 Emphasize forms of assessment that stimulate the individual learner to become self-reflective about his/her progress in the learning process, as well as about the learning process itself.

The model I have suggested is meant to be criticized and improved. Movement literacy is therefore now open for debate!

One aspect of such a debate would pertain to the very idea of models-based practice. Stolz (2014, pp. 151–152) argues that

> What I find to be particularly disconcerting about the discourse of models-based teaching is the inference that teaching in physical education involves the teaching of discrete bodies of knowledge in a rigidly non-negotiable specific way which can be followed like a 'blueprint' (see, for example, Metzler, 2011). As a result, the notion of 'models' creates unnecessary artificial boundaries that are logically problematic.

On the basis of this, Stolz would not agree with my attempt at outlining a pedagogical model for physical education based on a theoretical foundation that we both clearly value. Stolz is rather suggesting that physical education in general should be based on his conception of embodied learning.

One issue in this critique where I agree with Stolz is that embodied learning and phenomenological pedagogy have implications beyond the model I have suggested. Take two of the non-negotiable features of movement literacy as examples: I have argued that in movement literacy, one should avoid competition and avoid the normative ideals of skills traditionally found in motor skill acquisition or in sport skills. This, however, is not to say that the phenomenological perspective is irrelevant when pupils and teachers work with competition or traditional motor skill acquisition in physical education. First-person, subjective experiences are generated in both instances and it would, according to the educational philosophy of Dewey (1938), be valuable for pupils to reflect on these experiences. Therefore, the phenomenological perspective and pedagogy developed in this book is relevant to all aspects of physical education.

I am not entirely convinced about Stolz's (2014) argument that models-based PE leads to teaching of discrete bodies of knowledge. The strength of models-based practice is that it brings out specific pedagogical approaches that are more varied, nuanced and specific than the traditional one-size-fits-all way of teaching. What I find attractive about models-based practice is that in a subject characterized by a multi-activity approach with little progression and where the learning outcomes are not clear, the models-based approach provides specificity rather than being concerned with rigidly discrete bodies of knowledge. I also think it is clear from Kirk's (2013; 2010) work that even though a model must have some non-negotiable features, it should not be a rigid blueprint. A good pedagogical model must be described in a sufficiently loose way so that it can be adapted to local and national traditions and curricula.[2]

Another strength of models-based physical education is that it gives teachers tools to think with: when the focus is squarely on the activities (or even worse on the actions that constitute the techniques of specific activities), the highly different ways that activities can be practiced is ignored: running would be practiced in different ways and for different purposes in various pedagogical models. For example, in sport education running would follow the sporting logic of faster or longer, in health-based physical education running could be a means towards the end of leading a physically active and health life, and in movement literacy running would be an individual experience where the aim is for each pupil to find their own way of running. This is not to divide running 'into discrete bodies of knowledge', but to highlight the various qualities of running and the different practices of running.

The future of phenomenology and movement literacy

Finally, I would like to point out some areas where the work I have done in this book can be developed further. First, there might be a case of unclear use of terminology when it comes to the notions 'habit', 'skill' and 'experience'. Drawing on Merleau-Ponty, I have used habit to describe the practical knowledge involved in physical education. The same goes for the notion 'poise' (i.e. making the world of movement habit-able). However, some might object by saying that the knowledge objects in physical education are not habits, they are skills or techniques.[3] The truth of this assertion depends on the meaning we give to habit in relation to skill. As discussed in Chapter 3, in the phenomenological sense both habit and skill denote a flexible, situational, and adjustable ability to act, which also entails the possibility for creativity. As Ilundáin-Agurruza (2014) points out, habits are both limitations in the sense that they put restrictions on what we can do, but at the same time they are also positives in that they are the door to possibilities. In habits, 'we get intentional action rather than mere reflex acts, in today's parlance' (p. 3). For Dewey (1938, p. 35),

> the basic characteristic of habit is that every experience enacted and undergone modifies the one who acts and undergoes, while this modification affects, whether we wish it or not, the quality of subsequent experiences. For it is a somewhat different person who enters into them.

This means that habit is not a matter of reflex. Moreover, it is connected to experience and it has transformative potentials. I can say, for example, that I am in the habit of running, which means that I run regularly, but running is itself not a habit. It is a form of movement. However, I can say that I have a habitual way of running, which means that something about my way of running makes it distinctive and recognizable as my own way of running. It is this qualitative experience that is the aim of poise. Still, there is a need for more philosophical work that can clarify the relationships between the concepts 'habit', 'skill' and 'experience' in the area of physical education.

The perspective on habit, skill and experience is relevant for research about learning in physical education. Quennerstedt and colleagues (Quennerstedt et al., 2011; Quennerstedt, 2013) have drawn on the work of Dewey, in particular the notion of transaction,[4] in order to analyse learning as meaning-making in physical education. Quennerstedt et al. (2011) argue that with the transactional approach

> We can talk about learning in PE when the transactions in the educational situation are interrupted ... When everything proceeds without hesitation, we can either talk about habits or a habitual way of acting in a certain way in a certain situation. *This says something about our predisposition to act – what we have previously learnt.* When the transaction is interrupted – an indeterminate situation where students need to define the interruption as well as find an appropriate response – *we can talk about a changed predisposition to act, or, in other words learning.*
>
> (p. 163, italics added)

Thus, there are two aspects of experiential meaning-making that can be studied: what is already learned, i.e. pupils' habits of action, and the process of making meaning through reflection on experiences of confronting an indeterminate situation. Quennerstedt and colleagues (2014) in Sweden have developed a method for exploring learning in physical education that I find to have great potential for future empirical studies on habits, skill and experience. I further suggest that Shusterman's (2012) notion of pragmatic somaesthetics, i.e. the critical and comparative study of methods proposed to improve the use of the body, can be a useful analytical tool to study the various practices of learning and experiencing in the embodied practices of physical education.

Concerning futures: Kirk (2010) has outlined three possible futures for physical education: more of the same, radical reform or extinction. Radical reform involves the implementation of models-based practice. Somewhat pessimistically, Kirk concludes that more of the same is the most likely alternative in the short to middle term and extinction the likeliest outcome in the long term. Nevertheless, it is incumbent on researcher who would advance the radical reform option to develop the knowledge base that supports the reforms needed. Since I don't claim to have developed a pedagogical model that is final and ready to be implemented, there is a need to conclude this book by indicating some of the areas of future work.

First, I acknowledge that my contribution has been mostly theoretical and philosophical. There is a need to try out the ideas of movement literacy in actual physical education practice. I suggest that what is needed is action research where the pedagogical model I have outlined is developed by meeting the realities of physical education in a dialogical manner. Action research is not a matter of 'implementing an intervention', but of inquiring into the conditions of teaching and learning in physical education. Second, an area of both theorizing and empirical research that I have not dealt with in this book is embodied teaching. I have been concerned with pupils' experiences and how teachers can work with these experiences. How teachers embody pedagogy surely is important for physical education, but what it means to embody teaching is still an open question.

Notes

1 I have chosen the term *movement* rather than *physical* literacy for several reasons. The main reason is that physical literacy as developed by Whitehead has a wider application than a pedagogical model for physical education can have. Physical literacy is concerned with the whole life-span and a multitude of contexts beyond physical education. In addition, the term movement is better than physical due to the charges about dualism the use of the term physical evokes (Kentel and Dobson, 2007). However, I think it is unfair to criticize Whitehead for dualism given the emphasis she puts on the opposite in her texts.

2 As Kirk (2013, p. 979) states: 'The actual models used in any one programme of physical education is a matter of choice at school, local district or national level,

depending on how educational systems are organized. Considerations that would influence the selection of specific pedagogical models will include the appropriateness of the model to the age and stage of the learners, the sequencing of the models so that there is some cumulative and mutually reinforcing effect and, behind these factors, the broader educational values that schools, local districts or national systems seek to celebrate, reproduce, reconstruct and sustain.'

3 Habits like a healthy life style might be an exception, but I am not concerned with health education here.

4 As far as I can see, transaction and interaction cover the same phenomenon: "interaction' … assigns equal rights to both factors in experience – objective and internal conditions. Any normal experience is an interplay of these two sets of conditions. […] An experience is always what it is because of a transaction taking place between an individual and what, at the time, constitutes his environment' (Dewey, 1938, pp. 42, 43). Quennerstedt et al. (2011), however, note that Dewey, in his later work *Knowing and the Known*, co-authored with Bentley, claims that whereas 'inter-' means 'between', 'trans-' implies mutual or reciprocal. If so, then Dewey used interchange in both senses earlier, as should be evident from the quote just given.

References

Carr, D. (1981). Knowledge in practice. *American Philosophical Quarterly*, 18, 53–61.

Dewey, J. (1938). *Experience and education*. New York: Kappa Delta Pi.

Haerens, L., Kirk, D., Cardon, G. and De Bourdeaudhuij, I. (2011). Toward the development of a pedagogical model for health-based physical education. *Quest*, 63(3), 321–338.

Haydn-Davies, D. (2010). Physical literacy and learning and teaching approaches. In M. Whitehead (ed.), *Physical literacy: Throughout the lifecourse* (pp. 165–174). London: Routledge.

Ilundáin-Agurruza, J. (2014). John Dewey: experiential maverick. *Sport, Ethics and Philosophy*, 8(3) (August), 271–284. (Published online, 20 December, 1–14.)

Kentel, J. A. and Dobson, T. M. (2007). Beyond myopic visions of education: revisiting movement literacy. *Physical Education and Sport Pedagogy*, 12, 145–162.

Kirk, D. (2010). *Physical education futures*. London: Routledge.

Kirk, D. (2013). Educational value and models-based practice in physical education. *Educational Philosophy and Theory*, 45(9), 973–986.

Merleau-Ponty, M. (1963). *The structure of behavior*. Pittsburg, PA: Duquesne University Press.

Merleau-Ponty, M. (1968). *The visible and the invisible*. Evanston, IL: Northwestern University Press.

Merleau-Ponty, M. (2002). *Phenomenology of perception*. London: Routledge.

Quennerstedt, M. (2013). Practical epistemologies in physical education practice. *Sport, Education and Society*, 18(3), 311–333.

Quennerstedt, M., Annerstedt, C., Barker, D., Karlefors, I., Larsson, H., Redelius, K. and Öhman, K. (2014). What did they learn in school today? A method for exploring aspects of learning in physical education. *European Physical Education Review*, 20(2), 282–302.

Quennerstedt, M., Öhman, J. and Öhman, M. (2011). Investigating learning in physical education: a transactional approach. *Sport, Education and Society*, 16(2), 159–177.

Shusterman, R. (2012). *Thinking through the body: Essays in somaesthetics*. Cambridge: Cambridge University Press.

Stolz, S. (2014). *The philosophy of physical education: A new perspective.* London: Routledge.

Svenaeus, F. (2009). Vad är praktisk kunnskap? En inledning til emnet och boken. In J. Bornemark and F. Svenaeus (eds), *Vad är praktisk kunnskap?* (pp. 9–36). Stockholm: Södertörn Studies in Practical Knowledge.

Whitehead, M. (2001). The concept of physical literacy. *European Journal of Physical Education*, 6, 127–138.

Whitehead, M. (2007). Physical literacy: philosophical considerations in relation to developing a sense of self, universality and propositional knowledge. *Sport, Ethics and Philosophy*, 1, 281–298.

Whitehead, M. (2010). The concept of physical literacy. In M. Whitehead (ed.), *Physical literacy: Throughout the lifecourse* (pp. 10–20). London: Routledge.

Index